MENORCA

MENORCA

John and Margaret Goulding

THE WINDRUSH PRESS
GLOUCESTERSHIRE

Acknowledgements
The authors have received valuable assistance from Mark Foxon, Menorca resident and holiday rep *extraordinaire*, from long-term resident Dodo Mackenzie, who shared with them her intimate knowledge of the island, and from the staff of the Oficina Mobil Informació Turistica de Ciutadella. They would also like to thank Marjorie Blamey, Dee Darters for travel information, Christopher Saint for help with the sailing section of the book, and Ian Hepburn of the RSPB for expert advice on Menorcan birds. Special thanks are due to Sr Emili de Balanzó, Secretary General of the Fomento del Turismo de Menorca, for his patience in the face of endless questions and for giving so generously of his time.

First published in Great Britain by
The Windrush Press,
Windrush House,
Main Street,
Adlestrop, Moreton-in-Marsh,
Gloucestershire
1990

British Library Cataloguing in Publication Data
Goulding, John
  Menorca. – (Windrush island guide)
  I. Title   II. Goulding, Margaret
  914.67520483

  ISBN 0-900075-46-5

Typeset by DP Photosetting, Aylesbury, Bucks
Printed and bound in Great Britain by
The Bath Press Avon

Cover illustrations: (front) Cala Mitjana, (back) The taula precint entrance, Torre Llisá Vell

CONTENTS

For our parents

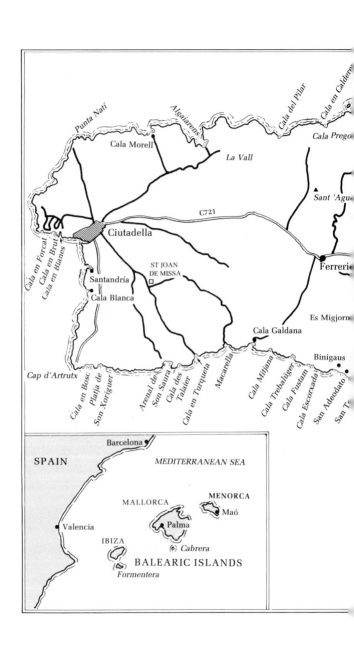

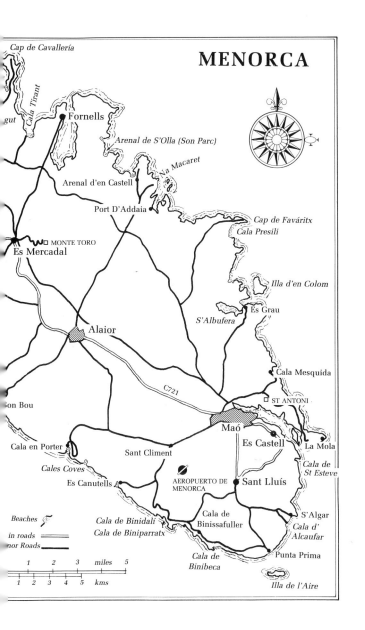

MENORCA

Cap de Cavallería

Cala Tirant

gut

● Fornells

Arenal de S'Olla (Son Parc)

Na Macaret

Arenal d'en Castell

Port D'Addaia

Cap de Faváritx
Cala Presili

✕▢ MONTE TORO
Es Mercadal

Illa d'en Colom

Es Grau

S'Albufera

Alaior

● Cala Mesquida

C721

▢ ST ANTONI

on Bou

Maó

● Es Castell ●

Cala en Porter ●

Sant Climent

Cales Coves

Es Canutells

AEROPUERTO DE
MENORCA

● Sant Lluís

La Mola ●

Cala de
St Esteve

Beaches

● S'Algar

in roads

Cala de Binidalí
Cala de Biniparratx

Cala de
Binissafuller

Cala d'
Alcaufar

nor Roads

Cala de
Binibeca

Punta Prima

| 1 | 2 | 3 | miles | 5 |

Illa de l'Aire

| 1 | 2 | 3 | 4 | 5 | kms |

INTRODUCTION

A staggering seven million holidaymakers from northern Europe visit the Balearic Islands each year, yet less than 10 per cent of them choose Menorca. This is as it should be, in the view of the 60,000 Menorcans: visitors are warmly welcomed, but this tranquil, unspoilt island is not dependent on tourism and has no wish to become so. Holiday accommodation is modern and comfortable, but small-scale and carefully limited; the brash resorts found on the other Balearics are completely absent.

Yet there are more beaches on Menorca than on Mallorca, Ibiza and Formentera together! The countryside, while lacking the mountains of its larger sister, is pastoral, rich in flowers and bird life, and criss-crossed by tracks which entice the walker and cyclist. Added to these natural attractions are the contrasting pleasures of the two major cities – the Georgian bustle of Maó and the more ancient dignity of Ciutadella – and a colourful history featuring over a dozen foreign occupations, three of them by the British; also the fascination of Menorca's unique archaeological heritage, typified by the spectacular T-shaped taulas and lofty talayots which can be seen not only in the depths of the countryside, but often right by the island's main roads.

Menorca, then, attracts the more discriminating visitor. A holiday on the island can be full of fun and activity: during the summer the warm sea is perfect for swimming and watersports of all kinds. But this island's magic appeal is its atmosphere of tranquillity and being at peace with itself: a place in which to unwind, relax and be refreshed.

A NOTE ON PLACE-NAMES

In recent years Catalan sensibility has made great strides on Menorca, and the tendency towards altering the Castilian Spanish names for streets and towns to their Menorquín variants has become pronounced. Although this trend is far from complete (and there are many instances of contradictory signs, etc., on the island at the time of writing), the use of Catalan nomenclature is now the official policy of the Balearic government and we have followed it wherever possible in this book. In most cases the relationship between the Castilian and Menorquín variants is obvious: Mahón becomes Maó, Ciudadela Ciutadella and Alayor Alaior. Greater difficulty is presented, however, by Villacarlos (now referred to as Es Castell) and San Cristóbal (now Es Migjorn Gran). Street names in the towns have been altered wholesale in recent years also; the latest edition of the Archaeological Map (see p. 6) gives the new versions, which many older maps do not, and is well worth purchasing.

GETTING THERE

BY AIR

Scheduled flights from Gatwick to Maó are operated by
Dan Air throughout the year: flights are on Mondays and
Fridays in summer (May to October) and on Saturdays only
in the winter. Monarch offer a similar service from Luton
on Mondays and Fridays in summer and Fridays only in
winter. For both services fares range from £86 (return) in
winter and £164–194 in summer. Flight duration is about
two hours. In summer it is often a better bargain to take a
charter flight: your travel agent can approach tour operators
for 'late availability' seats; alternatively these offers are
advertised in the newspapers or on Ceefax.

The Spanish airline Aviaco flies from Barcelona to Maó
5 times daily in summer and 3 times daily in winter; from
Palma de Mallorca 4 times daily in summer and 3 times daily
in winter; from Madrid twice daily in summer and daily in
winter via Palma; and from Valencia 5 times weekly in
summer. All these flights may be booked at travel agents or
at the following airports: Barcelona (tel: 93-3255829),
Valencia (96-1530325), Madrid (91-2058656), Maó (971-
356673/4), Palma (971-262649).

MAÓ AIRPORT

Maó airport is large, modern and efficient. On arrival, there
are adequate luggage carousels, good toilet facilities (including some for the disabled) and a free-flowing immigration
queue. Airport staff in green uniforms and black and white
scarves are on hand to answer enquiries. A large undercover
coach park is sited immediately outside the exit on the right
while on the left is the car hire terminal. There is a taxi rank
opposite the exit and a (sporadic) public bus service to the
centre of Maó.

In the departure lounge the traveller is made comfortable
in enormous padded chairs capable of accommodating one
and a half people. Recently opened is a substantial well-
stocked duty-free shop which sells Menorcan souvenirs as
well as the usual range of drinks, perfumes and tobacco. The
cafeteria, although spacious and adorned with prints and
trailing plants, offers no gastronomic delights and is frankly

disappointing; above this floor a gallery houses a restaurant and a further seating area. The view from this level stretches from Sa Mola right down Menorca's eastern seaboard. In common with restaurants in Spain, the airport keeps a *libro de reclamación* (complaints book), in which travellers may register any grievance against the airport, airlines or catering service.

BY SEA

If taking your car to Menorca, the recommended route is by Brittany Ferries from Plymouth to Santander: they sail twice weekly except during the period 20 December–15 January, when the service is suspended. Prices range from £55–62 per person one way (children half price) and from £57–106 for a car; the crossing time is 24 hours. Brittany Ferries are at Millbay Docks, Plymouth PL1 3EW (tel: 0752-221321, telex 45380) and at Estación Maritima, Santander (tel: 42-214500, telex 35913), or book through a travel agent. From Santander to Barcelona by road is 720 km. (450 miles); from Santander to Valencia is 713 km. (446 miles). The rail fare from London to Barcelona was, in summer 1989, £140.80 2nd class return and £198.20 1st class. Bookings should be made through British Rail Continental, PO Box 29, London SW1V 1JX (tel: 01-834-2345).

Compañía Trasmediterránea operate ferries from Barcelona to Maó as follows: Monday – 12.00 and 23.30; Tuesday – 12.00; Wednesday – 23.30; Thursday – 12.00; Friday – 23.30; Saturday – 23.45 (via Palma de Mallorca); Sunday –

The *Ciudad de Sevilla* leaves Maó harbour for Palma de Mallorca

16.30 (via Palma). The crossing time is 9 hours and single fares for passengers in 1989 ranged from 4550–11,440 ptas (children under 12 half price) and for cars from 7170–14,410 ptas.

From Valencia there is a weekly sailing at 23.30 on Saturdays, returning Sundays at 16.30: via Palma, it takes 9 hours for the first leg and 6½ for the second. From Palma a vessel departs for Maó weekly on Sundays at 09.00, arriving at 17.30: the reverse journey leaves Maó at 16.30 and arrives at Palma at 23.00; single fares are 3410–9070 ptas for passengers (children under 12 half price), 5000–10,000 ptas for cars. Passages on all these routes can be booked in the UK through the shipping company's agent: Melia Travel, 12 Dover St, London W1X 4NS (tel: 01-499-6731, telex 28887), or in Spain at the offices of Compañía Trasmediter-ránea: Maó – Nuevo Muelle Comercial, s/n (tel: 971-362950, telex 68888); Barcelona – Via Layetana 2 (tel: 93-3198504, telex 54629); Valencia – Avda Manuel Soto, 15-bajo (tel: 96-3676512, telex 62648); Palma de Mallorca – Muelle Viejo, 5 (tel: 971-726740, telex 68555).

In 1989, CATS line began a service from Ciutadella to Alcudia (Mallorca) and Barcelona with their fast catamaran *Leopardo*, which can carry 278 passengers but no cars. Their daily schedule in summer 1989 was:

dep.		arr.	
Alcudia	08.00	Ciutadella	09.00
Ciutadella	09.30	Alcudia	10.30
Alcudia	11.00	Barcelona	14.00
Barcelona	16.00	Alcudia	19.00
Alcudia	19.30	Ciutadella	20.30
Ciutadella	21.00	Alcudia	22.00

Fares were 4500 ptas return to Palma (inc. bus transfer from Alcudia), 9500 ptas return to Barcelona (children half price).

Three cruise companies include Menorca in their itineraries:

CTC (ex-Tilbury): 1 Regent St, London SW1Y 4NN (tel: 01-930-5833)

Seabourn Cruises (ex-Lisbon): 9 Hanover St, London W1R 9HF (tel: 01-629-1336)

Grandi Viaggi (ex-Genoa): Associated Oceanic Agencies UK Ltd, Eagle House, 109–110 Jermyn Street, London SW1Y 6ES (tel: 01-930-5683).

TRAVEL ON MENORCA

MAPS

Most of the maps of Menorca available in UK bookshops, whilst perfectly adequate for ordinary sightseeing, fall down when it comes to more adventurous exploration: their depiction of the countless rough tracks and farm roads on the island is distinctly erratic and even, in some cases, fanciful. The most commonly used map on the island is available only on Menorca (where it can be bought almost everywhere at a price of approx. 250 ptas). This is the *Archaeological Map of Menorca* by J Mascaró Pasarius (revised 1989), which shows most of the minor routes as well as having plans of all the towns. It has two slight disadvantages: it is not very sturdy, and will probably be in tatters after a fortnight's touring of the island; also, the marking of the archaeological sites themselves and the positioning of some of the place-names is somewhat imprecise and therefore potentially misleading.

Anyone seriously interested in exploring the more remote regions of the island, and particularly if on foot, is strongly recommended to invest in the military maps of the island (scale 1:25,000). A complete set of these maps (nine are required to cover the island) costs approx 3000 ptas, but is well worth it. The set is available from booksellers and stationers in Maó and Ciutadella (e.g. Cós 4, Cós de Gràcia, or Argos, Costa d'en Deià, Maó).

CAR HIRE

Firms offering car hire are plentiful on Menorca, both international and local. Prices are competitive, particularly off-season, but may not always include tax and insurance (other than third-party, which is obligatory); once these have been included some of the cheaper rates are less attractive. The largest local firm is Europ Betacar, who include comprehensive insurance and the 12 per cent tax in their prices. The following is a rough guide to what you might expect to pay for car hire (summer 1989 prices, the higher figure including comprehensive insurance):

	1 day	3 days	1 week
Seat Marbeila	3900–4700	8900–10000	15500–24000
Opel Corsa/Renault 5	4900–5300	9800–11150	17500–26000
Seat Ibiza/Ford Escort	5500–7200	11400–13000	19000–30000
Suzuki Jeep	7000–8900	15500–18000	35000–42000

Even in high season many companies have special offers (5 days for the price of 3, a week for the price of 5 days, etc.,) so these are worth looking out for, especially if you only require a car for a few days during your holiday.

A British or International driver's licence must be produced (photocopies are not acceptable); drivers must be over eighteen, and everyone intending to drive the vehicle must sign the contract if comprehensive insurance is included. Free mileage is invariably provided, and in many cases free delivery and collection to and from the airport or your hotel/apartment. Petrol is not included: the usual procedure is for the hirer to pay at the outset for any fuel supplied with the car; at the end of the period the hire firm will refund the value of whatever petrol remains in the tank in excess of that originally supplied.

DRIVING ON MENORCA

The network of metalled roads on Menorca is not extensive; most road excursions must start from and end at the main road between Maó and Ciutadella (C 721). This is a well-maintained road which, although busy and only single carriageway, presents few hold-ups even in summer. The speed limit on it and the handful of other main roads is 90 km.p.h., falling to 50 km.p.h. in towns. Where the C 721 goes through Alaior, Es Mercadal and Ferreries this 50 km.p.h. limit is strictly enforced: the radar speed trap at Ferreries, in particular, is notorious on the island. Other speed traps are south of Ciutadella on the Cala En Bosc road and between Maó and Sant Lluís. Car tax on Menorca is extremely low (about £15 per year), so investment in the roads is restricted; but at present, although the two main cities suffer from traffic congestion at times, driving on most of Menorca's roads is pleasant and easy.

The wearing of seat belts is compulsory except within towns and infringements can attract a 1000-peseta fine. (Like all traffic fines on Menorca, this is subject to a 20 per cent discount if paid on the spot.) It is, of course, sensible to wear belts at all times. Children under 13 should always ride in the back of the car. For motorcyclists, crash helmets are obligatory.

Menorca has many kilometres of unsurfaced road and tracks, the majority of them perfectly negotiable in a small car with the exercise of due care. Maps give very little indication of the state and grade of the roads, but seriously rutted stretches are fairly rare. Road signs are international; it is worth knowing, however, that '*Ceda el paso*' means 'give way' (to the left), and where this sign does not appear traffic from the right has priority – also that when a Menorquín cyclist or motorcyclist raises his left arm it may mean that he is about to turn right. It is usual to sound your horn when overtaking; a single unbroken white line down the centre of the road means overtaking is forbidden.

ACCIDENTS

The traffic police (*Guardia Civil de Tráfico*) are active on Menorca and lay much of the blame for accidents on tourists, who may become excessively relaxed on holiday, pulling in without warning to look at a map or take a photograph, and generally driving in a way they would never dream of at home! In 1988, 285 accidents were recorded on Menorca, with nine deaths and 358 injuries. If involved in an accident it is not obligatory to inform the police unless someone has been injured. It is, however, important to get a note of the name, address and registration numbers of any other drivers involved, together with their insurance details, and to contact your car hire firm without delay.

PARKING

Many parking areas in towns are '*Reloj Obligatorio*', with a time limit: this means that the time of arrival must be displayed in the windscreen; there may be a plastic or metal indicator in your car for this purpose, but otherwise it is quite in order to scribble the time (prefixed by '*Llegada*') on a piece of paper and display that. '*Carga y Descarga*' followed by times means that the space is reserved for unloading during the period shown but parking there is permitted at other times; '*Transporte autorizado*' by a parking space outlined in white means the space can only be used by a nearby business; and '*Vado permanente*' (often seen on garage doors) means no parking is allowed in front of the opening – an official sign that must be observed. There is no parking where red and white lines or yellow zigzags are painted on the side of the road. Parking meters were introduced in Maó in 1988 (60 ptas per hour); Es Castell operates a parking ticket system around Cales Fonts in the evenings.

PETROL

There are currently eight petrol (*gasolina*) stations on Menorca: three in Maó near the exits from the town for Ciutadella, Es Castell and Sant Lluís; two in Ciutadella, one on the main road at the end of the industrial *polígono* and the other (rather hard to find) in the Captius de Constantinoble; two on the C 721 (at Alaior and 2 km. west of Es Mercadal); and one on the Maó-Fornells road, about 12½ km. from Maó. Others are planned for Santandría and Sant Lluís. Except in high season they are open from 06.00–22.00 on weekdays, with one station opening on Sundays and at night (on a rota system). In July and August opening hours are extended, but considerable queues can form, especially at weekends, and it is sensible to keep your car topped up most of the time. Information on petrol station opening hours is published each month in the centre pages of *Roqueta* and on signs at the garages themselves. There are four grades of petrol available of which 96 octane ('super') is equivalent to 4-star; 90 octane is known as 'normal' and 98 as 'extra'. Diesel is *gasoleo* or *gasoil*, engine oil is *aceite*. In general fuel prices are 10–15 per cent lower than in the UK.

TAXIS

Taxis can be ordered by telephone from ranks on the following numbers: Maó (Pl. de S'Esplanada) 361283, (Pl. d'Espanya) 362891; Ciutadella (Av. Constitució) 381197; Alaior 371348; Es Mercadal 375027; Ferreries 373484; Es Migjorn Gran 370071; Sant Lluís 364083; Es Castell 362779. There are also 24-hour radio taxis in Maó (tel: 367111) and Ciutadella (tel: 381197). Prices are government-controlled on standard routes; for longer distances it is sensible to negotiate a price in advance. The minimum fare is 500 ptas, and examples of fares for typical journeys (summer 1989) were: Cala Galdana – Maó 2600 ptas; Punta Prima – Maó 1100; Arenal d'en Castell – Maó 1635; Cala Galdana – Ciutadella 1800.

BUSES

Transportes Menorca, SA, runs quite an extensive network of bus routes, but services are not particularly frequent, except between Maó, Es Castell and Sant Lluís and between

Ciutadella and its satellite villages. There are five or six buses daily between Maó and Ciutadella, calling at the three main inland towns. Services to the more remote seaside resorts are run mainly in the summer. Prices are extremely reasonable (e.g. Arenal d'en Castell – Maó 300 ptas, Punta Prima – Maó 120 ptas), and buses can be crowded in summer.

The bus company offices are in Maó at Avgda Josep María Quadrado 7, running northwest from the Plaça de S'Esplanada (tel: 360361) and in Ciutadella at Barcelona 8, south of the Camí de Maó before it meets the *contramurada* at Avgda de la Constitució (tel: 380393). In Maó buses leave from Pl. de S'Esplanada and Avgda Josep M. Quadrado (for Ciutadella); in Ciutadella local buses go from the northern end of the Plaça de S'Esplanada. The archaeological map shows where the bus stop is in each of the minor towns: in seaside resorts it is usually to be found near one of the larger hotels.

Full information about routes and times, which vary from month to month, is available from the offices of the bus company, from tourist offices and from hotel reception desks. The English language magazine *Roqueta* also prints an excellent summary on its centre pages each month.

Hitch-hiking is not illegal, but is not encouraged.

HOTELS AND RESTAURANTS

HOTELS

Full listings of the accommodation on Menorca can be obtained from the Spanish Tourist Office in London (see p. 26) or local tourist offices. Hotels on Menorca are given a star rating based on the proportion of rooms which have a bathroom, lifts, bar, air conditioning, etc: full details of the system are also available from Tourist Offices. Price tariffs should be displayed at reception and in each room. *Hostales*, more modest than hotels, may or may not provide meals apart from breakfast (*hostales residencia*); 1- and 2-star *hostales* should have a common bathroom for every 10–12 rooms.

Most hotels on Menorca close from October to April, exceptions being the Hotel Port Mahón, the Hamilton in Es Castell and the Residencia Capri, Maó. *Hostales* also usually remain open all year. Hotels on the island include:

MAÓ AND THE SOUTH-EAST

Maó
Hotel Port Mahón, Avda Fort de l'Eau: 4 star, smart, imposing, overlooking the harbour, central heating, garden, swimming pool and night club, open all year; 74 rooms (tel: 362600).

Hotel Residencia Capri, Sant Esteve 8: 3 star, bed and breakfast only, centrally situated, comfortable, central heating, open all year; 75 rooms (tel: 361400).

Hostal Residencia El Paso, Cós de Gràcia, 157: 2 star, convenient location, central heating; 40 rooms (tel: 361200).

Es Castell
Hotel Agamenón, Fontanilles, 18: 3 star, swimming pool, spacious rooms, popular with regular visitors, garden, landing stage; 75 rooms (tel: 362150).

Hotel Hamilton, Passeig de Santa Agueda 6: 2 star, open all year, overlooking the harbour, old-established, gracious and quiet, pool, central heating; 132 rooms (tel: 362050).

Hotel Rey Carlos III, Miranda Cala Corp: 3 star, pool and night club, overlooking harbour, central heating; 87 rooms (tel: 363100).

Del Almirante, Fonduco, Port de Maó: 1 star, individualistic hotel in Georgian villa once the residence of Admiral Collingwood, fine harbour views, pool, garden, central heating, tennis; 38 rooms (tel: 362700).

Sant Lluís
Residence Hostal Biniali, Suestra 50: 3 star, 100-year-old Menorcan house in quiet country S.W. of the town, comfortable and individual, pool, gardens, heating; 9 rooms (tel: 361724).

S'Algar
Hotel S'Algar: 3 star, low-lying with lovely gardens, overlooking the sea, pool, children's pool, disco; 108 rooms (tel: 361700).
Hotel San Luis: 3 star, pool, tennis, mini-golf, organized entertainment; 228 rooms (tel: 361750).

Cala d' Alcaufar
Hostal Residencia Xuroy: 2 star, on beach, landing stage; 44 rooms (tel: 361820).

Punta Prima
Hotel Pueblo Menorca: 1 star, pools, mini-golf, tennis, garden, games room, disco, lively entertainments programme; 538 rooms (tel: 361850).
Hotel Xaloc: 1 star, on the beach, pool, children's play area, mini-golf; 58 rooms (tel: 361922).

CIUTADELLA AND WEST COAST

Ciutadella
Hotel Patricia, Camí de Sant Nicolau, 90: 4 star, near the Borne, conference rooms, open all year; 44 rooms (tel: 385511).
Hotel Esmeralda, Camí de Sant Nicolau, 171: 3 star, overlooking the open sea at the mouth of the harbour, pool, good facilities for children, garden, tennis; 135 rooms (tel: 380250).
Hotel Playa Grande, Bisbe Juano, 2: 1 star, overlooks Cala des Degollador; 40 rooms (tel: 380793).
Hostal Residencia Ciutadella, Sant Eloi, 10: 2 star, bed and breakfast only, central yet quiet; 17 rooms (tel: 383462).
Hostal Mar Blava, Son Oleo: 2 star, overlooking Cala des Degollador, garden, landing stage; 18 rooms (tel: 380015).
Hostal Residencia Menurka, Domingo Savio 6: 2 star, central; 21 rooms (tel: 381415).
Hostal Madrid, carrer de Madrid: 1 star, restaurant,

friendly, pool; 11 rooms (tel: 380328).

Cala Blanca
Cala Blanca: 3 star, set in shady pine woods, children's play area, garden, pool, central heating; 147 rooms (tel: 380450).
Mediterrani: 3 star, new hotel near beach, pools, children's playground, tennis, entertainments programme; 180 rooms (tel: 384203).

Santandría
Poseidon Hotel: 2 star, 13 rooms (tel: 382644).
Ses Voltes: 2 star, on the beach, garden; 40 rooms (tel: 380400).

Cala En Bosc
Cala'n Bosch: 3 star, overlooking beach, pool, garden, disco; 169 rooms (tel: 380600).
Menorca Star: 3 star, overlooking yacht marina, very new, popular quayside restaurant, pool, garden, children's playground, entertainments; 199 rooms (tel: 385764).

Son Xoriguer
Hotel Club Falcó Sol: 3 star, village-style hotel, near beach, pools, fitness centre, disco, tennis, children's pool, children's playground, entertainments; 450 rooms (tel: 384623).

Cala En Blanes
Cala'n Blanes: 2 star, near small beach, pool, garden, mini-golf, disco, tennis; 103 rooms (tel: 382497).

Cala En Forcat
Almirante Farragut: 3 star, swimming pool, above small beach, disco, children's playground, tennis, mini-golf, many activities; 472 rooms (tel: 382800).
Los Delfines: 2 star, pool, garden, tennis; 92 rooms (tel: 382450).

SOUTH COAST

Biniancolla
Hotel Sur Menorca: 1 star, pool, garden, tennis; 238 rooms (tel: 361800).

Es Canutells
Hotel Mar de Menorca: apart-hotel scheduled to open May 1990 (tel: 350724).

Cala En Porter
Hotel Playa Azul: 1 star, pool, garden, superb position overlooking the sea; 126 rooms (tel: 367067).

Son Bou
San Valentín, San Jaime Mediterraneo: 4 star (opened summer 1989), elevated position in pinewoods overlooking the sea, specially designed rooms for disabled, air-conditioned, pools (indoor and out), gymnasium, sauna, tennis, children's nursery, heating; 214 rooms (tel: 372912).
Los Milanos Sol/Los Pinguinos Sol: 3 star, large twin hotels on beach, pools, tennis, mini-golf, entertainments programme; 300 rooms each (tels: 371175/371075).

Sant Tomás
Santo Tomás: 4 star, on beach, large pool, garden, mini-golf, sports activities, entertainments programme; 60 rooms (tel: 370025).
Lord Nelson: 3 star, pool, air-conditioned, central heating, garden, mini-golf, apartment block attached; 177 rooms (tel: 370125).
Los Cóndores Sol: 3 star, on beach, heating, pool, children's play area, lawns, mini-golf; 188 rooms (tel: 370050).
Hotel Victoria Playa: 3 star, large family hotel; 270 rooms (tel: 370200).

Cala Galdana
Audax: 4 star, rooftop swimming pool, disco, indoor games, tennis, Menorquín-owned (unusual); 244 rooms (tel: 373125).
Gavilanes Sol: 3 star, cliff-sized hotel on beach, disabled facilities, pool; 357 rooms (tel: 373175).
Cala Galdana Hotel: 2 star, indoor and outdoor pools, children's playground, disabled facilities, garden, sauna; 259 rooms (tel: 373000).

NORTH COAST

Fornells
Hostal Residencia Port Fornells: 2 star, pool, garden; 20 rooms (tel: 375073).
Hostal S'Algaret: 2 star, central; 23 rooms (tel: 375174).

Son Parc
Sol Parc: 4 star, apart-hotel, small-scale landscaped development, children's play area, many sporting facilities; 272 rooms (tel: 363840).

Arenal d'en Castell
Castell Playa: 4 star, indoor and outdoor pools, disco, sauna, tennis, children's play area, comprehensive amenities, gardens; 264 rooms (tel: 371450).

Aguamarina: 3 star, overlooking beach, shops, pool, gardens, children's playroom, tennis; 248 rooms (tel: 371275).

Topacio: 2 star, pool, children's playroom, entertainments programme, tennis; 276 rooms (tel: 371275).

INLAND

There are *hostales* at Es Mercadal (Jeni, Miranda del Toro, 81: 1 star, pool, restaurant specializing in Menorcan cuisine; 36 rooms) and Ferreries (La Perdiz, Maó, 14: 1 star, 27 rooms).

SELF-CATERING

Probably the majority of visitors to Menorca self-cater, and in recent years *urbanizaciones*, consisting of villas and apartments with ancillary supermarkets, shops, bars and restaurants, discos, sports facilities, etc., have sprung up in many parts of the island. They are ideal for a cost-saving holiday, especially for families with young children. Maid service can be expected at least once a week in most self-catering villas and apartments; in addition an introductory food pack is often provided, and there will be a reception desk able to summon taxis, dispense information and change foreign currency.

Most self-catering accommodation is fairly modern and of a high standard. Inevitably with a rapidly changing occupancy, furnishings tend to be practical rather than luxurious, and kitchens may lack certain items that British visitors tend to take for granted – notably a kettle (let alone an electric one), an oven or a grill. The lighting, too, is frequently inadequate: experienced self-caterers often take a selection of 60 watt and stronger light-bulbs on holiday with them (make sure they are screw-fitting).

Lists of self-catering accommodation may be obtained from the Spanish Tourist Office. In addition, a number of British firms offer villas and apartments on Menorca for short lets, among them: Beach Villas, 8 Market Passage, Cambridge CB2 3QR (tel: 0223-311113); Meon Travel, College Street, Petersfield GU32 3JN (0730-68411); Rentavilla, 27 High Street, Chesterton, Cambridge CB4 1ND (0223-323414) and Villaseekers, Romeland House, Romeland Hill, St Albans AL3 4ET. The following specialize to a greater or lesser degree in Menorca: Jean Harper Holidays, 20 Walton Road, Stockton Heath, Warrington WA4 6NL (0925-64234) – their subsidiary, Menco Ltd, deals entirely with properties at San Jaime; Martyn Holidays, Westleigh House, 390 London Road, Isleworth TW7 5AD (01-847-5855); and Patricia Wildblood, Calne, Wiltshire SN11 0LP (0249-817023).

CAMPING

There are several camping sites on Menorca, but only one meets the health and safety levels required to be registered as an official site; this is Camping Son Bou, reached by turning south off the main road 2½ km. east of Alaior and driving for about 3 km. towards the sea. This large site has a supermarket, tennis courts, mini-golf, children's playground and pool, restaurant, bar, swimming pool, telephones, laundry facilities, safe deposits and money changing facilities; there are access ramps and toilet facilities for the disabled. Tents can be rented – a tent that sleeps 2 is 750 ptas per day, while a chalet tent for 4–5 people is 1250 ptas per day. Other charges are:

15 June – 15 Sept	per adult – 475 ptas per night
	site for caravan/tent – 1750 ptas (inc. car)
	electricity connection – 300
1 May – 15 June/15 Sept – 30 Oct	per adult – 375 ptas
	site – 1050 ptas
	(Children under 2 are free).

The site is some 3 km. from the nearest beach at Son Bou. Reservations may be made or information requested from Apartado de Correos 30, 07730 Alaior (tel: 372626/372727).

A second camp site (unofficial as yet) lies beside the road from Ferreries to Cala Galdana: it has a pool, toilet facilities and a restaurant/bar (tel: 373095). Off-site camping is not allowed on beaches or within 1 km. of a town or village. Some farmers are willing to give permission to camp on their land; fire hazards loom large in landowners' minds during the summer months, however, so the majority discourage camping if they can.

FOOD AND DRINK

MENORCAN CUISINE

Menorca's gastronomy owes much to its history. Almonds, citrus fruits, saffron, nutmeg and cumin date from the

The Friesian cattle grazing all over Menorca today are a highly visible legacy of the British occupation

Moorish occupation, as does *cucusso*, a sweet dessert of honey, raisins and almonds that is also used to stuff turkeys at Christmas. From America, through Spain, come potatoes, tomatoes, maize and peppers. The French introduced their methods of making bread, pastries, fruit tarts and liqueurs. The British governor, Sir Richard Kane, left his mark also, by importing Friesian cattle and thereby initiating the dairy industry. Other British legacies include gin and the widespread practice of roasting meat, which is less prevalent in other parts of Spain; the Menorcans even adopted the word *grevi* from gravy.

Many Menorquín recipes have been passed down through generations: Most authentic of these are *sobrasadas* (spicy pork sausages), *oliaigua* or *oliaigo* (vegetable soup with oil, bay leaves and lots of garlic), *caldera Menorquina* (fish stew), *formatjades* (savoury pies), *codornices en salsa* (quails in sauce), *amargos* (almond shortbread) and *carquiñols* (almond biscuits).

Ensaimadas, huge coils of light bun mixture often served for breakfast, are in fact Mallorquín, though they are frequently presented in boxes as souvenirs of Menorca.

The invention of *salsa mahonesa* (mayonnaise) is sometimes attributed to the chef to the Duc de Crillon during the siege of Fort San Felipe near Maó; alternative versions credit its invention to the housekeeper of the Duc de

Richelieu, an earlier Frenchman who played a part in Menorcan history (he is said to have concocted it when required to disguise the taste of some meat that was less than fresh); or to a local peasant woman who, lacking garlic to make the traditional Mediterranean *alioli*, used the only ingredients she had to hand when she needed to dress a salad for the Duc. The sauce is intended to enhance many salad vegetables. Today it is also served with fish and often accompanies asparagus; its creamy flavour has none of the harshness of the bottled version.

The clean waters around Menorca are rich in fish and shellfish. The abundance of sea bream, bass, mullet, *dentón*, sea perch, eels, crabs and lobsters ensures that seafood is an important part of the islanders' diet. Boiling is the most popular way of cooking fish, the liquid being used for soup while the fish may be served with a mayonnaise garnish. Many composite fish dishes also grace the menu: top of the bill is certainly *caldereta de langosta*, an exquisite (and extremely expensive) lobster casserole or thick soup exclusive to Menorca. Visitors often visit Fornells to eat this, particularly the Restaurant 'Es Pla', which is patronised by King Juan Carlos; but delicious versions may be sampled elsewhere. Each restaurant guards its own secret recipe, but the staple ingredients are lobster, onion, tomato, garlic and parsley. Due to the prohibitive prices charged for this dish it may be preferable to sample the humbler but also delicious *caldereta de pescado/peix*, based on a variety of fish and shellfish. Distinctive among the seafoods listed on Menorquín menus are *datiles*, a kind of mussel visually resembling ripe dates. They may be served just with garlic, parsley and breadcrumbs or in a soup (*caldereta de datiles*). A similar soup is made from the locally popular *escopinya* (no English translation), a clam-like oyster substitute which is farmed in Maó harbour. Both *escopinyas* and red mullet are popularly used in baked fish dishes, usually on a bed of potatoes and covered with tomatoes. Another Menorcan favourite is snails (*caracoles*), usually cooked with garlic and herbs: you may well see islanders gathering them from the fields beside the road.

All kinds of meat appear on Menorquín menus, but the traditional *carne a la cazuela* (meat casserole) is made from pork and *sobrasada*, a reddish sausage of spiced pork paste. These *sobrasadas*, less piquant than their Mallorquín counterparts, are a common filling for the small savoury pies known as *formatjades*. Other sausage varieties you may encounter are *cuixot*, *salsitxa* and *carn i xua*; there is also a local variety of black (or white) pudding known as *butifarra*. Meatballs (*albondigas*) are usually minced beef or veal mixed with ham or bacon. In all but the most ethnic Menorquín restaurants, beef, lamb, veal, pork and chicken (maize-fed and thus rather yellow-fleshed) are served in international styles: the tourist can always eat the kind of meal with which he or she is familiar. Game has always been important to the Menorquín: partridge and quail both feature on island menus, and rabbit, often served with the typical garlicky mayonnaise '*alioli*', is also extremely popular.

Menorcan cheese is generally agreed to be Spain's best; the sharp-tasting *queso de Mahón* (Mahón cheese) is exported to peninsular Spain and other EEC countries. Traditionally, it is made in square loaves, which are suspended from grass ropes during curing. The centre of its manufacture is Alaior, home town of the dominant producer, Coinga (whose factory has a direct sales department). Small co-operatives elsewhere on Menorca also produce their own variations, usually marketed as 'Payes'. Menorquín cheese is soft and white when young, later becoming yellower and as hard as parmesan, with many intermediate stages of maturity. Although not cheap, the cheese has an unusual and delicious flavour and makes a very acceptable present to bring home. The processed cheese 'El Caserio' is a mixture of *queso de Mahón* and butter and is presented in wrapped triangular portions packed into shallow round boxes; this too is exported in great quantities.

Mahón cheese is the main ingredient of *greixera*, a cheesecake served in pastry shops. It also constitutes another filling for *formatjades*, little savoury pies on sale all over Menorca.

An ancient cheese-press preserved at a farm near Fornells

The island has also used its dairy produce to develop another spectacularly successful industry: that of ice cream manufacture. In 1943 the firm of 'La Menorquina', also based in Alaior, was founded by Don Fernando Sintes, and it has been concocting delicious creamy mixtures and mouth-watering fruit sorbets ever since. The former are presented in 'rustic' earthenware pots and the latter artistically encased in the frozen skins of the appropriate fruit (not only citrus fruits but even apples, peaches, melons and coconuts are used). What started as a small-scale industry on Menorca has become famous throughout Spain, and now 'La Menor-quina' is made under licence in Barcelona and Seville. Although it is sad in some ways to see the island factory's exclusivity end (especially if the original factory is to close), the Menorcans have cause to be proud of the immense kudos of the product that bears their island's name.

Gin was introduced to Menorca in the late eighteenth century by British sailors who divulged the recipe to a Mahonese businessman named Beltran. The firm he founded continues to produce the same drink to this day, making the spirit in the original stills and flavouring it with juniper. Today the windmill trademark of the firm of Xoriguer has a higher profile. Their best quality gin, 70 per cent proof and distinctly different in taste from London gin, is sold in earthenware bottles known as *canecas*, which have a thumb hole at the neck. Their distillery on the waterfront at Maó is open daily to the public, who are encouraged to sample the gins and gin-based liqueurs they produce. The most typical liqueurs are the dark, rather sticky '*palo*' (made from carob seeds) and the the lime-green '*hierbas*' (made from camomile picked on La Mola, the headland to the north of Maó harbour, and reputed to be good for stomach upsets); another is '*calent*', which includes aniseed, cinnamon and saffron and is usually served hot. A wide variety of other liqueurs is on sale at the distillery: most popular of all, however, is the cocktail of gin and lemonade known as *pomada*, which has a claim to be called Menorca's national drink. It is extremely refreshing and, although only 10 per cent proof, all too easy to drink in quantity; sometimes soda water is added to gin and lemon – the result is known as *pallofa*.

No wine to speak of is produced on Menorca, phylloxera having wiped out what vineyards there were on the island at the end of the last century.

RESTAURANTS

There are about 300 restaurants on Menorca – too many to

Delicious *paellas* are widely available on Menorca, as everywhere in holiday Spain

list them all. Most offer the standard tourist menus of Mediterranean Spain, and almost all desserts (*postres*) lean heavily on the products of La Menorquina. Several are owned by expatriate British. All offer a *menu del día* by law – usually costing between 600 and 1500 ptas. Most have English translations of the menu. It is worth noting that in the holiday resorts some restaurants have swimming pools which guests are welcome to use.

Prices vary comparatively little: only a few specialist dishes, notably the fish or lobster stews called *calderetas*, are really expensive; more ordinary meals will probably cost you much the same as they would in the UK. Eating hours are later than in Britain – lunch may easily begin at 14.00 and dinner at 21.00 or even later – but in the more touristic areas restaurants are usually ready to succumb to the demands of their Northern European guests for rather earlier meals! Outside the towns, many restaurants are open only between May and October. A few of the more unusual restaurants (either as regards quality or menu range) are listed below; most of these are rather more expensive than the standard resort eating places and, particularly in July and August, advance booking is advisable.

MAÓ (HARBOUR)

Rocamar, Fonduco 32: very popular, well-established seafood restaurant, owned by an opera singer, on the waterfront at Cala Figuera east of the city; closed Sunday evenings (tel: 365601).

Es Gregal, Moll de Levant 43: cool green and white décor and courteous service, popular, Greek-owned, seafood dishes change daily (see blackboard), some Greek dishes, harbour views (tel: 366606).

Cafe Alba, Moll de Levant 36: same ownership as Es Gregal, stylish, unusual menu, tapas (tel: 350606).

MAÓ (TOWN)

Chez Gaston, Sa Rovellada de Dalt 13: general menu, small and busy, reasonable prices (tel: 360044).

Pilar, d'es Forn 61: Menorcan cuisine, garden and terrace seating (tel: 366817).

Chequers, Sant Sebastià 15: off Plaça de la Miranda at the back of the market, imaginative international cuisine (tel: 350457).

El Greco, Carrer de ses Moreres 49: international menu, small and friendly (tel: 364367).

Ida y Vuelta, Plaça de S'Esplanada 39: popular, small garden terrace at the rear (tel: 366220).

Sa Parada, Plaça de S'Esplanada: excellent value for snacks right by the main bus stops, tapas.

THE SOUTH-EAST

Es Cap Roig, Cala Mesquida: fish restaurant just south of Sa Mesquida village (tel: 363715).

Picadero Malbùger, Sant Lluís road: converted farmhouse in countryside (tel: 363268).

Garden, Carrer Stuart 6A, Es Castell: above Cales Fonts, sophisticated menu, some expensive dishes and wines (tel: 369116).

Sa Taverna, Horizonte *urbanización*, near Es Castell: popular for its roast Sunday lunch, also vegetarian dishes and traditional English cooking, homemade puddings.

Scandals, on road south of Es Castell: English-owned, Spanish, English and Indian food, gardens, live music, traditional English Sunday lunch, and fish and chips on Thursdays (tel: 365313).

El Sereno: popular carvery in large old farmhouse reached on rough track due north of the airport runway, large garden, all you can eat for fixed price inc. wine (no phone, can book by leaving message in postbox at the end of the track).

INLAND

Bennetti's, San Macario 6, Alaior: international menu, fine old town house with lovely courtyard garden, evenings only (tel: 371400).

Es Molí d'Es Recó, Es Mercadal; in the prominent windmill by the C 721, very popular specializing in traditional Menorcan cuisine (tel: 375392).

Ca N'Aguadet, Carrer Lepanto 23, Es Mercadal; best (and busiest) specialist Menorcan restaurant on the island, interesting and unusual menu, must book (tel: 375391).

El Gallo, Cala Galdana road: Menorcan dishes and grills in old farmhouse, atmospheric and reasonable (tel: 373039).

S'Engolidor, Carrer Major 58, Es Migjorn Gran: tiny, typical Menorcan village house, authentic Menorcan menu, outdoor seating, unpretentious, reasonable and unusual, must book well ahead (tel: 370193).

Molí de Foc, Sant Llorenço 65, Sant Climent: unassuming Menorcan house in a side street, small but excellent French menu, lively atmosphere (tel: 364137).

Es Plans, on main road just west of Alaior between Son Bou and San Jaime junctions: international and English menu, friendly service, Sunday roasts, fish and chips Tuesdays, reasonable prices (tel: 372926).

CIUTADELLA

C'as Quintu, Plaça Alfonso III: traditional Menorcan town restaurant open all day, tapas, fish *calderetas* (tel: 381002).

Casa Manolo, Marina 103: one of several very busy restaurants along the harbourside, seafood specialities, booking essential in summer (tel: 380003).

La Payesa, Marina 67; another popular harbourside restaurant, fish and seafood (tel: 380021).

El Horno, carrer Forn 12: French and Spanish menu, basement restaurant, evenings only (tel: 380767).

Es Caliu, Cap D'Artrutx road: large, popular, beside coast road south of the city, specializes in charcoal grills (tel: 380165).

NORTH COAST

Es Pla, Fornells: probably the most famous restaurant on the island, large enclosure next to water with some outdoor seating, specializes in lobster *caldereta* (and occasionally visited by King Juan Carlos just for this dish which costs about £30 a bowl) (tel: 375155).

Es Cranc, Escoles 29, Fornells: very popular, although without Es Pla's view of the bay, similar menu (tel: 375242).
Tamarindos, Es Grau: new restaurant by water's edge, friendly service, simple lunches, relaxing atmosphere.
Sa Barraca d'es Carboner, Maó-Fornells road: converted charcoal-burner's hut, characterful staff, hearty helpings, attractive setting on the edge of woodland.
Alcalde, Arenal d'en Castell: popular, friendly, well-presented international menu.

SOUTH COAST

La Salamandra, Cala En Porter: popular, international menu, large open-air terrace, friendly service, live music, open noon to midnight daily.
La Finca, *urbanización* Torre Soli Nou: on the road between C 721 and San Jaime, converted country house, small international menu (tel: 372140).
Benamar, Cala Galdana: international menu, large but quiet, courteous service (tel: 373000).

NIGHTLIFE

It is often said that Menorca has not much to offer in the way of nightlife and that young people in particular will find little to do. While older holidaymakers may find it convenient to perpetuate this image (!), it has to be said that it is largely mythical. In addition to cinemas and theatres (see p.94–95) and numerous bars and restaurants, all the main

Cales Fonts in Es Castell is home to over a dozen popular restaurants

resorts have at least one disco, as do many hotels. Particularly if you have transport, it is possible to dance all night on Menorca if that is the way your fancy takes you.

Discotheques in the eastern part of the island include: **Lui**, on the road just before Es Castell from Maó; **Tonic**, in the Horizonte *urbanización*, near Es Castell; **Pacha** (very lively, in action till 3 a.m.), just before Sant Lluís on the road from Maó; **Sí**, Cós de Gràcia 16, Maó; and **Flistons**, San Jorge 10, Es Castell. In and around Ciutadella are: **Adagio's**, in the Son Oleo district to the south of the Cala des Degollador, and **Macho**, south of the city towards Santandría). There are also discos and several 'music bars' in the area around Ciutadella harbour, including **Es Pla**, **Zona B**, **Rincón de Martin**, **Disco Lateral**, **Aladino**, **Estels** and **L'Herba**.

Other nightspots are **Winstons** in Cala Galdana, **Zeppelin** in Ferreries, **S'Algar** in the *urbanización*, **España** in Alaior, **Neptuno** in Es Migjorn Gran, and, most unusual of them all, the **Xoroi** caves in Cala En Porter (see p. 157).

PRACTICAL INFORMATION

TOURIST INFORMATION

The main Tourist Information office in Maó is on the north-western side of Plaça de S'Esplanada at no. 40 (tel: 363790). Opening hours are 9.00–14.00 and 17.00–19.00 Monday to Friday, 9.30–13.00 Saturdays (closed Sundays and fiestas). In Ciutadella, there is an extremely helpful tourist information service (tel: 381050), run from a caravan which is parked in the Borne for most of the time, but also visits local resorts in the western part of the island in the evenings from 17.00–21.00 on different days as follows: Monday – Cala Morell, Tuesday – Cala En Bosc, Wednesday – Los Delfines, Thursday – Cala Blanca, Friday – Cala Galdana, Saturday – Santandría. In Britain, limited information about Menorca is available from the Spanish Tourist Office, 57–8 St James' St, London SW1A 1LD (tel: 01-499-0901).

TIME

Menorca, like mainland Spain, is usually one hour ahead of the UK; summer time, however, ends one month earlier than in Britain, so during October Menorcan time is the same as British time.

BANKS AND CURRENCY

The currency of Menorca is, of course, the Spanish peseta. The island is full of banks – indeed their proliferation in the towns is causing some concern to residents. All will change money and many offer mortgage services, etc., as well. Banks will change Eurocheques free, but charge 2 per cent commission plus tax on travellers' cheques and currency. Normal banking hours are 9.00–14.00 Monday to Friday and 9.00–13.00 on Saturdays (but some close altogether on Saturdays in the summer). In addition, the larger hotels will exchange foreign money or travellers' cheques (the rate is lower for currency than cheques), usually charging commission but no tax. Credit cards are widely accepted in restaurants and shops all over Menorca.

PUBLIC HOLIDAYS

National holidays in Spain are as follows:

January 1	Año Nuevo (New Year's Day)
January 6	Epifanía del Señor (Twelfth Night – an important holiday: on Menorca, 'three kings' arrive by sea to distribute presents to the children)
(movable)	Viernes Santo (Good Friday)
(movable)	Día de Pascua (Easter Sunday)
May 1	Fiesta del Trabajo (Labour Day)
(movable)	Corpus Christi (second Sunday after Whitsun)
June 29	San Pedro y San Pablo (St Peter and St Paul)
July 25	Santiago (St James, patron saint of Spain)
August 15	Asunción (Feast of the Assumption)
October 12	Día de la Hispanidad (Columbus Day)
November 1	Todo los Santos (All Saints' Day)
December 8	Inmaculada Concepción (Immaculate Conception)
December 25	Navidad (Christmas Day)

Shops and banks are generally closed on the above days. Additionally in Menorca the fiesta of Sant Antoni Abat (the island's patron saint) is celebrated on 17 January and that of Cincogema on 15 May; shops etc. are also closed in each of the towns on the island during most of the period when their own local fiestas are running (see pp. 96–98).

POST

Postboxes on Menorca are yellow with red stripes. Postal deliveries are not swift – allow about 10 days for a holiday postcard to reach its destination. Stamps are often available from the same sources as postcards. If this fails, some large hotels keep stock; alternatively stamps can be bought from state tobacconists (*estancos*, marked with a distinctive yellow sign), but often only if you have purchased your cards there, and post offices (*Correos*). Many hotels have post collection boxes.

The main post offices are: Maó – Bon Aire, 15 (tel: 363892); Ciutadella – Plaça d'es Born 5 (tel: 380081). There are also *correos* in Alaior, Es Mercadal, Ferreries, Es Castell, Es Migjorn Gran and Fornells – the street plans on the Archaeological Map (see p. 6) show their locations. Post offices are open 9.00–13.30. The current postage rate to EEC countries is 45 ptas, whether for letters or postcards.

(In Spain it is forbidden for the Post Office to open undelivered mail so it is sensible to put the sender's name and address on the back.) Poste Restante may be addressed to *Lista de Correos*, followed by the name of the town where it is to be collected. Telegrams may be sent from post offices.

TELEPHONES

There are public telephone boxes in most towns and villages; in addition many bars have telephones for public use (often with a meter showing the number of units used). The boxes take 5, 25 and 100 peseta coins. Phoning abroad is simple: after placing sufficient coins in the sloping groove, dial 07 and wait for the high-pitched continuous dialling tone. Then dial the code for the country (the UK is 44), then the regional code without the initial 0, then the number you require. The coins will drop into the body of the telephone as they are needed and any unused at the end can be retrieved. (Note that the small button to the left of the phone should never be pressed when there are coins in the rack at the top of the machine.) A reverse call charge is *cobro revertido* in Spanish. Calls are cheaper than the peak rate between 20.00 and 22.00 but cheaper still thereafter.

HEALTH AND MEDICAL CARE

Spain is a member of the EEC and visitors from other countries in the Community who have brought the necessary documentation (a form E 111 for the UK) can claim free medical treatment. In order to do so, however, it is necessary to take the form in advance to the Social Security Office (Instituto Nacional de la Seguridad Social) at Bisbe Gonyalons, 20, Máo (tel: 362456). There you will be given a 'cheque-book' (*talonario*) of medical vouchers. These can, however, only be used if you visit a Social Service Doctor, such as the Centro Medico Salus – in Maó at Miquel de Verí (tel: 366663) and near Ciutadella in the Los Delfines complex, at Apartamentos Delfín Park, Cala En Forcat (tel: 384117). There are, however, many private health centres on the island – most resorts have one, usually well-signposted, and hotels will have details; these charge on the spot for medical services, but holidaymakers who have taken out health insurance should not find this more than an inconvenience (be sure to take your flight ticket and insurance policy details with you to the clinic). Maó hospital is in Cós de Gràcia (tel: 361221), Ciutadella's at Plaça de Sant Antoni (tel: 381914); in emergencies, 24-hour medical help can be summoned by telephoning 364048.

There are plenty of dentists in Menorca, but treatment is expensive and not usually covered by holiday health insurance. If at all possible, it is better to wait until you return home for dental treatment.

Chemists (*farmacias*) display a green cross and are qualified to give advice on health as well as dispense drugs; they sell medicines and baby foods (not usually available in supermarkets), but not toiletries for which a *droguería* must be visited. The towns which have post offices (see above) all have *farmacias* also. Chemists are closed at weekends, but a rota system ensures there is always one open on the island (details of the duty chemist are displayed at each).

There are no dangerous snakes on Menorca: only mosquitoes present a potential hazard, and then mostly in summer. In summer, care should be taken to avoid sunburn: exposure to the sun should be increased only gradually at first, particularly between 11.00 and 15.00, and infants should be kept out of direct sunlight as far as possible. If you have a medical condition it is a sensible precaution to carry a letter from your doctor about your treatment, previously translated into Spanish.

LAVATORIES

There are scarcely any public conveniences (*aseos*) on Menorca. All bars and restaurants have them, however, and it is not essential to make a purchase in order to use their facilities: if you feel the need, you can always contribute a few pesetas.

LANGUAGE

Menorquín is not a language in its own right, but the local sub-dialect of Catalan, the Romance tongue spoken by about nine million people in eastern Spain and a small part of France. This, and not Castilian Spanish, is the mother tongue of most Menorcans and you are sure to hear them speak it amongst themselves. (They refer to it as speaking '*en pla*' – in plain language.) Greater regional awareness in recent years has shown itself in the campaign (by now largely successful) to alter Spanish place-names to their Menorquín version, causing some confusion for visitors: road signs and street names differ from what a map might lead one to expect, indeed at present there are plentiful instances of signs which contradict each other's nomenclature. Most Menorquín place-names are sufficiently similar to the 'old' Spanish names to be recognisable: possible exceptions are Maó (Mahón), Es Migjorn Gran (formerly known by its Spanish name of San Cristóbal) and Es Castell (formerly Villacarlos). Catalan-Castilian dictionaries may be bought in Máo, but this is not essential. Knowing a few Catalan words, however, may be useful or add to one's understanding of Menorca: thus, *es*, *sa* and *ses* all mean 'the', and *en* means 'of' (*ca'n* is 'house of'). Other Catalan words you are quite likely to meet include *tancat* (closed) and *obert* (open), *nou* and *vell* (old and new), *dalt* and *baix* (high and low), *avinguda* (avenue), *camí* (road), *carrer* (street), *illa* (island), *peix* (fish), *poblat* (village) and *estiu* (summer). *Bon dia* means 'good morning' and *benvinguts*, 'welcome'.

TIPPING

In general a small tip (*propina*) is expected in restaurants even when a service charge has been added. In bars it is usual to leave a few coins, especially if you have had waiter service (you will usually find that if you sit or stand at the bar you will pay 10–15 per cent less than if you are waited on at a table). Sometimes in restaurants and bars there may be a communal tip box (*bote*) by the till. As everywhere in the world, taxi-drivers and hairdressers expect a tip of 5–10 per cent and maids, hotel porters, cloakroom attendants, cleaners, etc., also appreciate a small gratuity.

ELECTRICITY AND GAS

At present Menorca's electricity comes entirely from Mallorca, via cables which arrive near Cap d'Artrutx; the large new power station you may see beside Maó harbour is inadequate and not fully operational (something of a local scandal). Voltage is 220 volts, with two-pin plugs; most British appliances work perfectly well though maybe a little less powerfully than at home.

Gas for cooking is distributed by Butano, SA. There is a regular delivery rota throughout the island, details of which are obtainable from the firm's offices in the main towns. There is also a depot on the C 721 (near the airport turn-off), which is open 12.00–13.00 and 16.30–18.00 daily (tel: 360202).

WATER

Surprisingly, water shortages on Menorca are rare, though restrictions on filling swimming pools with fresh water are sometimes applied; the limestone of which most of the island is composed is well suited to the bulk storage of the winter rains, which are usually sufficient to last the island and its thousands of visitors through the summer. No water is desalinated these days, but it can have a slightly brackish taste nevertheless. As in most parts of Spain the common practice is to drink bottled water, either *con gas* or *sin gas* (fizzy or still), which is widely available at little cost.

NEWSPAPERS AND RADIO

Menorca's daily newspaper is the *Diario Insular de Menorca*, Avenida Central 5, Maó (tel: 361458). Most newspapers from elsewhere in Europe are available in the main population centres, usually a day or two late and at about three times the original price. English-speaking visitors and residents are fortunate in having an excellent English language magazine on the island. This is *Roqueta*, published monthly from April to October and also in December; costing 150 ptas, it is edited from Apt. 201, 07780 Ciutadella (though the editor can also be reached via the English library at Costa d'en Deià, Maó). As well as general articles on restaurants, shops, etc., on the island, the magazine provides a great deal of practical information and full details of cultural and sporting events, fiestas and other activities and is well worth purchasing even if your visit to Menorca is short.

Menorca has its own radio station, Radio Popular de Menorca (Bisbe Vila 7, Ciutadella, tel: 380412). Radio Balearics (25.7 FM) broadcasts 'Listen Menorca' on Saturdays just after noon and on Wednesdays at 19.00. Frequencies on which the World Service of the BBC can be heard include 9.410 MHz from 04.00–07.30 and 16.15–21.15, and 12.095 MHz from 9.00–22.45 (GMT – add one hour in winter and two in summer for local Menorca time). From July to mid-September, ITN broadcasts are relayed on the Tele-Europa programme of Spanish national television (TVE) at 3 p.m., Monday to Friday.

POLICE

There are three police forces in Spain: the paramilitary Guardia Civil, in olive-green uniforms (and once with distinctive patent leather hats, but in recent years these are more rarely seen), who act as traffic police outside the towns; the brown-uniformed Policía Nacional, concerned with law and order in the larger urban areas; and the blue uniformed Policía Municipal, employed by the local authorities – their duties include traffic control, parking, etc. The Guardia Civil are based in Maó on the Sant Lluís road (tel: 361100) and in Ciutadella at Travesía de Gabriel Roca (380299); municipal police are based in or near the *ayuntamiento* of each town. In an emergency the '999' equivalent to telephone is 091.

CONSULATES

The nearest British consulate is at Plaza Mayor, 3d, Palma de Mallorca (tel: 712445), but there is an Honorary Vice Consul on Menorca at Torret 28, Sant Lluís (tel: 366439). The nearest US consulate is at Avda Rey Jaime III, 26, Palma (tel: 722660). Countries which have consulates on Menorca are: France – de l'Església 2, Maó (tel: 363889) and 9 de Juliol 13, Ciutadella (tel: 382781); the Netherlands – Pasaje J.B. Sitjes 4, Maó (tel: 362741); Italy – Norte 2, Maó (tel: 363393); and Germany – d'es Negres (Andreu) 32, Maó (tel: 361668).

BUSINESS SERVICES

The Centro Empresario Menorca (CEM) has recently set up an office in central Maó for businessmen who want a break but do not wish to be out of touch. It offers fax, photocopying and secretarial facilities, as well as a translation service (into six languages). Calls can be taken and messages sent to the businessman's resort by courier. Temporary office accommodation and conference rooms etc. can also be rented. The office is open 8.00–20.00 Monday–Friday (tel: 369163; fax: 362008).

PROPERTY PURCHASE

In certain parts of the island, salesmen of timeshare properties may be a nuisance. If you find their approach tempting, the essential thing to remember is to sign nothing until you have been given a written undertaking that you have the right to change your mind. Do not pay even the most minimal deposit until you are completely sure you want to proceed (and distrust any 'special discounts' or other inducements offered on condition you sign within a short period of time).

If possible, it is a good idea to insist on full written details of what is being offered to you, especially the type of tenure, and any hidden costs such as management charges that it may entail. Just because you are on holiday there is no need to rush into a decision that you would not consider making back home without thinking about it for a while, and preferably taking independent advice! Purchasing a timeshare in the Mediterranean is unlikely to prove an investment that appreciates dramatically, so be really sure you want to commit yourself. Once a purchase has been agreed, remember that a contract signed abroad is covered by Spanish law and a British court will not be able to help if there are any snags. Owning property in Spain, however, will always be attractive to many British people: there are a number of useful books available in the UK which can help you through the intricacies of Spanish property law.

LIBRARY

The English Library on the first floor at Costa d'en Deià 2, Maó (tel: 362701) welcomes temporary members (150 ptas per week, plus a small charge for each book borrowed). It has a collection of some 3000 books, also videos of English films are available for hire and greetings cards are sold. A notice board displays articles for sale and information about local events. The library acts as a meeting place for British and American residents in Menorca. It is open from 10.00–13.00 except on Sundays and fiesta days.

RELIGIOUS SERVICES

Catholic churches are to be found in every town and village on the island; services may be in Castilian or Catalan and most churches display notices showing the times of services and the language to be used, sometimes for all the churches on the island. There are Protestant services during the winter in Maó, at the Iglesia Evangélica, Carrer de l'Angel 2 (tel: 362757), and in Es Castell (Villacarlos), in the church of Nuestra Senora del Rosario, Carrer Victori, during the summer. In addition the Anglican chaplain of Palma (diocese of Gibraltar) holds services on the third Tuesday of the month in Santa Margarita, Carrer Stuart, Es Castell, at 11.00 a.m. Information about additional services is posted on a board outside the church, or information may be obtained from the English Library. Menorca has no synagogue.

GEOLOGY AND CLIMATE

GEOLOGY

Menorca is 48 km. long and between 8 and 19½ km. wide, with a total area of 700 sq. km. Geologically, it can be divided in two by drawing a line along the main road west from Maó as far as the Naveta d'es Tudons, then continuing the line northwards to Cala Morell. South and west of this line is a lowish undulating plateau of tertiary (Miocene) limestone; north of it are sections of red sandstone from the primary (Devonian) period, the most ancient rocks in the Balearics, alternating with (and overlaid by) secondary (Jurassic and Triassic) limestone.

The Devonian sector of the island is believed to be the tip of a lost continent which stretched from Corsica to the Catalan coast of Spain and northwards to southern France: the rock is identical to that of Catalonia and Provence. By contrast, the Miocene tableland of the south was once joined to Mallorca and Ibiza, the whole being a continuation of the Andalucian ranges. During the Cretaceous period, between 65 and 135 million years ago, the two sections joined to form the present island shape; Maó harbour represents the only point where perfect fusion never occurred, and the exceptionally long deep inlet there is the result.

Northern Menorca, or the '*tramuntana*' region, features low hills, wide valleys and a deeply indented rocky coastline with towering headlands. Notable among the large inlets are Fornells bay, Port d'Addaia, Cala Tirant and Cala de Es Grau: all of these have areas of wetland behind them, most importantly the freshwater lake of S'Albufera de Es Grau. The three highest points on the island are Monte Toro (358 m.), midway between Maó and Ciutadella, S'Enclusa (275 m.), 1½ km. north-west of Ferreries and Sant'Agueda (264 m.), 7½ km. north of Ferreries.

The south, or '*migjorn*', region is a rough but fairly low-lying platform of limestone, shading from white to ochre, whose long straight cliff is punctuated by ravines, small coves and longer stretches of white sand. There are streams, but the only one running throughout the year is the Barranc d'Algendar (p. 36), emerging at Cala Galdana.

All four coasts and many places inland are honeycombed with caves, both natural and enhanced by man. Five natural caves deserve an individual mention (clockwise from Maó): *Cova d'els Coloms de Alcaufar* – beneath the cliff on which the defence tower stands at the mouth of Cala d'Alcaufar: it is broad and tall with navigable water, and owes its name to the rock doves nesting there; *Cova d'en Xoroi* – a dramatic grotto with a colourful legend (p. 157), set high in the steep cliff at the eastern side of the mouth of Cala En Porter (has been converted into a bar and nightclub open during the summer); *Cova d'els Coloms de Binigaus* – comparable in size with a cathedral nave, this gigantic cave is in the eastern wall of the gorge behind Platja de Binigaus; *Cova d'els Inglesos* – marine cave in the northern coast of Sa Mola de Fornells, only reachable by sea; the interior is dome-shaped and the sea-bed reflects dazzling colours; *Gruta na Pulida* – the 'polished grotto' is the most notable and least known of Menorcan caves; an immense cavern under Sa Mola de Fornells, whose only entrance is from the sea on the northern side. A labyrinth of passages, chambers and freshwater lakes extends more than 3 km. inland. Discovered by fishermen in 1831, the caves have been explored by only a few people to this day: Juan Sans García of Fornells has produced a booklet, *Notas de Na Pulida*, which contains a plan of the whole cave system. In 1933 an approach was made to the landowner for permission to open an inland entrance, but this was refused and the matter dropped.

Menorca has some fine rock formations (clockwise from Maó): *Es Torn* – natural breakwater protecting Cala d'Alcaufar: an almost central hollow resembles the silhouette of a chef holding an enormous stewpot; *Sa Penya de s'Indio* – the profile of an Indian brave can be discerned when this sandstone rock is viewed from the northern side of the C 721 at km. 19/20 just east of Es Mercadal (parking and picnic area); *Es Pont d'en Aleix* – a limestone arch only visible from the sea between Calas Trebalúger and Mitjana; *Es Pont d'en Gil* – to the south of Cap de Bajolí north of Cala En Forcat: a small boat in full sail can pass through this limestone 'bridge'; *Cul de sa Ferrada* – sculpted sandstone headland to the west of Cala Morell; *Es Cap de Ferro* – at Cala Carbó, east of Algaiarens, an enormous red rock shaped like the head of a warrior; *Es Prego* – sandstone rock on an islet off Cala Pregonda which resembles a hooded monk.

Around 30 islets lie around the coast of Menorca – three of them in Maó harbour. The two largest are the Illa de l'Aire and Illa d'en Colom (see p. 149). Aire is the less interesting: low and featureless with little vegetation, its 300,000 square metres lie off Punta Prima. The rocks slope up to the south where a nineteenth-century lighthouse stands on cliffs some 18 m. high (the light is now automatic).

The island has been owned by the Morales Seguí family for 300 years (during the British occupation it was rented by a Mr Tugent and renamed Coney Island), but in 1989 was up for sale. At present it is uninhabited and the only house on the island has fallen into ruin. There are no boat trips to it, though there is a tiny harbour on the north side used by yachts.

THE ALGENDAR GORGE
(BARRANC D'ALGENDAR)

Finest of the thirty-six limestone gorges in Menorca, for 6 km. it runs between cliffs 50–80 m. high with many caves. Two streams which flow constantly and are fed by numerous small tributaries have carved their separate ravines and join together 1½ km. before the 'Cala Galdana' river meets the sea.

From Cala Galdana, a walk up the gorge starts just beyond the Cala Galdana Hotel. To walk from the upper end, drive up from the resort to the main (C 721) road, turn left for only 100 m., then left onto a tarmacked lane to the right of the entrance to the farm of Biniatrum; 3½ km. down the lane leave the car near a gate marked 'Algendar Vell'. Do not go through the gate but walk down a lane to the right, passing the house of Algendar Nou and following a footpath alongside a stream, past orchards and small market gardens, down to the point where the streams converge, then on to Cala Galdana. Birds of prey wheel above you, and small birds and butterflies dart in and out of the tall bamboos. Near the confluence of the streams an off-putting notice (*'Prohibido el Paso/Finca Privada/Cuidado con los perros'*) has recently appeared, but this is no legal prohibition and should not deter the intrepid, dog-friendly explorer!

Birds in great variety inhabit this gorge and it is not unusual to see red kites, booted eagles and Egyptian vultures. The wild flowers and the humid microclimate create ideal conditions for butterflies, while lizards sun themselves on the rocks. Currently causing much alarm among conservationists is a mooted plan to build an *urbanización* on the corniche between the ravines, and a marina upstream from Cala Galdana. Besides affecting the flora and fauna, these plans would increase the chance of contamination at the mouth of the river; already the rubbish tip of Ferreries threatens to pollute the area, but the authorities are committed to putting this right.

CLIMATE

Menorca lies at 40°N, and is 200 km. from the nearest point

of the Spanish coast and 29 km. NE of Mallorca. It has a true Mediterranean climate, though temperatures are more equable than in the other Balearics and places on the same latitude in mainland Spain. An average year sees less than a 25° variation between summer and winter temperatures, with 315 days of sunshine, 50 overcast and perhaps 80 on which some rain falls. The insolation averages 50 per cent throughout the year and never drops below 30 per cent even in December. Some variation in the weather is noticeable within the island: the south-east is the driest corner, while the heights of S'Enclusa and Sant'Agueda attract abnormally high rainfall. Ciutadella is slightly warmer than Maó.

The tourist season has a very definite duration: 1 May to 31 October. Normal summers are hot, dry and sunny: the maximum temperature ever recorded is 40° C, but the usual summer 'high' is 30°. It is least likely to rain in July and August (though a truly freakish day, 15 August 1918, produced 168 mm.). Humidity in summer is sometimes uncomfortable at around 70% and is fairly high all year round. The sea does not usually become warm enough for swimming until June, but once warmed remains comfortable until the end of October. May and September can be showery, but the wettest months are from October to March or, as local folklore has it, '*de Sant Miquel a Nadal*' ('from Michaelmas to Christmas'). Winter temperatures are mild, averaging 11° C during the day with perhaps a dozen frosty nights in the whole season. Snow is very rare: January 1985 saw the first fall for eleven years. (An all-time low of 2.8° C was reached on 3 February 1956.)

Perhaps Menorca's most criticized climatic characteristic is its winds: no less than eight distinct winds have local names, which as an earlier writer, Denis Taylor, has remarked, 'bespeaks a certain preoccupation with the subject'! These are: *Tramuntana* (north) – the most frequent wind, blowing for some 150 days a year; *Mestral* (northwest) – created by high pressure over France coupled with a depression in the Gulf of Genoa; *Gregal* (north-west); *Mitjorn* (south) – a gentle summer zephyr; *Llebeitx* (southwest) – warm, but can bring rain; *Xaloc* (south-east) – dry and desiccating sirocco, only blows in summer; *Llevant* (east); and *Ponent* (west). The *tramuntana* prevails in winter and is twice as strong in Maó as when it reaches Palma de Mallorca; rough seas follow in its wake. In summer it is less frequent but can blow up very suddenly, creating a hazard for small boats but freshening the high inland temperatures. The widespread destruction of the south-eastern beaches during the winter of 1988/89 can be blamed on the *llebeitx*, which is second only to the *tramuntana* in frequency. Not only were the beaches piled with stones and weed, the fields were covered in salt for miles inland.

Writing in the mid-eighteenth century, a British naval surgeon stationed on Menorca reported 'waterspouts are often seen' in conjunction with the autumn storms. This phenomenon is not commonplace today, but the weather reporter in *Roqueta* recorded seeing one off La Mola at the mouth of Maó harbour in June 1989.

AVERAGE TEMPERATURE TABLE

Month	Temp. range °C	Humidity %	Rainfall mm	Sunshine daily
January	8.0–14.0	77	64	3.5
February	7.9–14.4	76	49	4.6
March	8.4–15.5	76	50	5.7
April	10.2–17.6	77	47	7.2
May	13.5–21.3	71	30	8.5
June	16.8–25.2	67	19	9.8
July	19.8–28.3	65	7	11.1
August	20.5–28.6	68	30	9.6
September	18.5–26.2	73	70	7.2
October	15.1–22.1	75	105	5.7
November	11.2–17.8	77	92	4.3
December	8.8–14.8	77	85	2.9

Source: Centro Meteorologico Zonal, Palma de Mallorca

FEATURES OF THE MENORCAN LANDSCAPE

SHEEP AND CATTLE SHEDS (*Barracas/Ponts*)

A distinctive feature of the landscape are these ziggurat-like constructions in the form of a stepped pyramid from four to seven tiers high. Another practical application for the stone which Menorca so generously provides, these shelters are quite sophisticated structures: the exterior can often be climbed by means of stones projecting from the sides, while the interior, entered by crawling along a passageway under an arch composed of large slabs, usually consists of a surprisingly lofty dome some 3–4 m. high over a circular area of perhaps 7 m. in diameter. Sheep and cattle are protected in them from the harsh conditions of the windy Menorcan winter (and the blazing summers, too, when it is common practice on Menorca for cattle to be let out to graze

A typical Menorcan sheep-shelter

only in the cool of the night). Hard-wearing (one scarcely ever sees an example in disrepair), picturesque and beautifully constructed, most *ponts* appear to have been erected without benefit of mortar or cement, and particularly in the rather featureless landscape of the north-west of the island (where they proliferate), lend an exotic, almost Biblical air to the scenery.

QUARRIES (*Pedreras*)

Menorca's old buildings are built of limestone hewn from these immense pits. Most quarries are open to the sky, for example the one above Cala Mitjaneta which is seen on the walk from Cala Galdana; others are underground and more difficult to work. The stone is cut by machines in rectangular blocks, which are then subdivided as necessary on site. Thus the vertical-sided pits that result look like enormous cellars for some as yet unconstructed building. Many existing quarries were started by the Romans and have been gradually enlarged until the present century. Today, however, concrete is more widely used in construction work and limestone quarrying is in decline.

DEFENSIVE TOWERS (*Torres de Defensa*)

The squat towers positioned at irregular intervals around Menorca's coastline and, less prolifically, inland, were largely built as watchtowers or for active defence against pirates. Each is different in design and today, in disuse, they add an appealing feature to the landscape of Menorca. The inland *torres* date from the fifteenth century: they include that of Sant Lluís and the crenellated Torre de Son Saura in the south-west. These were erected by the landowners for the protection of their labourers: to raise the alarm, a horn would be sounded from the top. A constant watch for North African or Turkish raiders was kept from the coastal towers, one of the earliest of which is Torre de Torret north of Binibeca. Careful spacing enabled each look-out to communicate with the next, and all could signal to Monte Toro, whose garrison overlooked the whole island.

During the eighteenth century, tower walls were strengthened and artillery installed in the upper storeys of some of them. Thirteen such fortified look-outs remain standing and, in places, the bridleway linking them around the coast still survives: the 'Camí de Cavalls' is likely to enjoy a renaissance in our own century, this time for leisure purposes (see p. 106).

The English built the towers on La Mola (Port de Maó), also those of Sant Felip (Es Castell), Es Castellá (Santandría), Sant Nicolau (Ciutadella) and others at or near Sanitja, Fornells (one on Sa Mola and another on Illa Sargantanes), Port d'Addaia, Cala de sa Torreta and Sa Mesquida. The towers at Cala d'Alcaufar and Punta Prima were built by the Spanish after they took over the island in 1782.

FARMHOUSES (*Fincas*)

Throughout Menorca, the simple yet dignified architecture of the farmhouses is very noticeable. The oldest of them perch on the crests of hills, for protection against sea-borne raiders – examples are Santa Elisabet and So N'Ermita (p. 174), and Sa Torre Blanca (p. 66). Some incorporate towers, such as Torre Saura Vell (p. 185), Torre d'en Gaumes (p.

The fortified farmhouse of Torre d'en Quart, north of Ciutadella

72) and Torre d'En Quart (p. 182); all tend to be enclosed by dry-stone walls with rustic Menorcan gates.

Almost always facing south to combat the *tramuntana*, there are often no windows in the northern wall. The traditional Menorcan *finca* consists of a complex of interlocking buildings: the main house, usually whitewashed, may be two or three storeys high with a roof of red tiles; the chimneys are distinctive, each being capped with four tiles leaning against each other. Guttering down the side of the house may consist of similar tiles arranged in opposing steps so that rain splashes from one to the other before reaching the ground and draining into an underground cistern. In a two-storeyed house, the farmer occupies the ground floor, but in a three-storeyed one he may live on the first floor above a tenant. The living accommodation is often fronted by a wide-arched portico, the roof of which lends itself to drying fruit in summer; the top floor of the house is storage space.

Adjoining the main house may be a timber store, elevated laundry terrace and sewing room. Cooking used to be an outdoor task, and many older farms have a domed stone oven adjacent to the building and near the well. Outbuildings, often also adjoining, typically comprise a stable, sheep pen, granary and coach house (now a garage!). More removed from the farmstead are the cowshed, pigsty and straw loft, and a circular threshing floor of tiles enclosed by a rim of limestone blocks is never far away. Some of these farmhouses have been converted into luxurious private houses, while others retain features unchanged for generations: at Sant Rafel, just south of the Maó-Alaior road, for instance, is a shed containing a fascinating range of old farm implements (see Dodo Mackenzie's walk no. 9 in *More Walks in Menorca*).

DRY-STONE WALLS (*Tancas*)

The Menorcan terrain is exceptionally stony, especially in the limestone areas, and all over the island a network of dry-stone walls chequers the landscape. Said to have been introduced by the British governor, Sir Richard Kane, they were primarily built to delineate field boundaries and confine cattle, but also serve to clear the soil for easier ploughing and protect it from salt-laden winds. Many farmers have even enclosed trees within such walls. The technique of dry-stone walling has been passed from father to son; they are always two blocks thick, though the height is variable. The outer stones interlock in herringbone fashion and the whole is topped with heavy flattish stone. At

A pair of typical Menorcan gates

suitable places you will often find that individual stones project at different heights to form steps which enable people to climb over the wall. At a conservative estimate there are 15,000 km. of dry-stone wall on Menorca!

MENORCAN GATES

No visitor can fail to notice the charming and distinctive rustic wooden gates to many fields, farms and gardens on Menorca. Made of thoroughly seasoned branches of the wild olive tree whose natural curves are retained in the struts of the gate, they are wider at the top than the bottom, the historical purpose being to allow laden mules to pass through easily. The hinges of the gates are frequently wooden also, often simply an angled fork of olive-wood held in place by two of the stones in the adjoining wall – a system which works remarkably smoothly. There is, however, often a metal ring to hold a pair of gates together. The tradition of making these gates, which are completely weatherproof, is unique to Menorca, where only a few craftsmen carry on the tradition. One of these, Pedro Pons of Biniparrell (near Sant Lluís), is happy to demonstrate his craft to visitors.

WELLS (*Pous*)

Many of Menorca's wells are ancient: among the few remaining Moorish-influenced artefacts to be seen on the island, the pointed whitewashed stone arches that protect them are reminiscent of wayside shrines. The porous limestone that forms so much of Menorca ensures a plentiful supply of underground water and it is not difficult to spot these distinctive structures in the fields.

LIME KILNS (*Hornos de Calc*)

These now remain as historic monuments but the islanders remember them functioning only 25 years ago. Groups of 12 men worked each kiln under the direction of a leader. A pit of about $2\frac{1}{2}$ m. deep and 5 m. wide was surrounded by a rough stone wall 2 or 3 m. high. The stones destined to become lime (*piedras vivas*) were arranged in a ring around the central hearth and a stone roof, reminiscent of a talayot with chimney holes, built over the whole. Once the fire was lit it was tended night and day for up to a fortnight, the men working shifts. When the flames turned blue, the furnace was plugged and allowed to burn unfed for two or three more days. One firing would produce around 100 tons of lime for whitewashing the houses of the island. Now fallen into desuetude, you may see examples of lime kilns in all parts of Menorca; they are always in or near woodland for the easy availability of fuel.

NATURAL HISTORY

Preservation of the natural beauty of the Balearic Islands is overseen by an unofficial but very active conservation group; its headquarters is in Palma de Mallorca but it has branches in Maó (Isabel II, 42) and Ciutadella (cal Bisbe, 7). This organisation, known as GOB (*Grup Balear d'Ornitologia i Defensa de la Naturalesa*), brings important conservation issues to government and public attention and has done much to protect Menorca from overdevelopment. A periodical, *Socarrell*, published at irregular intervals, highlights current ecological topics: it is obtainable from larger bookshops for 200 ptas. Posters and leaflets are also distributed: in 1989 two of GOB's major concerns have been the threat of development at Cala Trebalúger and the Barranc d'Algendar; both of these proposals have been referred to the courts and, at the time of writing, decisions are anxiously awaited.

The group has also been responsible for the recent updating of the penalties for shooting protected birds: fines of up to one million pesetas may now be levied. Menorca's fishermen work on a small scale and use traditional methods: GOB's powerful influence has ensured that this situation continues. Summer 1989 also saw the Guardia Civil being given responsibility to protect flora and fauna and to stop illegal dumping, hunting and fishing.

FLOWERING PLANTS

In spring and autumn the fields, verges, woods and cliffs of Menorca are ablaze with flowers. Spring comes early, in February, and autumn lingers into December; only in the depths of winter are the flowering species dormant. Many field and wayside plants are instantly recognisable to a British eye, but, as in all islands, sub-species have developed to suit the environment exactly and some of these are unique to Menorca.

The catalogue below does not claim to be a complete list of Menorcan flowers, but it is hoped it will give an indication of what may be expected. As field guides, Anthony Bonner's *Plants of the Balearic Islands* and *Flowers of the Mediterranean* by Oleg Polunin and Anthony Huxley are recommended.

Allium ampeloprasum   wild leek. Tall plant with spherical heads of white or pink flowers on a thick stem. The whole plant has an onion smell. June–July.

Allium roseum   rose garlic. Dainty heads of pink flowers on stalks up to 40 cm. high: entire plant smells of garlic. April–June.

Allium triquetrum   pendulous, bell-shaped white flowers on triangular-sectioned stems. March–May.

Anthemis maritima   dune chamomile. Highly aromatic plant with yellow and white 'daisies' and fleshy leaves. June–August.

Arisarum vulgare   friar's cowl. Peculiar-looking plant with a stripy purple spathe (sheath) which bends forward to imitate a cowl. March–May and Oct–Nov.

Arum italicum   Italian arum. Like the British wild arum, except that the spathe is greenish-yellow rather than white. April–May.

Asphodelus aestivus   asphodel (*Asfodelo*). Tall plant growing on stony, over-grazed or infertile ground. The tubers are rich in starch and were used by shoemakers and book-binders to make glue. Pyramidal clusters of starry pink or white flowers with red veins. April–June.

Asphodelus fistulosus   asphodel (*Gamón*). Smaller plant of the same habitat as above, with similar flowers and rush-like leaves. April–May.

Asteriscus maritimus   sea aster. Similar in flower to the yellow marigold, a mat-like plant which grows only on the coast. May–July.

Barlia robertiana   giant orchid. Reddish to dull green cylindrical cluster of flowers; large and rather unattractive, but smells like lily of the valley. Feb–April.

Bellardia trixago   Somewhat reminiscent of the garden antirrhinum; pink and yellow flower. April–July.

Bellis annua   annual daisy. Like the British common daisy but with leaves up the stem. Dec–May.

Bellis sylvestris   southern daisy. Very like the British common daisy but much taller. Oct–April.

Cakile maritima   sea rocket. Prostrate plant of the sandy shores, with mauve flowers like lady's smock. May–Sept.

Calendula arvensis   field marigold (*Maravilla*). Smaller, wilder brother of the garden marigold. April–Oct, and sometimes through the winter.

Calystegia soldanella   sea bindweed. Pale pink flower with white stripes and kidney-shaped fleshy leaves. May–Oct.

Carlina corymbosa involucrata   flat-topped carline thistle. Very prickly yellow thistle growing to 50 cm. high. Widespread. June–August.

Centaurea balearica   Balearic centaury. Prickly low-growing 'cushion' of purple flowers. An endangered species, it still grows on Cap de Faváritx. May–July.

Centaurea calcitrapa   star thistle. Pink with smallish purple flowers having long yellow spines radiating from their bases. Aug–Sept.

Chrysanthemum coronarium   crown daisy (*Pajitos*). Handsome tall yellow or yellow and white daisy, often in large clumps on waste ground. April–Sept.

Cichorium intybus   chicory (*Anchicoria*). Pale to bright blue dandelion-like flowers on a tall plant: usually found on limestone. May–Sept.

Conium maculatum   hemlock. Well-known in Britain and recognisable by the purple dots on the stem. Highly poisonous. June–August.

Convolvulus althaeoides   mallow-leaved bindweed. Sprawls along the ground or climbs walls; pink flowers. April–August.

Convolvulus arvensis   field bindweed. Pink-flowered rambler distinguished by its arrow-shaped leaves.

Crepis triasii   yellow hawksbeard. Rosette of leaves forms flat against the cliffs; flowers small, yellow, several to a stem. April–June.

Crithmum maritimum   rock samphire. Greyish plant with pale yellow flowers found growing in rock crevices by the sea; edible.

Crocus minimus cabessedesii   Balearic crocus. White or mauve flowers in very early spring.

Cyclamen balearicum   Balearic cyclamen. Miniature cyclamen with white flowers and greyish mottled leaves; prefers damp places. June–Oct.

Cynara cardunculus   cardoon. Wild brother of the globe artichoke and similar in appearance. July–August.

Daphne rodriguezii   small relation of *Daphne gnidium* (see p. 50) found on the east coast of Menorca and on the Illa d'en Colom. May–Sept.

Daucus carota   Queen Anne's lace. The wild carrot; tall plant with white umbels of flowers and feathery leaves; familiar in Britain. May–Oct.

Digitalis purpurea dubia   foxglove (*Dedalera*). This variety is endemic and can be white or pink with purple spots; the island's most poisonous plant; may be seen near Sa Cudia Nova and at Binigaus. May–August.

Dorycnium pentaphyllum   very small pink flowers in clusters; leaves in groups of five up the stem; important in honey production. April–July.

Dracunculus vulgaris   dragon arum (*Serpentina*). Sinister-looking dark purple spathe with unpleasant smell; conspicuously veined leaves. April–June.

Ecballium elaterium   squirting cucumber. Grows on waste-ground and has fruits like small gherkins which explode when touched. The poisonous liquid and seed can be shot as far as 2 m.: protect the eyes if going near this plant. April–Sept.

Eryngium campestre   field eryngo. Not a true thistle, but very spiny. Green flowers surrounded by spear-like bracts. Prefers stony areas. June–Sept.

Eryngium maritimum   sea holly. Bluish-green plant with bluish globular flower heads which are also prickly. The plant resembles a prostrate holly and grows on sand dunes. June–Sept.

Euphorbia characias   large Mediterranean spurge. Green flowers with reddish-brown glands make this a spectacular spurge. It prefers stony ground. April–July.

Euphorbia paralias   sea spurge. Tall spurge with stiff stems; can grow out of sand dunes. May–Sept.

Ferula communis   giant fennel (*Cañaheja*). Can grow to 3 m. tall with umbels of $\frac{1}{2}$ m. diameter; florets are yellowish. June–Sept.

Foeniculum vulgare   common fennel. Can grow to 2 m., but never as robustly as *ferula communis*. Used in cooking.

Galactites tomentosa   purple or white, rather delicate thistle commonly seen in fields or on wasteground. April–July.

Gladiolus illyricus   field gladiolus (*Gladiolo*)/*Gladiolus Segetum*. Startlingly like a small garden gladiolus; bright pink flowers; former species is more common, but the latter bears larger flowers. April–June.

Glaucium flavium   yellow-horned poppy. Gold-yellow flowers and glaucous greyish-green leaves; usually found on shingle. May–August.

Helichrysum lanarckii cambessedesii   (*Siempreviva*) endemic to the Balearics and on Menorca confined to the slopes of Monte Toro; silvery rosette of leaves and dryish yellow flowers. April–July.

Hypericum balearicum   St John's wort (*Estepa juana*). An endemic species similar in appearance to the familiar *hypericum*, but sticky and resinous. May–August.

Leucojum aestivum pulchellum   summer snowflake. Very graceful narcissus bell-shaped white flowers edged with green. April–June.

Limonium capariense   statice (*Acelga silvestre*). One of ten species of statice or 'winged sea lavender' endemic to the Balearics. Bluish-mauve papery flowers. April–Sept.

Lobularia maritima   sweet alison. Round heads of white or pale pink flowers; a member of the cress family. Dec–August.

Lotus tetraphyllus   small plant with four leaflets and small yellow pea-type flower; found in woodland. April–June.

Matthiola sinuata   sea stock (*Alheli*). Pink or purple sweet-scented flowers and grey-green leaves; on cliffs. March–May.

Merendera filifolia   wild saffron (*Azufre*). Not the true saffron crocus but a tiny pink lily; rare but grows near Cala En Turqueta. Sept–Oct.

Mesembryanthemum crystallinum   mesembryanthemum. Creeping succulent found on rocks or coastal cliffs: the large white daisy-like flowers grow among 'frosted' fleshy green leaves. April–June.

Muscari atlanticum neglectum   southern grape hyacinth (*Jacinto de Penacho*). Familiar to British gardeners; grows on old walls and in fields. Mar–May.

Muscari comosum   tassel hyacinth. Two kinds of blue flowers borne on one stem; erect bright blue florets at the top and horizontally spreading dark blue ones further down; found on stony ground. April–July.

Narcissus serotinus autumn narcissus. Fragrant white flower with yellow centre and tallish stem; in woods and hedgerows. Oct–Nov.

Nasturtium officinale watercress (*Berros*). Grows, as in Britain, near streams and irrigation canals.

Ornithogalum arabicum Clusters of creamy white flowers with distinctive dark 'eyes' and yellow stamens; in rocky dry areas, notably Son Vitamina. April–May.

Ophrys apifera bee orchid. Furry reddish brown lip has two yellow spots at the base; overall shape resembles a bee. April–May.

Ophrys bertolonii Bertoloni's orchid. Showy flower with black velvety lip and pinkish-purple petals. March–April.

Ophrys bombyliflora bumble-bee orchid. Recognisable resemblance to the insect. March–April.

Ophrys fusca brown bee orchid. The most widespread orchid in Menorca. Velvety blue and brown flower. Jan–May.

Ophrys lutea yellow bee orchid. Yellow and green with a brown bee-like centre. March–May.

Ophrys speculum mirror of Venus. So named because of its reflective blue shiny centre with narrow yellow border. March–April.

Ophrys sphegodes atrata early spider orchid. Flower has an H-shaped centrepiece. Feb–April.

Ophrys tenthredinifera sawfly orchid. Very pretty pink and gold oval flowers with green veins. March–May.

Orchis tridentata toothed orchid. Conical cluster of pink- and white-spotted flowers which are fragrant; found in woodland. March–May.

Oxalis pes-caprae Bermuda buttercup. Pretty but invasive weed with umbels of yellow five-petalled flowers and leaves like a clover. Dec–May.

Paeonia cambessedesii Balearic peony. Magnificent deep red flower with yellow stamens; grows mainly in woodland. Rare. May–June.

Pancratium maritimum sea daffodil (*Nardo marino*). Fragrant white flower growing from sand dunes; both flowers and leaves resemble those of the familiar daffodil. July–Sept.

Papaver rhoeas corn poppy (*Amapola*). Turns entire fields scarlet in May and June.

Papaver somniferum opium poppy. Greyish waxy leaves and mauve or white flowers; formerly used in the Balearics for medicinal purposes. June–July.

Psoralea bituminosa pitch trefoil. Mauve or blue clover-like plant whose crushed leaves smell surprisingly of tar. April–July.

Reseda alba/lutea white/yellow mignonette. Both have slender spikes of flowers from May–Sept.

Rubia peregrina wild madder. Climber with curved thorns and greenish-yellow flowers; also very common in Britain. May–July.

Santolina chamaecyparissus magonica chamomile of Mahón. Very localized lavender cotton confined to the east coast. June–Sept.

Scabiosa atropurpurea maritima sweet scabious. Reddish-purple scabious also known as 'mournful widow'. June–Oct.

Senecio rodriguezii (Camomila del Mar). Attractive pale pink daisy with darker centre. Large toothed leaves with purple undersides. March–May.

Sinapis arvensis charlock. The familiar bright yellow 'wild mustard' which is a plague in cultivated fields. March–May.

Smyrnium olusatrum alexanders. Shade-loving plant with green umbels, trifoliate leaves and edible stalks. April–June.

Sonchus asper prickly sow thistle (*Lletsó*). Umbels of yellow daisy-like flowers on bristly stalks; known as 'milk plant', its stem contains a latex which can be used in salads. May–Sept.

Teuchrium chamaedrys wall germander. This member of the mint family has whorls of reddish-pink flowers and leaves like a miniature oak. May–Sept.

Trifolium stellatum star clover. Woolly heads with pink flowers and conspicuous bright red star-shaped calices. March–June.

Urginea maritima sea squill (*Cebolla albarrana*). A tall spike of white flowers appears in September from an enormous bulb. Broad glossy leaves follow in spring. August–Oct.

Urospermum dalechampii single pale yellow flowers with scores of petals as in a dandelion; stem and leaves are downy. May–June.

Vinca difformis periwinkle. Familiar pale blue-flowered prostrate plant usually growing in the shade. Feb–May.

TREES AND SHRUBS

When the first navigators arrived in Menorca they found a thickly forested island. The recession of these forests was caused directly by man felling trees to create space for cultivation or burning them for fuel; and indirectly by his introduction of domestic animals, particularly goats. Only 10 per cent of the island is wooded today: the most extensive areas of mixed woodland are in the north – La Vall, Arenal d'en Castell, Arenal de S'Olla (Son Parc), Sant' Agueda, S'Enclusa, south of Fornells bay and a very large tract extending from Port d'Addaia to Alaior. In the south, substantial pinewoods remain between Arenal de Son Saura and Platja de Binigaus; the last survivors of an ancient ilex forest crowd the gorge of Rincó de Rafalet.

The predominating island trees are Aleppo pine (*pino*), ilex (*encina*), mastic tree (*lentisco*) and myrtle (*mirto*). The list below is intended to be used only in conjunction with a field guide: most are described in Polunin and Huxley's *Flowers of the Mediterranean* and more fully in the excellently illustrated *Trees and Bushes of Britain and Europe* by Oleg Polunin.

Arbutus unedo   strawberry tree (*Madroño*). So named for its edible red fruits resembling strawberries. Flowers reminiscent of lily of the valley are often seen on the tree simultaneously.

Asparagus acutifolius   hardy asparagus. Scrambling plant with spiny leaves, bearing black fruit in summer.

Asparagus stipularis   asparagus (*Espárrago*). Rambling, thorny shrub with edible shoots in spring; grows in dry limestone areas.

Calycotome spinosa   thorny broom (*Retama espinosa*). Covered with glorious yellow flowers in spring, hiding its thorns which may be up to 5 cm. long.

Capparis spinosa   caper (*Alcaparra*). Very showy wall plant, having large white flowers with mauve stamens. The capers are the flower buds; the fruits at 5 cm. long, with crimson pith and purple seeds. June–Sept.

Ceratonia siliqua   carob or locust tree (*Algarrobo*). The only species on earth of its genus; capable of growing in very hot, arid conditions. Flowers and fruit sprout from the middle of a branch or from the trunk; the beans are borne in long pendulous pods. The fruits contain 50 per cent sugar.

Chamaerops humilis   dwarf fan palm. The only palm which is a native of Europe; found in woodland on parts of the north coast.

Cistus albidus   grey-leaved cistus (*Jara*). Showy pink flowers, up to 6 cm. across; the leaves scent the air in summer with a resiny fragrance. April–June.

Cistus incanus   pink rock-rose similar to *C. albidus*, but the leaves have longer stalks. Rather uncommon.

Cistus monspeliensis   narrow-leaved cistus. Small white flowers and sticky, aromatic, lance-shaped leaves. April–June.

Cistus salvifolius   sage-leaved cistus (*Estepa negra*). Rock-rose with large white flowers; not aromatic. March–June.

Clematis cirrhosa balearica   virgin's bower. Bell-shaped flowers which may be white or spotted with purple. Jan–March.

Clematis flammula   fragrant clematis. Similar to the British Traveller's Joy, but with larger and sweet-scented flowers. June–August.

Cytinus ruber/hypocistis   red and yellow respectively, these are parasitic plants with clusters of fleshy flowers and no leaves; sometimes found under cistus bushes.

Daphne gnidium   small shrub with fragrant white flowers and small black and red berries, both borne in summer. Should not be handled as the resin and fruits are poisonous.

Erica arborea   tree heath (*Brezo*). Grows 2–3 m. high and bears pale pink or white flowers in late winter and early spring. Abundant in patches of northern Menorca and on the hill of Sant 'Agueda.

Erica scoparia   green heather. Found in the wetter areas of the north; has a greenish flower, May–July.

Euphorbia dendroides   tree spurge. Can grow to 2 m. high and usually in a perfect hemisphere. Flowers bright green; the reddish stems contain a milky juice.

Globularia alypum   shrubby globularia. Low-growing shrub with brittle twigs, small leathery leaves and sweet-scented clusters of tiny blue flowers for most of the year.

Hedera helix   common ivy (*Hiedra*). Can grow with or without support. Sheep are fond of its leaves!

Juniperus oxycedrus   prickly juniper (*Enebro*). Very spiny grey-green shrub widespread in the scrublands. Oil from the unripe berries (known as 'cade') is used for skin complaints. The ripe berries are blue black.

Lavandula stoechas   French lavender (*Lavanda*). Familiar to all and used in perfume, it flowers in the spring.

Lonicera implexa   honeysuckle (*Madreselva*). Evergreen leaves and wonderfully fragrant flowers all summer.

Myrtus communis   myrtle (*Mirto*). Dark green shrub producing very fragrant white flowers with prominent stamens in late spring; a blue-black berry follows. When crushed the leaves of the myrtle exude a lemon-scented essence which is used in perfumes.

Olea europaea oleaster   wild olive (*Acebuche*). Grows on arid ground in full sun and bears an inferior fruit unsuitable for oil. Now a protected species due to diminishing numbers.

Pinus halepensis   Aleppo pine (*Pino*). Widespread over the island and capable of growing to 20 m. Often the trunk becomes twisted by the wind and occasionally grows almost parallel to the ground.

Pinus pinea   umbrella pine. Introduced by man and not common. Some fine specimens stand by the road between Ferreries and Es Migjorn Gran; yields pine nuts for cooking.

Pistacia lentiscus   lentisk or mastic tree (*Lentisco*). Occurs in every type of location and is recognisable by the powerful resinous scent emanating from its leathery leaves. The flowers are red or brown and the round fruits are black when ripe.

Quercus ilex   holm oak (*Encina*). Seldom exceeds 15 m. in height; yields acorns for pigs, wood for charcoal and tannin for medicines, setting dyes and tanning hides.

Rhamnus alaternus   Mediterranean buckthorn (*Ladierno*). Common in the areas of 'maquis', it is most easily distinguished in summer, when it bears glossy red, purple and black berries; a stiff-looking shrub with small shiny leaves.

Rosa sempervirens   wild rose (*Rosa*). White flowers in spring.

Rosmarinus officinalis   rosemary (*Romero*). Very well-known, grows on dry scrubland and can have blue, white or pink flowers all year round. As well as its uses in cooking, honey, infusions and perfume, it has antiseptic properties.

Rubus ulmifolius   bramble (*Zarza*). Well-known rambler; a safe refuge for nesting birds and a source of delicious fruit.

Ruscus aculeatus   butcher's broom. Small spiny shrub with bright red berries borne in winter; a native of Britain.

Smilax aspera balearica   Balearic sarsaparilla (*Zarzaparrilla*). Thorny rambler which often trails on the ground, tangling itself into a snare for the unwary walker; its young shoots may be eaten like asparagus.

Tamarix gallica   tamarisk (*Taray*). Tree or shrub with feathery grey-green leaves on red wood; spikes of delicate pink flowers from spring to summer.

Vitex agnus-castus   chaste tree (*Sauzgatillo*). Autumn-flowering deciduous shrub, whose flowers grow in fragrant violent racemes; once believed to be a preserver of chastity, it is also called 'Abraham's balm'. Grows most notably by the shore at Cala Ets Alocs, to which it gives its Menorquín name.

BIRDS

A range of habitats – woodland, marsh, cliffs, arable land and a freshwater lake – provide for a wide variety of birds, many of which nest on Menorca. In addition, the Balearics are a staging post for migrants who arrive and depart in their thousands each spring and autumn. Northbound birds mingle with southbound, offering great excitement for the bird-watcher. The majority of birds are typically European/Mediterranean, but a few come from Africa. Binoculars are a must for anyone interested in identification, and spring, when the birds are most active and musical, is a particularly rewarding time.

Recommended areas for observation are S'Albufera de Es Grau, where the area around the lake is now officially an ecological zone, La Vall, Fornells, Port d'Addaia and the gorges of the south. The north coast is richer in seabirds' nesting sites and is the only place to see the rare Audouin's gull: the Balearics provide its main European nesting place. Brightly coloured bee-eaters, hoopoes and blue rock-thrushes always enchant and the great birds of prey, red kites, eagles and osprey, astonish with their majesty.

The following list is merely for guidance; Ian Hepburn's *A Birdwatcher's Guide to Mallorca and the other Balearic Islands*, to be published in 1990, is recommended.

Audouin's gull   *Larus audonii*. Nearly as large as a herring gull, this rare and diminishing species is a paler and more elegant bird, distinguished by its red beak with a black band and yellow tip. The Balearics are one of its few nesting places in the world.

Barn owl   *Tyto alba (Lechuza)*. The white-faced barn owl with its eerie screech is fairly common; nests in towers and caves.

Bee-eater   *Merops apiaster (Abejaruco)*. Brightly coloured bird seen near sandy banks or dunes where it likes to build its nest; its back is chestnut, underparts jade green and throat bright yellow; feeds on wasps as well as bees.

Blackbird   *Turdus merula (Mirlo)*. Well-known to all, the blackbird sings in Menorca from January to August; hunted illegally for the table, it is not as bold as in the UK.

Blackcap   *Sylvia atricapilla (Curruca capirotada)*. Grey and brown warbler with a black head which usefully eats insects; the sweetness of its song is second only to that of the nightingale.

Black-headed gull *Larus ridibundus (Gaviota reidora)*. Very familiar in ploughed fields as well as by the sea, this gull is a winter visitor to the Balearics; it returns to northern Europe in March for the breeding season.

Black-winged stilt *Himantopus himantopus (Cigüeñuela)*. Unmistakable black and white wader with very long red legs; a summer visitor; can be seen in shallow ponds and marshes.

Blue rock thrush *Monticola solitarius (Roquere solitario)*. Handsome dark blue bird seen on cliffs or on top of buildings. Common on Menorca.

Booted eagle *Hieraaetus pennatus (Águila calzada)*. The smallest European eagle, around 50 cm. in length; used to be seen fairly frequently in the Balearics, but has now been hunted almost to extinction; may occasionally be seen in the wilder gorges of southern Menorca and the central hills.

Chaffinch *Fringilla coelebs (Pinzón)*. The commonest finch in Europe is widely resident in Menorca.

Common sandpiper *Actitis hypoleucos (Andarríos)*. Attractive brown and white wader which winters on the island; prefers small areas of fresh water to large expanses, and is also found in stagnant pools left by dried-up rivers.

Cory's shearwater *Calonectris diomedea (Pardela ceniaenta)*. Oceanic bird with a wide wing-span, greyish-brown back and white underparts; its habit is to skim the water and 'bank' like a plane; often approaches boats.

Cuckoo *Cuculus canorus (Cuco)*. Arrives in Menorca in March or April and usually chooses the nest of the Sardinian warbler; a voracious insect-eater regarded by farmers as a desirable visitor.

Curlew sandpiper *Calidris ferruginea (Correlimos zarapitin)*. Shore bird with a conspicuous down-curved beak, rather similar in appearance to the dunlin; a fairly common migrant, often seen with little stints.

Dunlin *Calidris alpina (Correlimos común)*. Brownish-grey wader familiar to British bird-watchers; a passage migrant, breeding in northern Europe and visiting Menorca in spring and autumn.

Egyptian vulture *Neophron percnopterus (Alimocha)*. Menorca is its only breeding place in the Balearics; it nests in the gorges of the south. It is entirely white, except for black wing tips, and has a yellow, black-tipped beak.

Goldfinch *Carduelis carduelis (Jilguero)*. This bird appears brighter than the northern goldfinch; seen typically in fields of thistle or in gardens of towns and villages.

Great tit *Parus major (Carbonero común)*. The largest of its family, the bird uses nesting boxes as in the UK.

Greater flamingo *Phoenicopterus ruber (Flamenco)*. A very recognisable bird, but its numbers are dwindling; an irregular winter visitor to the Albufera and now a protected species.

Greenfinch   *Carduelis chloris (Verderón)*. Familiar to the British birdwatcher, the greenfinch is a friend to the farmer as it eats insects and larvae.

Green sandpiper   *Tringa ochropus (Andarríos grande)*. A black and white bird rather than a green one! Legs olive-coloured; frequents small ponds and ditches rather than large stretches of water; a winter visitor.

Herring gull   *Larus argentatus (Gaviota argentea)*. Well-known large grey and white gull, having a bright yellow bill with a vermilion spot; apart from the rarely seen Audouin's gull, the only gull to breed in the Balearics.

Hoopoe   *Upupa epops (Abubilla)*. Unmistakable both when seen and heard; cinnamon-coloured with black and white striped wings and a prominent black and white tipped crest. Its call can be heard throughout the island in spring: 'hoohoohoo!'.

House martin   *Delichon urbica (Avión común)*. Blue-black and white bird, very gregarious and often seen in the towns, where it makes its nest under the eaves of houses; very common summer visitor to Menorca.

House sparrow   *Passer domesticus (Gorrión común)*. The common sparrow of Britain, equally common on Menorca.

Iberian yellow wagtail   *Motacilla flava iberiae (Lavandera boyera)*. Distinctive yellow-breasted bird which breeds on Menorca and is fond of feeding among cattle; also enjoys arable land and dry heaths.

Kentish plover   *Charadrius alexandrinus (Chortilejo patinegro)*. Commonest of the small wading birds which may be found inland as well as on the beaches; grey-brown upper parts, white underneath with black collar and face markings.

Kestrel   *Falco tinnunculus (Cernicalo)*. Resident falcon, about 34 cm. long, with reddish-brown plumage spotted with black, and a grey tail with black and white tip; often seen hovering over farmland; *Xoriguer* in Menorquín.

Lapwing   *Vanellus vanellus (Avetria)*. Handsome crested bird seen in large numbers in winter on cultivated land; a valuable friend to farmers as it feeds on insects and larvae.

Linnet   *Carduelis cannabina (Pardillo)*. Handsome finch with crimson breast; frequents the open countryside, usually in small flocks. Voracious insect-eater.

Little ringed plover   *Charadrius dubius (Chortilejo Chico)*. Pretty little wader which runs along the sand at the sea's edge; grey and white with black markings on face and neck.

Little stint   *Calidris minuta (Correlimos menuda)*. Very small red-brown wader which is a common passage migrant in spring and autumn; frequents marshes and salt flats.

Mallard   *Anas Platyrhynchos (Ánade real)*. Familiar wild duck with dark green head and white collar; some pairs nest on the island, others are winter visitors. Their numbers have been seriously diminished by hunting.

Marmora's warbler   *Sylvia sarda balearica (Curruca sarda)*

Grey warbler with upturned long tail; resident and common on the Balearics, but often unnoticed as it tends to skulk.

Marsh harrier *Circus aeruginosus (Aguilucho lagunero)*. Rust-brown bird of prey with bright yellow legs; fairly frequent in marshy areas of the island; a winter visitor.

Meadow pipit *Anthus pratensis (Bisbita común)*. Formerly preyed upon by agricultural workers, this small brown bird is now protected and flocks can sometimes be seen walking over cultivated land; also frequents damp marshland.

Moorhen *Gallinula chloropus (Polla de agua)*. A familiar water bird, resident in Menorca but much more secretive than its British counterpart.

Nightingale *Luscinia megarhynchos (Ruiseñor)*. A wonderful singer, heard during the day as well as night in spring and summer. Prefers wooded or marshy areas; often seen as well as heard.

Osprey *Pandion haliaetus (Águila pescadora)*. Magnificent bird, appearing white from below, but with brown back and tail. Nests on inaccessible cliffs and feeds on fish; for this reason has not been hunted by 'sporting' land-owners.

Pallid swift *Apus pallidus (Vencejo pálido)*. Similar to the familiar dark swift, but beige in colour and a strictly Mediterranean bird; in Menorca it is almost as common as the dark swift and nests under the eaves of houses.

Peregrine falcon *Falco peregrinus (Halcón común)*. Black and grey with definite stripes; a resident, nesting on cliffs and inland crags; feeds on pigeons, doves and starlings.

Pintail *Anas acuta (Ánade rabudo)*. Grey and white duck with a long dark pointed tail; a very common winter visitor, but a favourite of local marksmen.

Purple heron *Ardea purpurea (Garza imperial)*. Smaller than the familiar grey heron, darker and with a more snake-like neck and quicker wing-beat; visits the wetlands of Son Bou and Albufera during the spring.

Quail *Coturnix coturnix (Codorniz)*. Smaller than the partridge,

The lake of S'Albufera is now a designated nature reserve

this fat brown game bird nests in grass or growing crops; passage migrant but some pairs regularly breed near the Albufera and on arable land.

Raven   *Corvus corax (Cuervo)*. Easily identifiable by its size, it soars and nose-dives up the wild cliff-faces of the northern coast; its croak is very eerie.

Red kite   *Milvus milvus (Milano real)*. The most striking of Menorca's birds of prey; predominantly reddish-brown with a deeply forked tail; prefers hilly wooded country and nests on inaccessible cliffs in the south and centre of the island.

Red-legged partridge   *Alectoris rufa (Perdiz)*. Squat game bird, also common in the UK. When startled it rises suddenly from the undergrowth or cultivated land, its wings making a loud whirring.

Redshank   *Tringa totanus (Archibebe común)*. Shy wader recognisable by its long scarlet legs; a common winter visitor, frequenting the Albufera, where it swims as well as wades.

Reed warbler   *Acrocephalus scirpaceus (Carricero común)*. Rusty brown with a pale chest, this flitting little bird likes to sing from the top of a reed.

Robin   *Erithacus rubecula (Petirrojo)*. Well known on Menorca in winter; seen in pine forest, orchards, gardens – or anywhere!

Rock dove   *Columba livia (Paloma bravia)*. Blue-grey bird, the wild forebear of the domestic pigeon; fairly common resident, nesting in cliffs and caves; true to its name, it never perches in trees.

Sand martin   *Riparia riparia (Avión zapador)*. Brown and white bird, frequently seen in the air and often in flocks; some nest in sandy banks, but more usually a bird of passage.

Sardinian warbler   *Sylvia melanocephala (Curruca cabecinegra)*. Dark back and wings with a white throat and tail; prefers the dry areas of the island and draws attention to itself with an alarm call resembling the winding of a clock.

Serin   *Serinus serinus (Verdecillo)*. Somewhat canary-like finch seen in the pinewoods; its song is a jangling trill. Regular winter visitor.

Shag   *Phalacrocorax aristotelis (Cormorán Moñudo)*. Dark brown and black sea-bird whose feathers have a green and blue gloss; flies only a metre above the sea and is usually noticed when sitting on rocks, drying its outspread wings.

Short-toed lark   *Calandrella brachydactyla (Terrera común)*. Like a miniature skylark in all its habits; common on the island and sings very sweetly.

Skylark   *Alauda arvensis (Alondra común)*. The familiar skylark is a winter visitor to Menorca and is not heard or seen after April, when it flies north.

Snipe   *Gallinago gallinago (Agachadiza común)*. Brownish bird with darker head which visits the island in winter. Unfortunately hunted on the marshes and moorland, but numbers have not yet been seriously depleted.

Song thrush *Turdus philomelos (Zorzal común)*. Abundant winter visitor, but much wilder than in the UK due to the Balearic habit of killing thrushes for food.

Spotted flycatcher *Muscicapa striata (Papamoscas gris)*. Small brown and white bird usually seen sitting on a post or fence looking out for insects; after it has caught its prey it returns to the same perch.

Starling *Sturnus vulgaris (Estornino pinto)*. Too familiar to need description, it is a winter visitor to Menorca.

Stock dove *Columba oenas (Paloma zurita)*. Smaller than a wood pigeon, although similar, this is an autumn and winter visitor; rather uncommon.

Stonechat *Saxicola torquata (Tarabilla común)*. Black head, russet chest and white collar; probably more common in Menorca than in the other Balearics, this bird loves gorse and heathland.

Stone curlew *Burhinus oedicnemus (Alcaraván)*. Sandy brown, long-legged bird with unusually large yellow eyes; runs very fast and frequents open stony land or sandy patches; its cry is a strange wail.

Swallow *Hirundo rustica (Golondrina común)*. Spring migrant; the majority pass over the island in April and some stay to nest. They are seen again in great numbers flying south in late September.

Swift *Apus apus (Vencejo)*. Abundant summer visitor, perhaps most of all to Maó. This gliding, turning bird is incredibly regular in its dates of arrival and departure each year.

Thekla lark *Galerida theklae (Cogujada montesina)*. Fairly common in Menorca this lark has a distinct crest; unusually unafraid of man, it is frequently seen with its mate, singing from the tops of cistus or juniper bushes.

Tufted duck *Aythya fuligula (Porrón Moñudo)*. Black and white diving duck which visits the marshlands in winter; not hunted to excess.

Turtle dove *Streptopelia turtur (Tórtola común)*. Small brown and white dove with a soft purring call; hunted in season.

Water rail *Rallus aquaticus (Rascón)*. Nervous bird with chestnut back, grey face and underparts, black and white striped legs and a red bill; lives in marshlands and becomes very vocal in the evenings.

Wheatear *Oenanthe oenanthe (Collalba gris)*. Small grey and white bird with white rump and black and white tail; a summer visitor, breeding on the island; can usually be seen around drystone walls.

White wagtail *Motacilla alba (Lavendera blanca)*. Very long-tailed black and white running bird; a frequent winter visitor to the Balearics, it is seen most often near farms or in towns.

Wigeon *Anas penelope (Ánade silbón)*. Predominantly brown duck with yellow forehead and chestnut neck; winter visitor, liking sandy shores as well as the Albufera.

Willow warbler *Phylloscopus trochilis (Mosquitero musical)*.

Winter and spring visitor; small olive-brown bird usually noticed while singing in woodland areas.

Woodchat shrike *Lanius senator badius (Alcudón común)*. The only member of the shrike family which is abundant in the Balearics; nests in pines or orchards and impales small birds on thorns or barbed wire for later consumption.

Woodcock *Scolopax rusticola (Becada)*. Migrant from northern Europe; attractively barred plumage in shades of brown, affording excellent camouflage; very varied habitat: woods, orchards, 'maquis' and ditches. Hunted in season.

Wood pigeon *Columba palumbus (Paloma torcaz)*. Familiar bird to all birdwatchers, not as common in Menorca as in the U.K. Found mainly in pinewoods; very shy.

Wren *Troglodytes troglodytes (Chochín)*. Irregular winter visitor to Menorca. Its surprisingly loud song is often heard when the bird is concealed.

ANIMALS

All the mammals in the Balearics are descended from European and Peninsular species, except the hedgehog (*Erinaceus algirus vagans*), which was introduced from North Africa. First recorded in Menorca in 1901, it is smaller than its European cousin, has shorter spines, larger ears and is paler in colour. The indigenous rabbit, *Orytolagus cuniculus algirus*, is the same creature found in North Africa but has been in the Balearics for centuries: in his *Natural History* Pliny refers to the abundance of rabbits. In woodland glades you may see the Spanish hare (*Lepus granatensis*), which is smaller than the European animal and has reddish feet with a white stripe on top. Also living in areas of dense vegetation are the weasel (*Mustela nivalis*), Balearic dormouse (*Eliomys quercinus gymnesicus*), Balearic shrew (*Crocidura balearica*) and the woodmouse (*Apodemus sylvaticus*). Squirrels are now extinct, although their skeletal remains have been found; there are no moles on the island. Eleven species of bat make their homes in the inland caves. Dolphins play in the coastal waters.

Around 4000 years ago, Menorca's only large native mammal died out, following the advent of Neolithic man who hunted it to extinction; this was the Balearic antelope (*Myotragus balearicus*), whose bones have been found in caves in the west of the island.

REPTILES, AMPHIBIANS, MOLLUSCS AND FISH

Four snakes are found on Menorca: grass snakes, cowl snakes, ladder snakes and viperine snakes. Of these the latter are the most common. None of them presents any threat to the walker.

Lizards like to sun themselves on walls or bare rocks; those most usually seen on Menorca are the green wall lizards, known in Menorca as *sargantanes* and a favourite food of the hoopoe. They give their name to an island in Fornells bay. Some six sub-species occur in Menorca, most notably a black variety peculiar to the Illa de l'Aire. The larger star lizard, known as *dragó*, is scarce and in the Balearics only found in Menorca.

Both the land tortoise and the turtle survive, but in decreasing numbers; despite government protection, some unlawful killing of both creatures still goes on. The land tortoise conceals itself in the southern pinewoods and 'maquis'; turtles also prefer the south and are occasionally seen around Cala d'es Talaier and Cala En Turqueta. Giant land tortoises (*Testudo gymnesia*), distant relatives of the great tortoises of Indonesia, disappeared at the end of the last Ice Age; their remains have been found in caves beneath Cap de Bajolí north-west of Ciutadella.

Marsh frogs proliferate in the wetlands and, less numerous, tree frogs may be heard in the northern forests. Three species of toad, the natterjack, green and midwife, all exist in island sub-species.

Menorca is rich in snails (*caracoles*), some of which are edible. Their colour varies with the surrounding vegetation. Sometimes what appears to be a flower spike seen from afar turns out to be a cluster of snails.

The coastal waters are rich in marine life. The fish around Menorca are typically Mediterranean, often with names which do not translate into English. In rock pools and along the shore, many familiar sea creatures may be observed: mussels, clams, sea urchins, cuttlefish, sea anemones, hermit crabs, jellyfish and prawns.

INSECTS

Menorca's insect life is rich and varied, with many hundreds of different beetles and weevils providing food for the substantial bird population. The only insects likely to intrude on the holidaymaker are the mosquito, which haunts the marshes and S'Albufera in high summer, and the sheep tick, a parasite which can attach itself to the bare-legged walker, particularly in the Faváritx area of the north-east.

There has been no recent study of the butterflies of Menorca, but 50 years ago 30 species were identified by Professor H. Rebel. It is reasonable to suppose that their number may have diminished in the wake of widespread building for tourism. Even in midwinter, however, butterflies emerge on sunny days; in summer the wealth of wild flowers provides them with abundant nectar. Most frequently seen on the island are the Large White, Small White, Clouded Yellow, Red Admiral, Painted Lady, Swallowtail, Small Copper, Long-tailed Blue and Adonis Blue.

ARCHAEOLOGY

Even the most indifferent visitor to Menorca can hardly fail to notice some aspects of its unique archaeological heritage. The abundance of prehistoric sites on the island has led to its being described as a vast open-air museum, and, armed with a little information, the least archaeologically minded tourist will find that visiting them (especially the spectacular and photogenic standing stones known as 'taulas') can become quite addictive. All can be viewed without payment or permission; clearly, attention should be paid to closing gates etc., when visiting those on private land. A torch and stout shoes are useful.

The prehistoric remains on the island fall into three main groups:

TAULAS

Easily the most spectacular and visually appealing of the megalithic monuments, these are massive T-shaped constructions, formed by placing one large rectangular stone slab on top of another, vertical, one; the upright stones are wide, but quite slim, and can be as tall as 4 metres. At least 30 have been traced on Menorca, of which seven remain intact and complete – no mean achievement for artefacts that are about 3000 years old.

Taulas (the word simply means 'table' in Catalan) are unique to Menorca, though a few similar pillars, apparently late copies of the Menorcan version, have been found on Mallorca. How they were constructed and for what purpose has been endlessly discussed by scholars, but no firm conclusion has ever been reached on either score. Theories as to the method of their erection include the idea that the horizontal slab (which usually has an indentation hollowed out of the lower side to fit snugly onto the vertical) was placed over the vertical stone while both still lay on the ground, and that the whole massive construction was then laboriously raised into a previously excavated hole, possibly by ropes which were wetted over and over again so that their shrinkage as they dried would gradually hoist the taula into a vertical position.

As to their purpose, it has been suggested that sacrifices were made on the top (but how did the priest manage to get up there?); alternatively, that they represent a stylised version of a bull and may have been venerated as images of a deity, or simply as cult objects. Older theories that they may have supported some sort of roof, now vanished, have been discounted. The only certainty can be that their function was religious and that almost every settlement had one, invariably sited in a 'precinct' whose entrance faced south and was placed directly in front of the taula. Some of these precincts have survived in part, and all seem to have included a series of niches in the encircling wall, separated by columns.

Today only one taula (Torre Llisá Vell) has an intact wall surrounding its precinct, complete with the entrance. But all of them have a peculiar magic. Particularly early in the morning or in the slanting light of evening, a taula precinct is an awesome place where the imagination can be given full rein.

TALAYOTS

There are at least 200 of these on the island, and doubtless there were once many more; usually sited on the highest ground available, their main function is generally assumed to have been to serve as defensive watchtowers (which is what their popular name on Menorca, *talaia*, means), and it seems that every prehistoric settlement had at least one: often it is all that now remains of a village. Talayots consist of conical heaps of stone, the outside being constructed of massive stones, while inside smaller ones are used. Usually there was a small entrance in one side (most often the south-facing), with a corridor leading to the centre of the talayot where there might be a small or in some cases (as at Sant Agustí Vell, see p. 73, or Torre Vella d'en Lozano north of Ciutadella) quite a sizeable chamber (whose purpose is not known). Many of these inner constructions have collapsed over the centuries, and some talayots may never have had them, being designed solely as watchtowers, but it is known that some had ramps within and even staircases.

The talayots of Menorca can be up to 10 metres high with diameters between 15 and 20 metres. Almost all the surviving examples are built in the truncated cone shape and it is impossible to guess whether originally there was some sort of wooden superstructure on the top (some authorities suggest it might have constituted the chief's dwelling place). Most were built between 1300 and 800 BC and this era in Menorcan prehistory, corresponding roughly with the Bronze Age, is accordingly known as the 'talayotic period.' Talayots occur in Mallorca also, though on the larger island they tend to be smaller; there are also similar structures on Sardinia ('*nuraghi*' or 'giants' tombs') and Corsica ('*torri*'), supporting the view that early influences on the Balearics came largely from the Near East, rather than from the Iberian peninsula.

Today, many talayots are extremely overgrown and in many cases it is difficult to distinguish them from other heaps of stones, which the Menorcan farmers have been forced to make simply to clear their fields for cultivation.

NAVETAS

Sometimes called '*talayetas*' in Menorca, navetas are similar to talayots but usually smaller and of a more distinctive shape: this somewhat resembles that of an upturned boat, whence the name given to them by early archaeologists. Most navetas were used as burial places; they often had two storeys, in the upper of which the dead were left gradually to rot, the bones being transferred to the lower chamber when the process was complete. The restored naveta at Es Tudons, which has been called the outstanding monument of the Balearic Bronze Age, is the best example, but there are other quite well-preserved navetas at Rafal Rubí Nou (see p. 69), Biniac, Llumena, Torralbet, Torre Llisá, Son Mercer de Baix and Cotaina, most of these sites lying in the Alaior area. Altogether some 45 survive on the island.

The basic structure of a naveta is an oval or horseshoe-shaped building with sloping sides made by bringing the

The restored naveta of Es Tudons, one of the oldest buildings in Europe

courses of stone used in the construction gradually together until the space between could be covered by large roofing slabs. There is an entrance (almost always in the straight end) which leads to a small vestibule or chimney in which one may either go under a massive lintel or over it to reach the upper storey. The chambers inside are usually oval, faced with medium-sized stones of fairly regular shape and sometimes containing shelves or ledges. There is little doubt that they were used for burials: the remains of over 100 skeletons from various periods were found in the naveta at Es Tudons. Navetas can look rather like small talayots when they have fallen into decay; usually, though, they are sited in open country outside the settlements they served.

Other prehistoric monuments on Menorca include caves, of which there are a vast number, both natural and man-made; the majority of these were used for funerals and they often occur in groups (there are over 30 such complexes on the island) as at Cales Coves (see p. 71). In the pre-talayotic period (5000–1300 BC), of course, natural caves must have been used as dwellings also: in some caves near Ciutadella bones of the *Myotragus balearicus,* a type of small antelope which was the island's only indigenous mammal when the first settlers arrived but had become extinct by about 2200 BC, were found. Underground caves (known as 'hypogeums') were also cut into the rock in this earlier period, again for burial purposes, and other interments took place in stone sepulchres made of large flat stone slabs in one of which a hole had been carved to form an entrance. Later generations constructed altogether more elaborate caves, often with enlarged rectangular entrances incorporating a decorative surround: inside these there might be more than one room and even windows.

Also to be seen on the island are the remains of several quite large villages, such as Son Catlar and Torre d'En Gaumes. In addition to talayots, taula precincts and extensive walling, the remains of wells and housing can be examined at several sites, including the semi-subterranean rooms containing 'Mediterranean columns' (i.e. composed of several stones increasing in size towards the top) which are known to archaeologists as 'hypostyle chambers': the pillars support large flat roofing slabs and the rooms were either used as living space or for livestock or grain storage, etc.

Of course, all these stone constructions were not built at once, and the 'talayotic period' on Menorca is reckoned to have lasted some 500 years. Nevertheless the wealth of megalithic remains on the island is quite staggering, and the more remarkable so when one reflects that it was all the work of a population which is unlikely to have exceeded 5,000 people at any time.

There is one further category of ancient building to be seen on Menorca. This is the early Christian church, of which there are excavated examples at Son Bou, Fornells and Torelló. The architectural inspiration for these basilicas seems to have come from North Africa and they were probably built in the fifth–sixth centuries AD.

PRINCIPAL ARCHAEOLOGICAL SITES

Most of the sites can be incorporated in one or other of the routes described in pp. 140–85. They are listed here in roughly geographical order (from east to west), to enable interested visitors to combine a visit to some of them with other expeditions on the island.

TREPUCÓ

Perhaps the simplest (though not the shortest) route to this site is to leave Maó on the Es Castell (Villacarlos) road, and, just after the Villacarlos sign, turn right onto a minor road signed 'Talayot Trebuco 2.1'. Continue straight on along this country lane and follow signs to the right at a T-junction, where the talayot comes into view; the site is reached along a turning to the left (signposted) after a high cemented wall; there is limited parking in the lane by the entrance, but it is possible to drive right up the rough track leading to the talayot and park in one of a dozen spaces between it and the encircling wall. Trepucó can also be reached directly from Maó (straight on out of the city from the end of the Cós de Gràcia) or through the Horizonte development or from the Maó-Sant Lluís road by taking a left turn (signposted) about 2½ km. from the centre of Maó (1½ km. north of Sant Lluís), then turning left when this road meets a T-junction and left again at the next opportunity (note that the narrow lane going past the entrance to the site is one-way going south).

The talayot at Trepucó is constructed of massive stones, and both it and the nearby taula can be seen from within the city limits of Maó. Its proximity to the capital has meant the site has suffered considerable damage through the centuries: the wall surrounding the talayot was built in 1782 by the French army attacking Fort San Felipe in order to protect its cannon batteries (during this campaign the French commander, the Duc de Crillon, is said to have used the top

The taula precinct at Trepucó near Maó, with the talayot behind

of the taula as a command post!). Unfortunately the rear face of the taula has had to be reinforced by a concrete support; nevertheless, with a vertical stone some 4 m. high Trepucó is the tallest surviving taula on the island. Also to be seen on the site are a second, smaller talayot and the remains of several round buildings around a circular courtyard. First excavated by a team from Cambridge University in the 1930s, it appears that the original talayotic village at Trepucó continued in occupation as late as medieval times, so many of the original buildings show signs of having been converted by later generations.

SA TORRETA

This is a spectacularly sited yet little visited complex of remains to the south of Cap de Favàritx, and one of the relatively few talayotic settlements in the northern half of Menorca. To get there, take the Maó-Fornells road (PM 710). At the 8 km. post you will pass the small church of the Ermita de Fátima on a small hill to your right; 750 m. further on take a right turn signed 'Faro de Favàritx'. After just over 2 km. turn right again, continuing for 600 m. to a T-junction, at which you turn left onto a track; slightly less than 1 km. further on there is a gate, after which the track swings sharply to the right and climbs a small bluff before reaching the farmhouse of Sa Torre Blanca. It is possible to leave the car here and climb the wall by a stile of projecting stones; now cross the farmyard to a similar stile on your left, from where the talayot is clearly visible close to the farmhouse.

A well-preserved precinct with a raised entrance huddles beneath it, enclosing a complete taula some 4 m. high with an unusually small horizontal stone. From the top of the talayot there are good views to seaward of an ancient tower with the Illa d'en Colom behind. Scattered around are many other traces of the prehistoric settlement, the whole of which is perched on quite a high bluff with splendid views in all directions (Monte Toro looks particularly mountainous from here). A visit to this site, which has only been recently cleared of throttling vegetation, can be conveniently combined with an enjoyable walk (No. 8 in Dodo Mackenzie's book *More Walks in Menorca*, no. 3).

The spectacular taula at Sa Torreta

TORELLÓ

This massive talayot is for many visitors the first evidence of
Menorca's fascinating archaeological heritage that they see
– one of the largest on the island, it is clearly visible from the
airport (which, indeed, threatens to engulf it). To get there,
take the airport road from Maó (heading for Sant Climent
and Cala En Porter, and passing, incidentally, the two
talayots of Cúrnia on the right) and about 50 m. after the
airport turn-off (over a bridge) take a sharp right hand turn
(signed 'Talaiot de Torelló' and 'El Sereno') onto a rough
track on which you bear left as it passes the lights at the end
of the airport runway. The talayot is unusual in having its
entrance high up on the southern side. It can be climbed
from the far side for an extensive view of the south coast;
other ruins, including a second smaller talayot, can be seen
in the surrounding fields. Several bronze statuettes were
found when this area was excavated, and a large hoard of
Roman coins.

Further along the same road is another archaeological
treasure, the remains of the palaeo-Christian basilica of Es
Fornás de Torelló with an impressive mosaic floor which is
in a remarkable state of preservation. First discovered by a
farmer ploughing his land in 1956, the floor is now roofed
over and fenced in for protection, with a raised viewing
platform. The lively mosaics show peacocks at the altar end,
as well as lions, birds and geometrical motifs. Similar in plan
to the basilica at Son Bou (p. 158), the building probably
dates from the fifth–sixth century AD.

TALATÍ DE DALT

This site is very near the main Maó-Alaior road, reached by
a turning off it to the left just west of the 4 km. sign. Park in
a lay-by (signposted) on the left and climb the nearby wall
(steps provided): the site is some 100 m. along the path.
There is a good view of the area from the talayot, sited as
usual on the highest ground available. The taula precinct
below contains a complete taula with a fallen pillar leaning
against it (which is generally agreed by scholars to be an
accidental fall rather than a support for the taula itself), and,
in the outer wall, a columned chamber half-submerged in
the ground. The horizontal stone of this taula, measuring
$4 \times 1.53 \times .68$m, is the largest surviving example on the
island. Talatí de Dalt is quite an extensive site, as can be seen
from the surviving fragments of the extremely thick walls
which once surrounded it. Two other hypostyle rooms in a
good state of preservation are visible close together to the

The taula precinct at Talatí de Dalt

left of the taula precinct (viewed from the talayot) and a little further away, as well as several ruined buildings and caves.

Continuing along the lane after visiting this site, and going straight over the crossroads for just under 1 km. will bring you to Montple, where the remains of two megalithic sepulchres can be seen, one of them only a few yards from the lane (on the left). Returning to the minor crossroads and this time turning left will take you back to the main Maó-Alaior road near the site of Alcaidus, where there are three ancient wells. You are now exactly opposite the turning for the two navetas at Rafal Rubí Nou.

RAFAL RUBÍ NOU

This site also is easily accessible from the main Maó-Alaior road and is reached by taking a right turn at a crossroads about 700 m. west of the 6 km. post (there is a transformer just before the turning on the south side of the main road). It is possible to park some 200 m. up this road and enter the field on the left by a wooden gate. Here there are two well-preserved navetas close together. The smaller one has only a single storey, though its roof and chimney survive; the larger has a lower storey in good repair, with a shelf at each end and the lintel giving access to the upper storey still in place.

TORRALBA D'EN SALORT

The most northerly of a series of prehistoric settlements best reached from the road running south from Alaior towards

Cala En Porter (well-signposted, this road leaves the main C 721 just west of its entry into Alaior and east of the turning to the Coinga cheese factory), the site of Torralba d'En Salort is in fact bisected by the modern road, which reaches it some 3 km. south of Alaior. There is space to park on the right of the road, where the perfectly preserved tapering taula stands in a precinct of which much is missing, though enough survivies to make clear its outline and extent. The area around contains the remains of several other structures, some of them possibly pre-talayotic.

The site, the main parts of which date from between 1000 and 900 BC, is regarded as representing the high point of talayotic culture. It has still been only partially excavated, but early results indicate that it was almost continuously occupied from the eighteenth to the second centuries BC. Objects found here by the excavators included a bronze figure of a bull and several terracotta heads of the Punic goddess of fertility, Tanit. To the left of the road, the as yet unexcavated talayot gives a good view of the site, and about 30 m. back along the road towards Alaior there is a columned building well-hidden and partly underground.

TORRE LLISÁ VELL

Continuing south towards Cala En Porter, you come to a crossroads after about $2\frac{1}{2}$ km.; here turn right and proceed for about 400 m., parking where convenient by the drive to the farm. Here the farmer has painted helpful red 'T' signs on walls and gateposts; follow these along his drive, then left past the farmyard and left again at two gates. Shortly afterwards a right turn through a gap in the wall brings you to the taula precinct on your left. Unique on Menorca in having retained its surprisingly thick encircling walls and entrance arch almost complete, this taula provides an authentically thrilling experience as you stoop low to enter the precinct and the taula looms before you. The view southwards towards the sea is dominated by the huge talayot of So Na Caçana.

SO NA CAÇANA

A little further south on the Cala En Porter road there is yet another rewarding archaeological site, reached through a gap in the wall (with cattle grid) on the right just before the next 30 k.p.h. sign. As well as two talayots, So Na Caçana had two taula precincts and many other buildings. Clearly it was an important religious centre and it is impossible to guess why two such large sites as this and Torre Llisá Vell should have grown up so close to each other. Only recently excavated, one taula precinct has an unusual flattened shape with circular niches within; the second precinct has a very high lintel and clearly visible niches round the precinct. Its taula has a double upright, but neither of the taulas here has retained its horizontal stone.

CALES COVES

South of So Na Caçana, the road shortly meets the main Maó-Cala En Porter road. Here a right turn takes you to the coast; a left turn, followed by a right a few hundred metres afterwards, leads to the fascinating site of Cales Coves. After passing through a small development the road ceases to be metalled and deteriorates quite rapidly as it continues downhill towards the sea. In the cove at the bottom, once a flourishing port, there are over a hundred burial caves in the surrounding cliff faces, almost all of them invisible from the sea.

The caves to your left as you arrive are the oldest: it is possible to scramble up to inspect some of them if you are so minded. Most probably date from the ninth–seventh centuries BC, and are characterised by their round entrances and low roofs. On the right of the cove is a large natural cave known as Des Jurats (with an iron railing in the front), which contains a mass of barely decipherable Latin inscriptions. Continuing round the small headland brings a further ravine into view, both sides of which are again riddled with caves. Mostly of a rather later date, these have larger entrances and some have decorative façades; a few incorpo-

Prehistoric caves in the cliffside at Cales Coves

rate a patio and even windows, with niches and ledges within. They date from between the fourth century BC and Roman times. There are still more caves in the slope above; the more athletic may find it rewarding to scramble up behind the small house and inspect some of them.

In the summer, and especially at weekends, several of the caves at Cales Coves have in recent years been occupied by 'hippies' and other campers.

TORRE D'EN GAUMES

Torre d'En Gaumes is the largest excavated prehistoric settlement on Menorca and well worth a visit; furthermore, a metalled road runs round part of it, so that it is one of the few sites that can be inspected by the elderly or disabled. It is reached by taking the road to Son Bou just west of Alaior (at the 13 km. post on the C 721), from which the site is signposted to the left some 2½ km. further south; at this point the three large talayots are already visible. Follow the signs left at a fork and just past the elegant farmhouse there is a parking area on the right.

Following the road from the car park along the top of the site takes you past two large talayots on your left (which may be climbed for a good overall impression of the settlement) and a smaller one on the right; the road then descends and bears left towards the taula precinct. Here the horizontal stone has fallen off, revealing the large slot hollowed out of it to fit over the top of the vertical (though some experts think this hole has been subsequently enlarged). A bronze helmet and statuette of the Egyptian god Imhotep were

A pillared chamber at Torre d'En Gaumes

The sepulchre at Ses Roques Llises

found in this precinct. Past the taula precinct the road continues down the hill past walls and various unrecognisable structures, ending in a turning circle next to which is a well-preserved, pillared ('hypostilic') building; one of the best surviving examples, this structure vividly displays the building methods of the talayotic civilization.

There is a lot more to explore on this site if you have time, including the remains of many circular houses, some caves and a flat area ingeniously scored with channels designed to catch water and conduct it to large reservoirs via a series of small pits in which any sediment would be deposited.

SES ROQUES LLISES

Just south of the site just described is a pretalayotic sepulchre said to be the finest surviving example of its kind. To reach it drive along the narrow lane south from Torre d'en Gaumes for 700 m., where there are steps projecting from the wall to your left. Unfortunately the farmer has recently put up a '*prohibido pasar*' notice here and laid brushwood on top of the wall to discourage visitors. If you are undeterred, climb the wall and turn half-left: the sepulchre stands alone in a field about 150 m. away from you. Essentially a large stone box with an entrance at one end reached by a passage, the sepulchre is reckoned to be 3500 years old.

SANT AGUSTÍ VELL

Some 1400 m. south of Es Migjorn Gran, on the road to Sant Adeodato and Sant Tomás (and after passing the somewhat less interesting talayotic settlement of Santa Monica to your left), a sandy track to the right (not signposted) leads to the farm of Sant Agustí. When the track forks near the farmhouse, take the right fork (away from the house); after 500 metres go through a gate and the incongruous sight of two Council litter bins standing proudly beside a field (one wonders how often they are emptied!) is the clue that you have reached the site. This settlement contains a large talayot with an unusually large chamber within; the roof incorporates beams of olive wood and is supported by three splendid Mediterranean columns. A further room backs onto the talayot. The farm stands on the edge of the deep gorge of Binigaus, which is full of caves including the enormous Cova des Coloms. On the far side the palatial farmhouse of Binigaus Nou is prominent. It is quite a scramble to get into the gorge (best attempted from further back along the track towards the farmhouse) but, once down, there is a pleasant walk along it to the beaches at Binigaus and Sant Adeodato.

TORRE LLAFUDA

This site is reached via the narrow road to the farm of Son Sintes, running southwards from the main C 721 between Ferreries and Ciutadella approximately 300 m. west of the 37 km. mark. After 500 m., go through the farmyard of Son Sintes (this involves opening and closing two sets of gates) and continue past a pair of stone pillars until you reach a second pair, with the arched tunnel to a large cave near the road on the right. Park here and climb the small rise behind the cave, where you will come upon the large talayot on the highest ground, some massive defensive walls of great height a little further on, and, romantically hidden among the trees between the talayot and the road, a taula precinct with a complete taula only 1.7 m. high; the overgrown and secluded setting of this precinct makes it one of the most atmospheric of them all. The site also includes burial caves and the remains of circular rooms, etc., but has been little excavated.

TORRE TRENCADA

Back on the main road, continue west towards Ciutadella and 200 m. after the 39 km. mark turn sharp left beside a wood; at the T-junction turn left and after 2 km. left again onto the track leading to the farmhouse. Park along the road near the farmer's sign and enter the field on your left, where the taula is already visible; the path towards it passes the entrance to a large cave. In the precinct itself, the (complete) taula has a reinforcing stone at the back; the talayot behind

The taula at Torre Trencada

is as usual on the highest ground, distinguishable from the many heaps of stone in the area by its height and by the size of the blocks. The farmer clearly takes trouble to keep the site from becoming overgrown and has even constructed a picnic area of large stone slabs on a raised platform nearby.

NAVETA D'ES TUDONS

Probably the most visited of all the prehistoric sites on Menorca, Es Tudons is the only naveta in almost perfect condition, and this is because it was restored in 1975 (except for the top, since no one can be certain what this would have looked like). The naveta has its own car park clearly signposted on (and visible from) the south side of the Ferreries-Ciutadella stretch of the C 721 just west of the 40 km. mark. From the car park it is a pleasant stroll to the monument, along a track which in spring is lined with poppies, chamomile daisies, wild gladioli and other flowers.

The naveta (said to be the oldest architectural structure still standing on Spanish soil) can easily be entered on hands and knees. Horseshoe-shaped, it is 14 m. long, with a maximum width of 6.4 m., and consists of two oval chambers one above the other, the upper floor being reached from a small lobby or chimney just inside the entrance passage; the roof of the lower chamber is made of massive flat slabs, with a huge lintel. Further along the track, past the naveta, the entrance to a large cave can be seen on your left.

SON CATLAR

To reach the large prehistoric settlement of Son Catlar it is necessary to leave Ciutadella on the Cala En Turqueta road or Camí de Sant Joan de Missa. Proceed into the city until the T-junction with the *contramurada*, where you turn left, taking the third left (Carrer Sor Agueda) after the road has made its first swing to the right. This brings you into a small square (the Plaça de Jaume II); go round the square, exit at the opposite corner and follow this road out of town. After 2½ km., just past the farm of Son Vivó, take the right fork and follow this road for a further 2 km. until you reach the farm of Son Catlar (there is a transformer on the right just opposite). Park by the road about 200 m. further on and enter the field on the left of the road. The enormous extent of the walls encircling the village (some 864 m. in all, with straight stretches up to 200 m. long) begins to become apparent as you approach, watching out for a pre-talayotic burial cave (or 'hypogeum') facing you about 30 m. from the road and a little to your right. You may find it instructive to walk right round the walls before entering the settlement; some of the blocks used in its construction are immense, and there are several gateways, only one of which has been cleared. On the eastern face, the four towers made of smaller, more regularly shaped stones are Roman additions. Several talayots are visible, one built into the angle of the wall at the south-east corner, and another against the eastern wall which has the remains of a columned building adjoining.

Inside the walls, the village occupied an area some 160 m. wide. Among the labyrinthine ruins the remains of many buildings can be discerned, some of them circular, as so often on Menorca. But in general the site is severely overgrown and outlines have been further confused by farmers dumping unwanted rocks from their fields on top of the ancient remains. The most easily recognisable feature is the taula precinct which is about 100 m. in from the walls a short distance to the right of the point where you first approached the village.

HISTORY, ECONOMY
AND INDUSTRY

The history of Menorca is a fascinating one. Few territories of its size anywhere in the world can have been subjected to such a variety of invasions and influences. Occupied in turn by early Iberians, 'Sea Peoples', Phoenicians, Carthaginians, Greeks, Romans, Vandals, Arabs, Catalonian Aragonese, British and French, before finally becoming a part of Spain, Menorca's story is a microcosm of the history of the Mediterranean, with additional elements which make it unique.

Yet it must be the distinctive character of the Menorcans themselves which best reflects the legacy of their island's multifarious past. More tangible relics are hard to identify, since each occupying power used the building materials of its predecessors. Her prehistoric monuments aside, Menorca's oldest buildings date from only a few hundred years ago.

PREHISTORIC MENORCA

The first inhabitants of Menorca probably arrived from mainland Spain via Mallorca. There is archaeological evidence which suggests this may have been as early as 4000 BC or even earlier, though the first clear evidence of a human presence on Menorca dates from 2000 years later. At this time men were living in natural caves on the island; simple pottery was made, animals domesticated and tools of bone or flint were being used. The *Myotragus balearicus*, a small antelope indigenous to Menorca and Mallorca, which before the coming of man had completely lacked natural enemies (to the extent that evolution had shifted its eyes to the front of its head, unlike those of most deer which need a wide field of vision to alert them to possible predators), had already been hunted into extinction. Possibly by around 1500 BC, the first man-made structures were being built in Menorca: navetas (see p. 63), simple dwellings of a similar design (called 'naviforms' by archaeologists); and excavated, sometimes multi-chambered, caves more advanced than the natural caves that provided shelter for the earliest inhabitants.

This era is referred to by the archaeologists as the 'pre-talayotic period'. It came to an end fairly decisively around

1300 BC, when it seems that a new wave of immigrants arrived, probably from the eastern Mediterranean (the Aegean, Crete and even Egypt have been suggested) and probably via other Mediterranean islands (Sardinia, Corsica and Malta all show evidence of a similar new culture arriving at this time). These peoples used bronze and they seem to have introduced the concept of the 'talayot' (see also p. 62). Hence the era 1300–800 BC on Menorca is referred to as the 'talayotic period'. During it, megalithic constructions were built all over the island (but with a great preponderance in the south), and by 1000 BC these were becoming quite sophisticated. The islanders now would mostly have been living in walled settlements around their talayots, with taula precincts (see p. 62), pillared rooms ('hypostyle chambers', see p. 64) and often quite extensive fortifications.

By about 800 BC the talayotic culture was declining (though some of the settlements seem not to have been finally abandoned until as late as 50 AD). As the Iron Age began, Menorca was being regularly visited by the biremes (two-tiered galleys) of the Phoenicians who were adventurous seafarers from Tyre and Sidon (modern Syria). Their trading links extended to southern France, Spain and even Cornwall; and Menorca provided a useful staging post. The Phoenicians were skilled at navigating by the stars and their attention is said to have been drawn to the island by the fires seen on it by night. At any rate, they gave Menorca its first known name, 'Nura' (Fire). They set up trading posts at Ciutadella and Maó, and also at the little inlet of Sanisera (Sanitja today) on the western shore of Cape Cavallería (see p. 167).

Little evidence of the Phoenician presence remains today, however, any more than it does for the next group of visitors, who from around 500 BC began to supplant them (Tyre fell to Alexander the Great in 332 BC.) These were Phocian Greeks from the eastern Mediterranean and they founded colonies, probably based around some of the prehistoric villages. Their name for the island was 'Meloussa' ('Island of Cattle' – a name which the modern visitor will find appropriate!), but apart from a couple of statues, some coins and plentiful pottery fragments (including a fine beaked jug), no trace of their occupation survives; the lack of metal on the island may have discouraged large permanent settlements. (These Greeks are also said to have given Menorca and its neighbours the name 'Balearics' from the Greek word *balein*, to throw with a sling, a skill for which the people of Menorca seem to have been celebrated throughout the ancient world; but the presence on Sardinia of a tribe called the Balari may give a clue to the true origin of the name.)

THE FIRST INVADERS

The first more hostile invasion was that of the Carthaginians, who arrived from North Africa around 400 BC. The Menorcan slingers were able to prevent a full-scale occupation, but many enlisted with them as mercenaries in the Punic Wars fought by Carthage against the newly emerging power of Rome. The Carthaginians founded towns on the sites of present-day Ciutadella and Maó, naming the former 'Jamma' ('West Town'). According to Pliny, Maó was named after Magon, the last Carthaginian commander, who wintered in the town in 206 BC, but it is equally likely that the name derives from the Semitic word *maghen* (meaning 'shield' or 'defence').

After the defeat and final destruction of Carthage by the Romans in 146 BC, it was not long before the safe anchorage at Maó attracted the new rulers of most of the western Mediterranean, and in 123 BC Menorca was once more invaded. Under the consul Quintus Cecilius Metellus, the Romans easily overcame the resistance of the islanders, and gave Menorca a new name, Balearis Minor or Minorica.

The Romans stayed for more than five hundred years, during which time they built perhaps as much as 85 miles of road, and set up military strongpoints throughout the island, including the fortress of Sant' Agueda, where traces of their engineering can still be seen. The Balearics became a Roman province and Portus Magonis (Maó) gained increasingly in importance, being granted the status of a *municipium* with its own local government. Agriculture improved, and Menorquín slingers continued to fight all over the world as mercenaries (possibly even in Britain). Most importantly, however, Christianity was introduced towards the end of the Roman era: a letter written by Bishop Severo of Menorca to the Christian world survives from 417 AD, and, although the basilicas at Fornells (p. 165), Son Bou (p. 158) and Torelló (p. 68) date from the Byzantine period, it is reasonable to suppose that at least one centre of Christian worship must have existed on the island at this time.

Other remains of the Roman era include various inscriptions, the remains of villas (for example at Sanitja, see p. 167), a mosaic pavement from the Illa del Rei (now in Maó museum), jewellery, coins and a few statues, one of which, a head of the young Tiberius, is now in the Bibliothèque National in Paris. We know from inscriptions that there was a Roman theatre on Menorca, but no trace of it remains. The Menorcans continued to live in talayotic villages but began to adopt Roman ways. At first, Menorca was incorporated in the province of Tarraconensis based on Tarragona, but the Balearics became an independent province in 402.

The Roman era was brought to an end by the invasion of the Vandals in 427, who pillaged the island and persecuted Christians. (The Bishop of Menorca, Makarius, was summoned to Carthage during this period and never returned: he may have been martyred. He was to be the last bishop of the island until 1795.) After the great Byzantine general Belisarius overthrew the Vandals, Menorca became part of the Byzantine Empire in 533. Christianity was restored and an era of peace and prosperity followed, but the new order was comparatively shortlived: by the early years of the eighth century the invincible sweep northwards and westwards of the Arabs of North Africa had embraced almost all of Spain, Menorca included.

MOORISH MENORCA

For the first two hundred years, however, Menorca was only nominally Moorish. Islamic raids were frequent but no resident governor appeared on the island until the tenth century. The island gained a new name, Minurka, (Ciutadella became Medina-Minurka) and gradually the Moslem element in the population grew. In 902 the Balearics were formally incorporated into the Caliphate of Córdoba, passing, when that authority broke up, into the kingdom of Denia; subsequently the islands were taken over by the strict but tolerant Almoravid dynasty from North Africa, and after them by the harsher Almohades.

Thus for almost five hundred years Menorca was a Moorish island and Islam its main religion. Today, however, traces of this epoch in Menorca's history are few and far between (certainly far fewer than those that remain from the comparatively brief period of British occupancy). The Menorquín fondness for horses is perhaps an Arab legacy, as are numerous place-names, e.g. Cala Galdana (Oued-el-Ana) and all those beginning with 'Bini' ('place of the sons of ...'), 'Al' ('the') or 'Rafal' ('a large property'). Traces of the Moors remain in Sant'Agueda, their main inland fortress (though for much of the occupation it was used more peacefully, as a summer retreat for the local aristocracy), but there is very little even in Ciutadella, which under the Moors became a city of some luxury; most of Moorish Ciutadella was destroyed by pirates and other later centuries. The tower of the cathedral was probably once a minaret.

THE MIDDLE AGES

Menorca's modern history begins in 1287 when the young King Alfonso III of Aragón in mainland Spain conquered the island, drove out the Almohades and restored Christianity. Mallorca had been wrested from the Moors 57 years earlier by Alfonso's grandfather Jaime I, but Menorca was not occupied at that time due to a shortage of troops. Instead, Jaime had tricked the Menorcan Moors into thinking he was about to invade with a large force by the cunning expedient of lighting a large number of fires on the hills of northern Mallorca. Daunted by the apparent size of his army, the rulers of Menorca agreed to become his tributaries, but some years later betrayed the plans of Jaime's brother Pedro III to attack the Moorish cities of North Africa to their compatriots there. Pedro died shortly after, but not before swearing his son to take revenge on the island.

This son was Alfonso, then aged 21 but already an experienced commander. The young king's invading fleet was dispersed by bad weather and he was forced to land on Rabbit Island in Maó harbour (later renamed the Illa del Rei) with only 20 ships and await reinforcements. When these arrived, he landed on La Mola, driving the defending Moors along the north side of the harbour and, although outnumbered four to one, finally defeating them in a bloody battle on the flat land to the north-west of the city known as 'dels Verges'. This was on 17 January (the Feast of Sant Antoni Abad, who became the patron saint of the island). The Moors retired to Sant'Agueda and surrendered the island four days later.

The vanquished were treated with surprising harshness: all but the few rich enough to pay a large ransom were sold into slavery and some were simply taken out to sea and drowned. Ciutadella was declared the capital of the island under the Aragonese crown and work started at once on converting the great mosque there into a Christian church dedicated to the Virgin Mary. It is estimated that the Moorish population before the conquest may have been as large as 25–30,000, so their expulsion left the island severely depopulated. New settlers were imported from Catalonia and Alfonso ('the Liberal') awarded extensive estates to his followers and to the religious orders.

Alfonso died aged only 25 in 1291, before he could marry Eleanor, daughter of Edward I of England, to whom he was engaged. The next Aragonese king to take an interest in the island was Jaume II of Mallorca, who divided the island into seven administrative parishes and gave it a Bill of Rights, the *Carta Puebla*. Markets were instituted at Maó, Es Mercadal and Ciutadella, and firm administrative foundations established – yet there is no evidence that he ever visited Menorca! Later generations of the Mallorcan dynasty quarrelled with their Aragonese cousins and the line of Mallorcan kings ended with the death of Jaume III at the battle of Lluchmayor in 1349. Thereafter the Balearics were officially incorporated in the Crown of Aragón. From now on they were governed from Barcelona; administration was slack and a period of decline ensued.

THE SIXTEENTH AND SEVENTEENTH CENTURIES

The next two centuries were dismal. Plague, smallpox and cholera were rife, and droughts and famine frequent. The population declined to a point where it was decided to permit convicts from the mainland to settle on the island in exchange for a pardon. There was also bickering between Ciutadella and Maó, leading at one stage to a small civil war. Moslem piracy, too, was a thorn in the island's side, strangling maritime trade; economic stagnation and emigration ensued and even agriculture was increasingly abandoned. At one low point the populations of Maó and Ciutadella together numbered a mere 3,000.

But even worse was to come. In 1535 the dreaded pirate Khair-el-Din Barbarossa entered Maó flying false Christian colours; too late, the inhabitants realised his true identity, and after bloody resistance the town fell. Maó was virtually destroyed and 800 captives (over half the population) were sold into slavery. A few years later it was Ciutadella's turn. In 1558 the Turks under General Mustafa and Admiral Piali (oddly, a Hungarian Christian by birth), attacked the city. The citizens' defence was heroic (it is commemorated by the obelisk in the Borne), but unavailing. Ciutadella was sacked (its historical records being destroyed in the process) and large areas of the countryside laid waste. This time no less than 3,452 prisoners were taken away to the slave markets of Constantinople. So devastated was the city that the governor's residence was a cave.

After these demonstrations of the vulnerability of the Balearics, work began on fortifying Menorca: the fort of San Felipe (designed by Juan Bautista Calvi, an Italian who had also built the city walls of Ibiza) was begun on the southern side of Maó harbour, with smaller forts at Ciutadella and

The Plaça d'es Born, Ciutadella, with the obelisk commemorating the sack of the city in 1558

Fornells. Some coastal settlements were evacuated in favour of inland sites, and many of the defensive towers that stand today on the Menorcan coast date from this period. Nevertheless by 1570, when less than one thousand families remained on Menorca, the plight of the islanders was so bad that Philip II proposed that the Balearics should be evacuated completely.

Piracy continued to dominate life on Menorca until well into the seventeenth century; Britain, too, was to find it troublesome as her trade with India grew in importance, and the harbour of Maó attracted her as a base in which her ships could shelter from the winter storms. Oliver Cromwell is said to have first drawn attention to the advantages of Menorca, but it was Charles II who negotiated with the Spanish crown for the right to use Maó harbour in 1644. From then on British ships called regularly at the port, and this is the period when Samuel Pepys became familiar with Menorca, through the reports of Richard Gibson, his former secretary, who became victualling officer in the port. Maó, then, grew in importance, becoming the dominant town on the island by the end of the century; but Ciutadella remained the capital, a fact which caused continuous friction among the islanders.

THE TURBULENT EIGHTEENTH CENTURY

With the new century, Menorca at last emerged from

neglect and isolation to become once again one of the strategic 'hot spots' of the western Mediterranean. The War of the Spanish Succession, which began in 1702, found the Balearics on the side of Charles III of Austria, and Menorca revolted against the Bourbon King Philip V. The uprising was put down with harsh reprisals by French troops acting on Philip's behalf in 1707. It was now that the British first played a leading part in Menorca's colourful history. A permanent base in the Mediterranean was needed for British ships and Maó seemed ideal: in addition to the natural advantages of its harbour, it was well placed for keeping a watch on the main French naval base at Toulon. In 1708, therefore, the Duke of Marlborough resolved to annex the island, and in September of that year a British fleet under Sir John Leake arrived off the Illa de l'Aire. Some 1200 marines under the command of Major-General James Stanhope (a grandson of the first Lord Chesterfield) were landed with considerable difficulty at Cala d'Alcaufar on 14 September and by the end of the month the British were in control, sustaining only 40 casualties. Most of the people of the island, smarting from the harsh regime imposed on them after their fruitless revolt, welcomed the invaders; only the fairly small number of defenders in Fort San Felipe held out for any length of time.

Officially, the British had taken Menorca in the name of their ally Charles III. The following year, however, Stanhope succeeded in persuading the king (despite Menorquín protests) to cede the island to Britain as security for expenses incurred on his behalf, and at the end of the war the Treaty of Utrecht in 1713 ratified British sovereignty over both Menorca and Gibraltar. The second Duke of Argyll arrived as governor and the first of three periods of British dominion over Menorca began.

The island they had acquired was impoverished and run down: the farms were large but neglected, and society was divided by the recent conflict and top-heavy with greedy churchmen and impecunious grandees. Initially the main concern of the British, however, was with defence: a new fortress was constructed on La Mola, Fort San Felipe was reinforced to become one of the most impregnable bastions in all Europe and the Marlborough Redoubt was built on the opposite side of Cala Sant Esteve. Stanhope had reported home that 'England ought never to part with this island, which will give the law to the Mediterranean both in time of war and peace'.

But internal concerns were not neglected for long, and one of the most significant events in the history of modern Menorca was about to occur: the arrival on the island of

Colonel Richard Kane as lieutenant-governor in 1712. A professional soldier who had served in Flanders and Canada, he was an exceptional administrator who grew to love the island and took immediate and imaginative steps to improve the lives of its inhabitants.

Kane's first significant contribution to Menorca was to build a road. Financed by a tax on alcohol and built by British soldiers, the Camí d'en Kane was a solidly constructed, straight highway some 10 m. wide which ran from Fort San Felipe, via the three main inland towns, all the way to Ciutadella. (The protests of the landowners through whose estates it passed were ignored.) Much of Kane's road still exists today: it ran to the north of Alaior, but from Es Mercadal to Ciutadella followed more or less the same route as that taken by the modern C 721. As a first step, the marshy area at the head of Maó harbour had to be drained – it was converted into orchards and market gardens and a monument to Kane stands there to this day.

Kane also moved the capital from Ciutadella to Maó, producing a rapid expansion of the latter city; indeed it outgrew its walls within a few years and Kane had most of them demolished; he also carried out extensive town planning and improved the facilities of the port. Schools were opened and a naval hospital was built on the Illa del Rei (renamed 'Bloody Island' by the British) which remained in use until 1964.

But from the islander's point of view the most important of Kane's legacies may have been quite different; during the years under Spain Menorcan agriculture had been severely neglected. Kane imported the seeds of new strains of crops, and fresh breeding stock of cattle (Friesian and Charollais) and sheep; also poultry from France, new varieties of apples and plums (locally called '*quen*' even now) and for fodder the sainfoin which grows to this day on the island. As a result, production of wine, vegetables and chicken increased by 500 per cent during the first forty years of the British occupation. Kane even instructed the farmers in crop husbandry and checked on food prices daily at Maó market.

Inevitably, there was occasional friction between the Menorcans and the British soldiery imported to rule over them. In particular, the Church remained resolutely hostile to the occupation forces: as Catholics, they resented Protestant rule and the loss of many of the privileges they had previously enjoyed. Based in Ciutadella, they and their fellow-citizens were also embittered by the decline in their city's importance following the transfer of the capital to Maó. But in general, the governorship of Sir Richard Kane, who died in Menorca in 1736, was seen to be beneficial for the people and his name is still honoured on the island. The British occupation completed the process of bringing Menorca into the modern world: its legacy included not only new buildings, improved communications and increased prosperity, but better education, cultural advancement, administrative order and a new concept of political liberty.

In 1756 Britain and France were again at war, and almost the first hostile act of the French was to invade Menorca with a large force under the Duc de Richelieu. Despite adequate intelligence of the French intentions, the British Admiralty and government were taken by surprise: there were only three British ships in the Mediterranean and security on Menorca itself had become lax. The Governor, General William Blakeney, was a jovial octogenarian, and although the defences of Fort San Felipe were formidable (especially its famous labyrinth of underground passages, some communicating with Maó harbour and Cala Sant Esteve, which made it possible for the entire garrison to remain underground), the strength of the force within it was minimal, while Ciutadella and Fornells were scarcely defended at all.

Richelieu landed at Santandría and Ciutadella, where the Anglophobe citizenry welcomed him as a liberator, and was able to advance on Maó without a shot being fired. Arriving outside the walls of Fort San Felipe on 23 April, he embarked on a siege that was to last ten weeks. The defenders' only hope was for the arrival of reinforcements from Britain and these were indeed on their way, but only after many delays and much confusion. A small fleet of seventeen warships under the command of Admiral Byng had reached Gibraltar on 2 May and was now making its way towards Menorca. Byng, a meticulous but unimaginative and irresolute commander (he was said to have gone

Ruins of Fort San Felipe

The 'fishing village' at Binibeca Vell

Cala Galdana from the cliff top   (below) High summer at Arenal d'en Castell

View from the cliffs at Cala En Porter

The superb beach of Arenal de S'Olla (Son Parc)

Ciutadella harbour

A typical Menorcan farm

The ruins of a palaeo-Christian basilica near Fornells

The pine-fringed beach of Cala Macarella

Little-visited Cala En Turqueta

The northern beaches of Cala Pregonda (top) and Cala Algaiarens (above) are assiduously protected from development

(left) Menorcan gate on the path up to the fortress of Sant'Agueda   (right) The Algendar gorge   (below) Olive trees shade the taula of Torre Llafuda

Cala de sa Torreta, a remote beach to the north of Es Grau

Cales Coves

(left) Grey-leaved cistus near Cala Pilar
(right) Mesembryanthemum on Cap de Faváritx

Pair of hoopoes (© *Eric & David Hosking*)   (right) Bee-eater
(© *Dennis Bright, Swift Picture Library*)

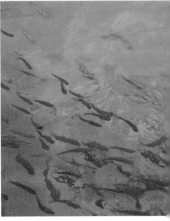

(left) Tortoise near Cala Mitjana   (right) Sardines at Cala
Trebalúger

into battle with a copy of the *Admiralty Fighting Instructions* in his hand), anchored off Cap de Faváritx on the 19th, where he was confronted by the French fleet under the Marquis de la Galissonnière; but after an inconclusive engagement he retreated to the open sea, having apparently decided that the fort could not be saved and that it was more important to defend Gibraltar than to risk a further battle with the French in which ships might be sacrificed unnecessarily. Not unnaturally discouraged by this turn of events, the defenders of the fort held out a little longer before being overwhelmed by a massive French attack and surrendering on 29 June. The loss of Menorca caused an outcry in Britain, culminating in the disgraceful court-martial and execution of Admiral Byng, as Voltaire had it, '*pour encourager les autres*'.

On Menorca, seven years of French rule followed. A young Breton, the Comte de Lannion, became governor, conducting an efficient administration which was generally popular with the Menorcans (already well-disposed to their fellow-Catholics). Public hygiene was improved and the pleasant town of Sant Lluís, the chief legacy of the French occupation, constructed on grazing land south of the capital. The end of the Seven Years War in 1763, however, brought back the British under the terms of the Treaty of Paris (in which France also ceded Canada, Florida and part of the West Indies).

This was a less happy period of occupation. The first governor, Lord James Johnston, was haughty and grasping and his rule was marked by droughts and epidemics. His successor, General Mostyn, did rather better. During his governorship the military township of Georgetown (now Es Castell) was founded overlooking the harbour. Es Migjorn Gran (San Cristóbal) was founded a few years later. The inhabitants of Menorca now numbered some 26,000, so new housing had become a pressing need. A third governor, General Murray, sought to alleviate unemployment by licensing some fifty Menorquín sailing ships as corsairs: the islanders showed great aptitude for this calling and within a few years the 'Mahonese pirates' enjoyed a reputation as fearsome as that of the Barbary pirates of earlier centuries.

The second period of British occupation lasted only 19 years. By 1778 Britain and France were at war again, and four years later Menorca was to change hands once more, this time to become Spanish. The expedition against it was led by the Duc de Crillon, who landed at Cala Mesquida with 3,600 men and met no resistance on his onward march to Fort San Felipe. Inside the fort General Murray had some 1800 able-bodied troops; once again reinforcements were urgently requested, but in vain: British forces were largely deployed in America at this time, and the small relief expedition that was mounted in England had to be deflected to assist with the defence of Gibraltar, also under siege. Meanwhile further Spanish reinforcements arrived; a sustained bombardment of the fort began and conditions within it deteriorated rapidly. On 4 February the English garrison surrendered after a siege lasting almost six months which left Fort San Felipe in ruins.

On 23 March Menorca came officially under the Spanish monarchy, with the Conde de Cifuentes as governor. The Conde was a popular ruler, but the Menorcans' delight at being reunited with Spain was short-lived. New taxes and regulations were imposed and, worst of all, Catalan, which had been the only language used by the native population since 1287 and in which a flowering of Menorquín literature had taken place during the preceding century, was supplanted by Castilian. On the positive side, however, the Vatican gave Menorca its first Bishop for twelve centuries in 1795. One of the chief (and least explicable) achievements of the new regime was the complete destruction of Fort San Felipe; this marvel of military engineering was completely razed within two years (the Spanish government apparently thought this would make Menorca safer from future invasion). That this was a serious misjudgement was to be demonstrated a mere sixteen years later, when Britain, fresh from Nelson's victory over the Napoleonic fleet in the Battle of the Nile, once more felt the need for a strategic base at Maó and launched yet another invasion. This time the landing (under Sir Charles Stuart) took place at Port d'Addaia; it found the Spanish authorities in disarray and Stuart was able to advance on Es Mercadal, from which

Port d'Addaia today

central base both major cities were taken without difficulty or loss of life within nine days.

The third and last period of British occupation lasted only four years, but was perhaps the most harmonious of all. Sixteen years of interference and incompetent rule from the mainland had left Menorcans in a mood to appreciate the greater freedom and prosperity brought by the British: Maó harbour was busy with a constant succession of British ships and as many as 12,000 English soldiers visited the island over the four years. From this period come the myths surrounding Nelson's visits to Menorca and his supposed residence with Lady Hamilton at Sant Antoni ('The Golden Farm') on the northern shore of Maó harbour; in fact the famous admiral appears to have spent four days in Maó in 1799, but he was on his own and he did not leave his ship.

English influence on island life reached a peak at this period. Chippendale and Sheraton furniture were imported, while gin, English puddings and (of all things) gravy (*grevi* in Menorquín) found a place in the local cuisine. Bow windows (*boinders*) became a popular architectural feature, and countless words of English origin entered the language which remain in use to this day: examples include *escrú* and *tornescrú* (screw, screw-driver), *mervels* (marbles), *xel* (shell), *punx* (punch) and many others. Even All Fools' Day, celebrated in Spain on 28 December, is observed on 1 April in Menorca!

Only with the Treaty of Amiens on 25 March 1802 did Menorca finally come to rest under the Spanish crown, and even then it was a close thing: it seems that Britain was chiefly determined that France should give up any interest in Egypt and was willing to sacrifice Menorca to this end; finding that France had already evacuated Egypt before the treaty was ratified, however, the British saw no further need of the sacrifice and secret orders were rushed to the last governor of Menorca, Sir Henry Cleophane, to delay handing over the island to the Spanish. Had the orders arrived in time Menorca might have been British to this day; but they arrived two days too late.

With the departure of the British, Menorcan prosperity waned. Refugees flooded in, fleeing from the upheavals caused by the Peninsular War in Spain, and there were shortages. Menorca itself remained unscathed by the war, ironically because the British fleet maintained a presence there (under Nelson's second-in-command Lord Collingwood) for its protection. Nevertheless a period of emigration began, to Algeria, South America, California and Florida (where descendants of Menorcans live still). In 1815 an important link with America was forged when the US

Mediterranean fleet began to use the Illa Plana in Maó harbour as a training station; this base was maintained for some 25 years and, until the Naval College at Annapolis opened, most American midshipmen received their training at Maó. American links were strengthened in 1867, when the first admiral of the American Navy, Admiral David G. Farragut, hero of the Civil War and the son of an emigrant from Ciutadella, visited the island.

During the nineteenth century Menorca's population grew until its agriculture could no longer sustain it. Further emigration took place, and a few industries were started – notably the shoe industry in Ciutadella, begun by Don Jeronimo Cabrisas y Caymaris, a native of that city who had emigrated to Cuba and made his fortune there before returning to his homeland. The arrival of steamships brought a decline in the fortunes of Maó harbour, though the opening of the first inter-island ferry service in 1852 improved communications. Before the end of the century the richer Menorquín families were building small seaside holiday homes in such places as Santandría, Na Macaret and Cala Mesquida, early forerunners of the *urbanizaciones* of today.

Menorca's next brush with history came in the Spanish Civil War of 1936–39. Unlike its Balearic neighbours, the island declared for the Republicans, despite the fact that the general in command of the local garrison at the start of the war was pro-Franco. His troops mutinied, and in the ensuing civil strife the cathedral at Ciutadella and the sanctuary on Monte Toro were damaged, while the prehistoric caves became hiding places for wanted men. The island was heavily blockaded and there were shortages of some items. As Franco's Nationalists gained the upper hand on the mainland, Menorca became the last redoubt of Republicanism, attracting the acquisitive attentions of Mussolini, who planned to subdue the island. This alarmed General Franco to the extent that he approached the British for help in retaining the island as part of Spain; ironically, it was thus a British ship, the HMS *Devonshire*, that brought Franco's envoy into Maó to negotiate the island's surrender in 1939 a few weeks before the official end of the war.

MENORCA TODAY

The twentieth century has seen great changes in the Menorcan countryside and in the lives of the people who work on it. Probably less than 10 per cent of the population could now be described as peasants, and these spend much more time in the various towns and villages of the island than their grandfathers did. The cultivation of cereals has declined, too, in favour of the intensive rearing of cattle for the export of meat and, above all, cheese.

In this century, the towns of the island have expanded dramatically – almost all the building outside the *contramurada* in Ciutadella, for example, is post-war, while the Es Castell suburb of Horizonte is almost a new town.

TOURISM

Tourism in the Balearics began as early as the 1930s in Mallorca, but it was much slower to take off in Menorca, and even now the people affect a 'take it or leave it' attitude. The island enjoys the second highest average income per capita in all Spain, so there is justice in the argument that Menorca's economy rests on firm enough foundations without tourism, and that anyway most of the jobs it provides are taken by immigrant workers from mainland Spain, especially Andalucía. Nevertheless, during the boom years following the opening of the new airport, the number of visitors to the island increased from 186,727 in 1968 to 702,430 in 1975 – more than doubling the island's population during the peak season. A rash of new hotels and holiday developments sprang up all over the island, earning fortunes for many landowners, particularly those whose estates lay near the coast. Happily, since 1975 more rigorous controls, particularly on high-rise building, have been introduced and further excesses should be avoided.

AGRICULTURE

Still the mainstay of Menorca's economy, agriculture employs a large percentage of Menorcans as farmers or market gardeners. Dairy farming is the most important activity: Friesian cattle (and a smaller number of Charollais) graze the lush pastures and produce the milk which is used to make the famous Menorcan cheese and ice cream – both products, like the local beef and veal, which Menorca produces in quantities far in excess of local needs. The Friesians' ancestors were imported in the eighteenth century by the British governor, Sir Richard Kane (see also p. 85), who was also responsible for introducing crop rotation and other technical improvements to the agriculture of Menorca. Today, the island has excellent grazing, freely watered in dry weather; during the summer heat the cattle and sheep retreat to the elaborately constructed dry-stone shelters (*barracas* or *ponts*) which are such a feature of the Menorcan landscape.

Lucerne and sainfoin (*enclova* in Menorquín) are grown for silage, and a small amount of mixed cereals is still harvested in May and June. Market gardens produce onions, tomatoes and other salad vegetables, and some soft fruit is commercially grown, including strawberries. The season is about ten weeks ahead of the UK.

The south of the island, although stonier, is more intensively cultivated than the north, just as it has been since the talayotic era: the lighter soil retains warmth better. Today as always, the stones and rocks in the fields are gathered into heaps and used to construct dry-stone walls (*tancas*), which help to reduce erosion and protect the soil from the salt-laden winds. There are also large farms in the less exposed areas of the north, where modern methods can to some extent overcome the irregular fertility of the area. Irrigation of the fields is a major concern, and has been ever since the Moorish occupation, from which period date many country wells in use today. Overall there is no shortage of water on the island, even when the population more than doubles in summer.

Menorcan farming is sophisticated, making use of modern techniques and machinery. Improved irrigation and greater mechanisation mean that farmers need fewer workers. Today's visitor will be struck by the absence of peasant cottages in the countryside: instead, one sees large isolated farmhouses, obviously built many years ago and apparently perfectly capable of farming without outside aid the large tracts of land that surround them. It is rare to see peasants in the fields: yet only a generation ago, colourful bands of agricultural workers were a common sight.

It is probably unexpected to find an almost total lack of vines on the island; there used to be vineyards on Menorca but a plague of phylloxera at the end of the last century brought the industry to an abrupt halt.

INDUSTRY

The two main light industries on Menorca are shoemaking and costume jewellery, which together employ a large proportion of the population. In both industries much of the work is done by home workers. Ciutadella, where the shoe industry was founded, traditionally concentrates on ladies' shoes, Alaior on men's. There are also a number of workshops and small factories producing furniture on the island.

Since 1970, all industrial development in Maó has been confined to the *polígono industrial* (industrial estate) to the west of the city, and Ciutadella's industry is similarly zoned

CULTURE AND FOLKLORE

ATENEU DE MAÓ

This very active scientific, literary and arts association is the cultural nucleus of the whole of Menorca. It comprises a museum, art gallery, substantial library and reading room, and runs courses on a wide range of subjects: lectures open to the public are held in the library. *Revista de Menorca*, a cultural review of historical, artistic and scientific matters, has been published annually for over a hundred years. The Ateneu is at Sa Rovellada de Dalt 25, Maó.

ART

In Maó, exhibitions can be seen at the following galleries: Museu del Ateneu, Sa Rovellada de Dalt 25 (open 18.30–21.00); Casa de Cultura de Sa Nostra, S'Arravaleta; Dalt y Baix, Sant Jordi 31 (open 18.00–21.00); and the Centro Ministerio de Cultura, Vassallo 33 (open 16.00–21.00). The permanent art collection was previously housed in the Casa de Cultura, Plaça de la Conquesta 8, but this has been closed for several years: it is hoped that it will reopen in the summer of 1990 in the cloisters of the Convent of Sant Francesc (Plaça de Monestir). Occasionally exhibitions are held above the Claustre del Carme (covered market). In Ciutadella, art forms part of the collection of the Museu Municipal in the Plaça d'es Born (also closed for restoration at the time of writing); other paintings hang in the Salort Palace (see p. 175), in La Cauxa, Bisbe Vila 5 and Verge del Carme 'Sa Nostra' on the Camí de Maó. There are smaller galleries in 9 de Juliol, Santa Clara and Roser. In Es Migjorn Gran the Galería Migjorn at Sant Llorenç 14 exhibits the work of both local and expatriate artists from 1 May to 31 August.

Art exhibitions are infrequently held in other towns: watch for posters outside the Casa Cultural, Alaior, Musupta Cusi, Sant Climent, and the town halls of Es Mercadal, Sant Lluís and Es Castell.

Menorca's most eminent artist was the eighteenth-century portraitist Pascual Calbo Caldes, who painted at the court of the Empress Maria Teresa of Austria. Sir Joshua Reynolds painted on the island during a five-month stay in

1749, but few of his Menorcan works have been traced.

CINEMA

The Teatro Principal de Maó, Costa d'en Deià 46 (see p. 95), is frequently used as a cinema. Other screens in Maó are at Nuevo Alcazar, Santa Anna 27; Salón Victoria, San Roque 30; Consey, Sa Rovellada de Dalt 9. Ciutadella has four cinemas: OAR, Avgda Capital Negrete 1; San Miguel, Ses Andrones 32; Artístico, Plaça d'es Born; and Alcazar, Avgda de la Constitució 20. There are also the España in Alaior, the Centro in Es Mercadal, and the Astoria in Ferreries. Films are occasionally shown in the Museu de Ateneu (p. 93); there is a film society in Ciutadella, Cineclub Casino, 17 de Enero, whose screenings are on Thursdays at 20.30. At all cinemas the programme usually begins at 21.00, but check the posters.

LITERATURE AND SCHOLARSHIP

Menorca's most celebrated writer was D. Angel Ruiz Pablo (1865–1927) of Es Castell, who wrote poetry and prose in both Spanish and Catalan. An unusual and respected work, *De re cibaria*, written by the lawyer and intellectual Pedro Ballester in 1923, is by no means only a cookery book: in it recipes are interspersed not only with the history of Menorcan cuisine but with philosophy, religion and social comment. In preparation is a gargantuan work by a group of writers and scholars: compilation of the *Enciclopèdia de Menorca* began in 1977 and the first section was published two years later. It is envisaged as being ultimately an eight-volume work: one volume, 'Geografia', is published, but many sections of future volumes are on sale in bookshops.

Menorca has made a considerable contribution to Catalan culture: indeed historians of the literature refer to the late eighteenth to early nineteenth century as the 'Menorca period'.

MUSEUMS

The Museu de Menorca has for many years been housed in the Casa de Cultura in Maó; but the building was unsuitable and required restoration, so it was decided to rehouse it in the cloisters of the church of Sant Francesc, which have been converted for the purpose. At the time of writing, the conversion work is almost complete and it is hoped the transfer of the collection itself, which is primarily of archaeological interest, can be completed by summer 1990. In the interim it is, unfortunately, not open to the public. A it happens, the museum at Ciutadella, housed in rooms of the ground floor of the *ayuntamiento*, is also closed for restoration.

The Ateneu has its own museum, containing an enormous collection of marine specimens as well as a map archive (open 18.30–21.00). At Sant Lluís there is a small agricultural museum (p. 153).

MUSIC AND DANCING

Both Maó and Ciutadella have annual music festivals, which attract world-famous performers. These are prominently advertised on posters and banners in the towns; the local press, including the English-language *Roqueta*, gives listings of concerts. In Maó, the International Music Festival takes place in August: concerts are held in the Teatro Principal and the church of Santa María and start at 22.00. Ciutadella has its Festival d'Estiu (Summer Music Festival) in July and August: performances begin at 21.30 and take place in the memorable setting of the cloisters of the old Seminary (Claustre del Seminari), Bisbe Vila. Recitals are given on the celebrated organ in Santa María, Maó, both in conjunction with the International Music Festival and every weekday in July and August from 11.45–12.15 (admission 200 ptas).

Jazz can be heard every Tuesday from 21.30 in the Casino de San Clemente in the village of Sant Climent (tel: 360053). Visitors to the island who can play or sing are always welcome to join in. Other live music is available nightly at Cala Corb in Es Castell and in some of the 'music bars' (many of them caves) around the head of Ciutadella harbour.

Menorca's own folk music originated in Aragón and was 'imported' in the thirteenth century. The songs can have religious, mythical or amorous themes, while the accompanying dance is a kind of fandango. Es Mercadal has its own version of this, known as the '*jota*'. A surprising legacy of the eighteenth century is highland dancing, which is still practised in Es Castell; this dates from the occupation of the town by Scottish troops. Pop concerts take place at irregular intervals in the Polideportivo, Polígon Industrial, Maó, and dancing to various groups can be enjoyed weekly at the Claustre del Carme, Maó (see local press for details).

THEATRE

The Teatro Principal at Costa d'en Deià 46 in Maó is the oldest opera house in Spain and has over 80 boxes. Built in

1824 to the design of an Italian architect, it is now rarely used for its original purpose; it chiefly functions as a cinema, though operas are staged during the week of the city's fiesta and occasionally at other times. Ciutadella has two theatres: Teatro Municipal d'es Born, Plaça d'es Born 2 (tel: 380176), and Teatro Salesiano, Maria Auxiliadora 10 (tel: 380007). Posters in the city advertise forthcoming dramatic productions.

FIESTAS

The local fiestas on Menorca are spectacular events. All are held between June and September, so most summer visitors to the island are likely to coincide with one or other of them: the opportunity to witness one should not be missed.

Pre-eminent among them is the Fiesta de Sant Joan, held at Ciutadella from 21–23 June. This ancient and unique festival is revered as a cornerstone of Menorcan tradition. Recalling archaic fertility rites in some of its aspects, it is said that the fiesta was instituted by a group of Knights of the Order of St John who came over with Alfonso III and converted existing semi-pagan rites to a celebration of their patron saint. It takes place on the Saturday and Sunday before the Feast of St John and the feast day itself (Midsummer Day, 24 June). The fiesta is run by a group of citizens known as the *Junta de Caixers*: of these, the *Caixer Senyor* represents the nobility, the *Caixer Capellà* the church and the *Caixer Pagès* the people. On the Sunday before the festival the *junta* patrols the streets all day, inviting the people to the fiesta and collecting donations on two big trays; they are preceded by a *Fabioler* (herald) with whistle and drum, and by a young man covered in lamb skins and carrying a live lamb adorned with ribbons and flowers on his shoulders as a representation of St John the Baptist: this Sunday is known as '*Diumenge d'es Be*' ('Sunday of the Lamb') for this reason. On St John's Eve the *junta* lead a horseback procession; they go thrice round the Borne (the '*Caragol*'), while youths crowd and jostle the richly caparisoned horses, running under them while their riders make them step and prance on their hind legs to the traditional *jaleo* music. At about 7 p.m. the cavalcade proceeds to the chapel of Sant Joan de Missa, 10 km. away, for a blessing and the singing of traditional songs. Thereafter, further horseback processions go through the narrow streets until well into the night, the riders occasionally encouraging their mounts to go right into the front doors of the houses. Another cavalcade with *caragols* ushers in the festivities on St John's Day itself; this time the people throw

Civic dignitaries observe the frenetic scenes at the Ferreries fiesta

hazelnuts, said to represent kisses, into the path of the horses. In the afternoon there is a special mass in the cathedral, after which the procession reforms and spectacular tournaments are held down by the harbour. The fiesta ends, very late, with a firework display in the Borne.

All the other towns of any size hold fiestas during the summer, in emulation of Ciutadella's. Usually the week before the fiesta itself features a series of minor events – concerts, dances, sports competitions, chess tournaments, clay pigeon shooting, art exhibitions, regattas in bizarre variety – culminating on the fiesta days with a carnival procession with floats and bands, and several cavalcades through the town. At all the fiestas, the young men delight in taking risks as they leap under the rearing horses, traditional rosewater (*aigu-ros*) is sprayed on the people and enormous quantities of *pomada* (gin and lemon) consumed till the ground is ankle-deep in plastic cups. A firework display brings each fiesta to its end. Menorcan fiestas are noisy, exhilarating and occasionally dangerous; but they are unique and very memorable.

Fiestas in other towns in Menorca take place as follows:

Es Mercadal, Fiestas of Sant Martín	July 15–17
Fornells, Fiestas of Sant Antoni	July 22–23
Es Castell, Fiestas of San Jaime	July 25–26
Es Migjorn Gran, Fiestas of Sant Cristófol	August 9–11
Alaior, Fiestas of Sant Llorenç and Sant Climent	August 12–14 August 19–21
Ferreries, Fiestas of Sant Bartolomé	August 23–25
Sant Lluís, Fiestas of Sant Lluís	August 26–28
Maó, Fiestas of Nuestra Señora de Gràcia	September 6–9

Dates may vary from year to year. *Roqueta* gives full details of times and events for each fiesta in the relevant month's issue.

Another festival is celebrated at Ciutadella on 17 January every year – that of Sant Antoni Abad, which commemorates the reconquest of Menorca in 1287: the children of the city are each given a palm leaf.

SPORTS AND ACTIVITIES

SPORTS

BOWLING

There are two alleys at Europa Bowling, urb. Cala En Bosc.

BULLFIGHTING

Not really a part of the Menorquín culture; there is no bullfighting on the island, despite the presence of a large but rather down-at-heel Plaza de Toros in the southern outskirts of Ciutadella.

CANOEING

Canoes may be hired at a few beaches, e.g. Arenal d'en Castell, Cala Galdana, Sant Tomás and Arenal de S'Olla (Son Parc), for between 600 and 800 ptas an hour.

CRICKET

The Menorca Cricket Club (MCC!) was formed six years ago and membership was 5000 ptas a year in 1989. The club plays on the football pitches of the San Luis Hotel, S'Algar, and of Es Castell, but are trying to raise money for a permanent cricket pitch. Matches are played against teams from Britain, Mallorca and Ibiza: dates and times are advertised in *Roqueta*, Menorca's English-language magazine.

CYCLING

Once off the main roads, the cyclist can explore the Menorcan countryside in peace; it is a particularly popular activity in the flatter western parts of the island. There are miles of minor roads and bridleways, some of them impracticable with a car; while it is true that these are often potholed, they frequently lead to remote beaches or little known prehistoric sites. Naturalists will find a bicycle ideal transport, enabling them to see more wildlife than they would from a car.

An excellent little book of cycle tours, produced by GOB in 1989, is sold on the island: *Menorca en velo*, by Llorenç Sastre (250 ptas). It is written in Catalan, but complete translation is unnecessary as the maps, distances and times are quite clear.

Bicycles may be hired at the principal resorts: expect to pay about 400 ptas per day, 1500 ptas per week (including tax and a baby seat if required).

DIVING

Diving is officially prohibited in Menorca, but despite this there are eight diving schools on the island. With tuition in German there are: Centro de Buceo, Cala Galdana; Intersub Tauchen, Hotel Almirante Farragut, Cala En Forcat (tel: 382800); Tauch Centre, Hotel Poseidon, Cala Santandría (tel: 384725); and Nautic Punta Prima (tel: 361854). In English: Menorca Country Club, Playas de Fornells (tel: 375160); Club S'Algar Aquasport, S'Algar (tel: 363881); and in the Son Parc *urbanización*. The Club Falcó at Platja de Son Xoriguer offers tuition in both languages. Of these only the Club S'Algar Aquasport has a decompression chamber.

Diving is, of course, an expensive sport: one dive might cost approx. 3000 ptas, plus 650 ptas for the hire of a boat; and a beginner's course of ten lessons costs 20–30,000 ptas including the hire of all equipment. Divers may be required to join the Spanish Diving Club (FEDAS), so take two passport photographs, photocopies of pages two and three of your passport and the page of your log book which shows your qualification. In addition to ordinary travel insurance, supplementary cover is advisable.

The enjoyment of this sport is enhanced in Menorca by the wealth of caves to explore, the multi-coloured reef fish and the remains of wrecks. *NB It is dangerous to fly less than 48 hours after diving.*

FISHING

The waters around Menorca teem with fish, and the rocks at the mouths of the *calas* will reward the amateur with rod and line. Day trips out to sea in fishing boats can sometimes be arranged: it is worth enquiring at any harbour.

FLYING

Sightseeing excursions and lessons are available at the Real Aero Club de Mahón, 3 km. south of Maó on the Sant Lluís road.

FOOTBALL

Sporting Mahón play on Sundays in the Estadio Mahones on the Sant Lluís road near the south-east corner of Plaça de S'Esplanada.

GOLF

The nine-hole Club de Golf Son Parc (tel: 352250/363840) was opened in 1977 and forms the nucleus of the Son Parc *urbanización*. The course has a par of 70; in 1989, green fees were 3600 ptas per day, 18,000 for a week, 45,000 for 30 days (which do not have to be consecutive); club rental was 1,000 ptas per session. A reasonable standard of dress is expected. Instruction is available and a practice area with driving range is planned for early 1990. A shop and restaurant adjoin the clubhouse, in a renovated farm building. Although relatively short (2714 m.), the course offers many hazards and strategically placed greens.

Regular competitions are held and matches played against teams from the UK and Mallorca; plans for a further nine holes have been submitted to the authorities in Palma de Mallorca.

HORSE RACING AND TROTTING

Flat racing meetings are held on Sundays at the Hipódromo Municipal de Mahón (by the Sant Lluís road) at 17.30 in summer and 11.30 in winter; also at the Hipódromo, Torre del Ram, north-west of Ciutadella. At Maó, there is an English commentary.

At both meetings there are also trotting races. In these the jockey sits in a small well-sprung cart, and the horse is permitted only to trot: if it 'breaks' (gallops) and thus gains ground it is disqualified, though it may continue if the jockey is able to restrain it and resume trotting. A horse is allowed three such 'breaks' and bets are taken. This sport still flourishes in the USA, but is dying in Europe. Menorca is the only Spanish venue.

HUNTING

Much of the land on Menorca is 'Coto Privado de Caza' (i.e. hunting rights are private), but a few km. north of Alaior on the road to Arenal d'en Castell the Ministry of Agriculture has a hunting reserve: 'Coto Social de Caza'. Permit-holders may hunt partridge, rabbit, turtle-dove, quail, woodcock and thrush in season. Applications for permits to hunt on

Menorca should be addressed to Servicio Nacional de Pesca Fluvial y Caza, Calle Goya 25, Madrid. Allow several weeks.

KARTING

Meetings are held at the Real Aero Club de Mahón on the Sant Lluís road on Sunday afternoons and evenings.

PARASAILING

Only available in high season at Platja de Son Xoriguer, where the price in 1989 was 3000 ptas per flight, with a 10 per cent discount for parties of four.

PEDALOES

Can be hired at a cost of between 600–800 ptas per hour at many beaches, including Arenal d'en Castell, Binibeca, Binimel-lá, Cala Blanca, Cala En Blanes, Es Canutells, Cala Galdana, Punta Prima, Cala En Porter, Cala Tirant, Sant Tomás, Son Bou and Arenal de S'Olla (Son Parc).

RIDING

Picadero Binixica (tel: 368055) on the Maó-Cala En Porter road at km. 7 is a British-owned riding school open every day from 9.00–13.00 and 17.00–20.00 except Sunday afternoons. A similar establishment is Picadero de Menorca on the main road west of Alaior at km. 15. As well as riding it offers horse and cart rides, pony rides, island tours, breaking and livery.

Near Ferreries, some 500 m. down the road to Cala Galdana there is a regular 'equestrian show' including demonstrations of the training methods used for the prancing and controlled rearing that is the most spectacular feature of island fiestas, displays of four-in-hand carriage driving and of Andalusian horsemanship. The show takes place on Wednesdays and Sundays at 20.30: entry costs 800 ptas (including free *pomada*), with children admitted free.

SAILING

For the boat-owner, Menorca is a paradise: the many coves which are difficult to reach from the land present the yachtsman with no problem. Although Menorca has only a small proportion of the berths and moorings available in the Balearics, its wealth of sheltered inlets offers safe anchorages in idyllic surroundings, often away from all trappings of tourism.

Anyone negotiating these waters should carry a copy of *East Spain Pilot*, by Robin Brandon (published by Imray, December 1988): chapter 7 deals with the Balearic Islands and details the procedures for legal entry as well as navigation. The temptation is to relax and take less care in the Mediterranean where there are no tides and few currents. However, the *'tramuntana'*, a fierce north wind originating in France as the *mistral*, can blow up out of a clear blue sky. Submerged reefs can be another hazard and careful chart-reading is recommended when entering harbours and *calas*. Weather forecasts are obtainable daily at 06.00, 11.00 and 17.00 from the Central Office of the Meteorological Institute for the Balearic Islands, whose telephone number is given in *East Spain Pilot*.

Maó and Ciutadella both offer berthing and repair facilities. Maó is one of the world's largest natural harbours extending inland for 6 km. Chandleries, shops and workshops line the waterfront; the yacht club, the Club Maritimo de Mahón, has basic facilities. Nearer the mouth of the harbour the town of Es Castell also has a yacht club, the Club Nautico de Villacarlos, overlooking the cove of Cales Fonts. Ciutadella's harbour is 1½ km. long; it becomes overcrowded in summer and a new marina is planned. The Club Nautico is inadequate for the number of summer visitors.

On the north coast of the island, the Bay of Fornells resembles an enormous shallow lake; it contains two islands, and is 4½ km. long and up to 1½ km. wide. The small Club Nautico is at Ses Salines on the western side: there are very few moorings and the anchor holding is 'moderate' as the bottom is grass on sand. Further east is Port d'Addaia, a deep narrow fjord between wooded hills. One of the most sheltered (and beautiful) havens in the Balearics, it is a natural 'hurricane hole'. Although buoyed for safe passage, the entrance requires care in approach and can be difficult in windy conditions. There is a launching ramp, crane, repair shop and contiguous growing *urbanización* with attendant facilities. The nearby resort of Na Macaret has a small mole and round the headland of Cap de Faváritx to the east is the sheltered but very shallow harbour of the fishing village of Es Grau. At the extreme south-western corner of Menorca, the resort of Cala En Bosc has a busy marina, reached by a channel which goes under an arched footbridge.

Other sheltered anchorages are (clockwise from Maó) Cala de Sant Esteve (very narrow), Cala d'Alcaufar (can be crowded), Illa del Aire (except in a southerly wind), Cala Binibeca (open to south-west wind), Cala Biniparratx (very narrow), Cala Binidalí (narrow), Cala Es Canutells, Cales Coves (forked inlet, Stone Age caves), Cala En Porter, Cala Trebalúger, Cala Galdana (resort), Calas Macarella and Macarelleta, Cala En Turqueta, Arenal de Son Saura, Cala Santandría (can be crowded), Cala Morell (launching ramp), Cala Pregonda (daylight only because of rocks at the entrance), Arenal d'en Castell (resort), Cala Molins and the Illa d'en Colom.

'SKI-BOB'

This relatively new addition to the watersports scene can also be called a 'ski-bus', a '*duarry*' or a 'sausage', the last name being the most descriptive. Six or so people sit astride an inflatable cylinder and are towed at speed around the bay; part of the fun is to be capsized *en route* and for this reason life-jackets are usually provided. The average price is 6–700 ptas per ride with children half-price. Ski-bobs operate at Arenal d'en Castell, Cala Galdana, Son Xoriguer, S'Algar, Son Bou and Son Parc.

SQUASH

Courts can be found at Binibeca Vell, at the Club Tenis de Ciutadella in the urb. Los Delfines, Cala En Forcat, and at the Squash Club, Ferreries.

TENNIS

Many of the larger hotels have tennis courts. Other courts are: Las Dunas, Sant Tomás (tel: 370118); Club Tenis de Ciutadella, urb. Los Delfines, Cala En Forcat; Casablanca, Cala En Blanes; Club OAR, Avgda Negrete, Ciutadella; bar/restaurant Xauxa, Cala Blanca (tel: 385287); Europa Bowling, urb. Cala En Bosc; Club Tenis Alayor, Camino s'Atalaia (tel: 371589); Club Tenis Binisafua, Binissafuller; Club Tenis Mahón, c. Trepucó, Maó (tel: 360576); Tenis Es Plans, west of Alaior (tel: 372926); and at urb. Horizonte, Es Castell. There are also courts attached to the golf club at Son Parc. In all these venues you can expect to pay approx. 1000 ptas per hour, with racquet hire for 50 ptas.

WALKING

Menorca offers excellent walking country, especially in late spring and early summer, when the weather is not too hot for exertion and the birds and flowers are at their most profuse; October and November are also good walking months. There is no space in this book to cover walks in detail, but thankfully this is not necessary, for there already exists an admirable series of booklets on walks in Menorca by Dodo Mackenzie, a long-term resident of the island who has carefully researched a number of circular walks in all quarters of Menorca. These are graded according to difficulty, with full map references, the distance to be covered and detailed descriptions of the route. Book 1 is unfortunately out of print, but Book 2, *12 Walks in Menorca* and Book 3, *More Walks in Menorca*, are widely available in the island's shops for a few hundred pesetas and cannot be recommended too highly to anyone interested in exploring the more remote parts of the island and experiencing the beauty and tranquillity of its countryside. Serious walkers would be very well advised to purchase a set of the military maps of Menorca (see p. 6) in addition.

Locked gates can be a problem for walkers, but often they do not mean that the way is barred to pedestrians: look for stones projecting from walls which form a stile enabling you to climb the wall. Notices may be off-putting, too: '*camino privado*' or '*camino particular*' usually mean 'no vehicular access'; '*coto privado de caza*' means 'private hunting rights' merely; '*entrada prohibido*', however, conclusively means 'no entry'. If in doubt about a sign encountered on a well-established track, it pays to ask permission of the landowner or farmer (if you can find him!): Mrs Mackenzie has found this usually leads to friendly permission.

Discouraging signs may confront the walker in Menorca, but a friendly word with the landowner often produces permission to proceed

In 1331 a path, the Camí de Cavalls, was constructed right around the perimeter of Menorca; it was partially restored by the French during their occupation in the eighteenth century. Since then it has fallen into disuse, been ploughed up or built over. Marvellous news for walkers, however, is that it is now the island government's intention gradually to reopen and reinstate this ancient right of way.

WATER SCOOTERS (*Motos acuáticos*)

Slightly less powerful than jet-skis, these noisy inventions have recently appeared on the beaches of Cala Galdana, Son Bou, Sant Tomás, Arenal d'en Castell, and Son Parc.

WATER-SKIING

Not as popular as it was, but the sport may be enjoyed at Cala Galdana (at 13.00 only – telephone 373267 to book), Son Bou, Ses Salines de Fornells, Arenal d'en Castell, S'Algar and Son Xoriguer. For obvious reasons, the sport is forbidden in the harbours of Maó and Ciutadella.

WINDSURFING

Menorca's sheltered coves are ideal for the learner: having mastered the art, more exposed beaches await the enthusiast. Tuition is often, but not always, available where boards are for hire. Several resorts offer courses: at Platja de Son Xoriguer, beginners are taught for two hours a day on a simulator before taking to the water (a week's tuition cost 14,000 ptas in summer 1989). Official 'schools' are at Arenal d'en Castell (Aquasport Menorca), Cala Galdana, Ses Salines de Fornells (children and older people welcomed), Playas de Fornells (Menorca Country Club), Son Parc, Cala Tirant, Sant Tomás, Son Bou, Cala Torret (Club Nautico de Urb. Binibeca), S'Algar, Port d'Addaia and Punta Prima (Nautic Punta Prima). Boards can be hired without tuition at Arenal de Son Saura and Platja de Binimel-lá.

EXCURSIONS

COACH EXCURSIONS

There is a range of these available in almost every resort; information about them is most easily found at the larger hotels. Typical coach trips are the 'island tour', usually comprising Maó (including boat trip round the harbour), Binibeca and the south-east coast and Fornells (approx

2500 ptas), a drive up Monte Toro and a visit to Ciutadella. There are also various evening excursions, to harbour restaurants in Ciutadella and to barbecues and other touristic events at various venues inland. Viajes Ebusus, Plaça de S'Esplanada 3, Maó, is worth visiting for these and several other excursions.

BOAT HIRE

Dinghies or catamarans can be hired at Arenal d'en Castell, Cala de Binibeca (Club Nautico), Cala de Binisafuller, Cala Galdana, Playas de Fornells (Menorca Country Club), Fornells (Ses Salines), Port d'Addaia, Platja de Punta Prima (Nautico Punta Prima), Platja de Sant Tomás, Platja de Son Bou, S'Algar and Cala Tirant. The average price is 2000 ptas per hour plus 1000 ptas for instruction.

Small motorboats seating up to nine people may be hired at these beaches: Arenal d'en Castell, Cala Galdana, Son Bou, Sant Tomás, Punta Prima, Arenal de S'Olla (from the Sol Parc Hotel), Son Xoriguer and S'Algar. Expect to pay at least 3000 ptas for an hour and 12,000 for a day (8 hours). From the Club S'Algar Aquasport, S'Algar (tel: 363881), a magnificent 6-berth Regal 320 Commodore power boat can be hired for around 24,000 ptas per day. This takes 6-10 passengers, is capable of 40 knots and can circumnavigate Menorca or visit Mallorca without refuelling. The Club S'Algar has many other vessels available for hire from a Menorcan *llaut* to a Furia 332.

BOAT EXCURSIONS

In addition to the various boats making regular tours of Maó harbour (p. 145), there are organised excursions exploring sections of the coastline from a number of resorts. Days, times and routes vary with demand and the season, but information can usually be found prominently displayed at the waterfront of the relevant resort or in a bar nearby. Boats which make a full-day trip along the coast between Cap d'Artrutx and Cala Escorxada leave from Cala Galdana and Cala En Bosc; from Ciutadella boat trips sail down the west coast and round as far as Arenal de Son Saura and Cala En Turqueta; some boat excursions are available from S'Algar; and from Na Macaret and Port d'Addaia the north-east coast can be explored. Full-day trips often include a *paella* and *sangría* lunch and might cost 2500–3000 ptas per head. Several resorts also have glass-bottomed boats which make short trips around the local coast.

Trips to the Illa d'en Colom are operated on a shuttle service from Es Grau between mid-May and September in the motorboat *Arc* (400 ptas return). You can ask to be landed on one of two beaches and to be collected any time up to 8 p.m. (so far as we know, no one has been yet inadvertently left behind on the island overnight). More information from the bar Ca'n Bernat in Es Grau.

It is also possible to make an excursion to Mallorca. The fast catamaran run by CATS Line leaves Ciutadella harbour regularly for Alcudia in northern Mallorca, journey time about 45 minutes (see p. 5).

CHILDREN'S MENORCA

Menorca is a very suitable holiday destination for families with young children. The most obvious attraction is the wealth of beaches with safe bathing and fine sand. There are plenty of beach toys on sale at the resorts; some beaches even have a kiosk on the sand.

The larger package-tour operators lay on in-hotel children's activities, often in the form of a club with a 'uniform' of T-shirts and badges; these are supervised by an experienced adult who takes full responsibility for three- to eleven-year-olds, taking them on picnics and nature trails, and organizing games and quieter indoor activities such as film and video shows. Such hotels usually provide baby-sitting or a baby-listening service.

Older children will enjoy hiring bicycles and pedaloes, going for ski-bob rides and perhaps learning to windsurf. Young people of all ages can get a thrill from the corkscrew water slides: the largest is at Club San Jaime near Son Bou

The waterslide at Club San Jaime, Son Bou

beach (150 ptas for two runs); others are at Cala Blanca and Cala Galdana, where the Tobogán pizzeria also has a mini-golf course. Such courses also feature at some of the larger hotels, as do outdoor table tennis tables. The *urbanización* at Son Parc has a playground in the woods with slides, swings and climbing frames.

In Maó, before or after a boat trip round the harbour, a visit to the Aquarium on the waterfront (Moll de Ponent) is free.

DONKEY TREK

There is a 'Donkey Safari Park' 15 km. north of Maó on the Fornells road – take care when approaching as the entrance is on a tricky bend just before the Son Parc turning. The 'park' comprises a small zoo and a snack bar and provides organized donkey rides through the woods. These take place between 12.30–13.30 and 17.30–19.30 and are often arranged in advance by package tour companies. Horse-riding lessons and trails can be arranged at the island's riding schools (p. 102), and the equestrian show held on Wednesdays and Sundays on the Cala Galdana road (500 m. after the junction with the C 721) is fun to visit: children get the opportunity of a donkey ride in the intervals.

The Menorcans welcome children in even the smartest restaurants: it is not unusual to see local children dining with their parents quite late at night, or asleep in a pushchair alongside the table.

SHOPPING

In leather goods, costume jewellery and, above all, shoes, Menorca has a good deal to offer the discriminating shopper, both in the cities of Maó and Ciutadella and in the various large emporia (often called 'boutiques' or even 'factory boutiques') to be found beside the major roads; the latter purport to charge 'factory prices'. There are no branches of the large national Spanish department stores.

Shoes can be of very high quality (you may be told that the late Princess Grace of Monaco *always* came to Menorca for her shoes). An important manufacturer is Rubrica, who have a factory with attached showroom on the main road 1 km. east of Ferreries (open 9.30–13.30, 16.00–20.00 Mon–Fri, 16.30–19.30 Sats). A large selection of men's and women's shoes are for sale here at prices somewhat below what you would expect to pay for similar quality in the UK. The various designs are displayed by size and there is no

Shopping street in Maó

pressure to buy. Tours of the factory can be made by prior arrangement. Shoes are also sold at the more general showrooms of Es Plans on the C 721 between Maó and Alaior (they also have leather wear and jewellery). Other shoe shops are Calzados Torres, Camí de Maó 35, Ciutadella; Calzados Davo, Joan Huguet 21, Alaior; Grabados Alaior, Ctra Nueva, Alaior; and La Torre, Jose María Quadrado, Ciutadella, and S'Arravaleta 17, Maó. It is still possible to have a pair of shoes handmade to measure if you think of this early enough in your holiday.

Costume Jewellery is fast becoming one of Menorca's main industries. Much of it is exported to South America and may not appeal greatly to British tastes, but prices are reasonable and if you do see a piece that takes your fancy you may be fairly sure that you are paying a great deal less than you would at home. As with shoes there is a selection for sale at roadside shops such as Es Plans (similar establishments are Novus, Llonga and Leo in the industrial estate east of Ciutadella). In Ciutadella the factory of Hijos de Bernardo Marqués (opposite the start of the old Maó road) has a large showroom (open 9.00–13.00 and 16.00–20.00 daily except Saturday afternoons); other jewellery specialists around the city are the supermarket 'El Super' on the southern fringes and Freijomil and the Bisutería Marqués in the industrial *polígono*. Every year at the end of May, Menorca hosts SEBIME (Semana de Bisutería de Menorca), a major costume jewellery exhibition/trade fair held at Maó exhibition centre, Polígon Industrial de Maó.

Pottery and porcelain is another local craft: examples can be seen at Cerámicas Lora on the Maó waterfront. On the main road west of Ferreries (between the 35 and 36 km. posts), the enormous castellated Castillo Menorca shop carries a large range of Lladró porcelain figures and the cheaper variant, Nao. They also sell shoes, handbags and other leather goods, jewellery, Majorica and Orquidea pearls and lace (all from Mallorca) and souvenirs of all kinds. Castillo Menorca is open daily except Sundays from 9.30–13.30 and 15.00–20.00. The Lladró porcelain is housed in a separate building, where there are elaborate set pieces at prices exceeding 100,000 ptas as well as more affordable items.

Leather goods are widely available: as well as the large roadside shops, Patricia and Center both have branches in Ciutadella and Maó, selling a wide range of locally made shoes, bags and clothing.

Other acceptable souvenirs of Menorca include the delicious hard **cheese** *queso de Mahón*, Spain's best, which is widely available or can be purchased direct from the Coinga factory in Alaior; it usually comes in square loaves (sometimes with the grass ropes from which it was suspended during the curing process still attached). When fresh the cheese is creamy and strong-tasting; after a few weeks it hardens to become a little like mature cheddar and if left still longer (3 or 4 months), it darkens and becomes crumbly, much like parmesan. Other Menorcan food products are **macaroons** (*amargas*) from Es Mercadal and, of course, Menorcan **gin**.

Model boats are made in a small factory in Sant Lluís: its products can be found for sale in Maó. Such items as lace doilies, etc., dolls, glassware, and objects made of olive-wood usually come from Mallorca or the mainland.

Well worth a visit is the English-owned Picture House (Casa de Cuadros) housed in a converted coach house 2 km. west of Maó on the C 721. Opened in 1988, it sells paintings (mostly by Menorcan residents of several nationalities), as well as pottery and craft items, dried flowers, books and hand-printed 'designer' T-shirts (open daily in season except Sundays, 9.30-19.30).

In general, **shopping hours** on Menorca are 9.30-13.00 and 17.00-20.00; most shops close on Saturday afternoons. Small supermarkets abound in the tourist areas, which often open for longer hours than this during the season. There are two very large modern supermarkets, one each in the industrial estates outside Ciutadella and Maó.

Market days on the island are as follows: Maó – Tuesday and Saturday; Alaior – Thursday; Es Mercadal – Tuesday; Ferreries – Tuesday and Friday; Ciutadella – Friday and Saturday; Es Castell – Monday and Wednesday; Es Migjorn Gran – Wednesday; Sant Climent – Tuesday and Friday; and Sant Lluís – Monday and Wednesday.

Clothing sizes

Shoes

Men–British	7	8	8	10	$10\frac{1}{2}$	11
American	$7\frac{1}{2}$	$8\frac{1}{2}$	$9\frac{1}{2}$	$10\frac{1}{2}$	11	$11\frac{1}{2}$
Continental	40	41	42	43	44	$45\frac{1}{2}$
Women–British	3	4	5	6	7	8
American	$4\frac{1}{2}$	$5\frac{1}{2}$	$6\frac{1}{2}$	$7\frac{1}{2}$	$8\frac{1}{2}$	$9\frac{1}{2}$
Continental	36	37	38	39	40	41

Shirts (Men's)

British and US	14	15	16	17	18
Continental	36	38	41	43	45

Women's dresses

British	10	12	14	16	18	20
American	8	10	12	14	16	18
Continental	40	42	44	46	48	50

BEACHES

There are beaches for all tastes on Menorca – over a hundred of them; most are sandy, and they range in size from large stretches such as the 2½ km.-long strand at Son Bou to tiny coves with room for only a couple of sunbathers. They vary, too, in their accessibility, and several fine beaches can only be reached via private land, the owners of which can be less than enthusiastic about visitors, especially in the high season.

The following selection of beaches is divided into two sections. First, those that can easily be reached on metalled roads with a car: these tend, naturally enough, to be at the centre of holiday resorts and most have car parking and a range of facilities on and around the beach itself. The second group of beaches can in some cases (but not all) also be reached in a car, but only by means of rough tracks with the possibility of a certain amount of walking when the car can go no further. Within each section the beaches are arranged in an order that follows the coast clockwise from Maó. The map references refer to the 1:25000 military maps (see p. 6): the purchase of a set of these is recommended to those interested in exploring the more inaccessible beaches.

The star system we have used is entirely subjective and should not be taken too seriously; with so many beaches to choose from, it seemed valuable to highlight the very best, particularly where access is arduous and a hint as to whether the goal is worth the effort may be appreciated!

Safety flags: those beaches which are manned by the Red Cross (*Cruz Roja*) display flags indicating the prevailing conditions. A green flag means swimming is permitted, yellow that it is dangerous but may be attempted with caution, and red that it is forbidden.

Nudism is officially not allowed and there are no designated naturist beaches; nevertheless there are plenty of remote areas where it is practised with impunity, so this is a matter for personal judgment.

EASILY ACCESSIBLE

CALA D'ALCAUFAR★★
Situated 4½ km. south-east of Sant Lluís, and just south of S'Algar, this picturesque haven is well hidden from the road. There is in fact no parking by the

The beach at Cala d'Alcaufar

beach and very limited space in the village. A quaint, steep street, lined with fishermen's cottages and small holiday homes, winds down to a long curving inlet with a tiny harbour, sheltered from all winds except the east and southeast. The surrounding limestone cliffs are low and flat-topped and contain a cave opposite the village which invites exploration. A Martello tower crowns the southern headland, under which a boat may easily enter the spacious grotto of 'Els Coloms', named after the hordes of rock doves which frequent it. The cave has two entrances, both of them navigable, separated by a wide pillar. The northern promontory culminates in a single enormous rock known as 'El Torn'.

The beach is narrow but deep and the sand hard-packed and rather gritty. Bathing is safe for children in the very shallow water, but better for swimmers from the rock platforms further away from the beach. Umbrellas and sunbeds may be hired from the bar/restaurant; there is a Red Cross post here.

Cala d'Alcaufar has been pop-ular since the last century as a summer retreat for the people of Sant Lluís, many of whom keep their boats here: indeed, bathers may have to pick their way between the boats before reaching open water! The resort has hardly grown and remains reasonably quiet in high season. There is one hotel, the Xuroy, which was Menorca's first tourist hotel. An expensively constructed bridge of local stone spans the stream and marshland behind the cove. The road across it has yet to be made up and leads at present only into wild scrubland to the south, but an extension to Punta Prima is planned. Between the foot of this bridge and the back of the beach lies the village football pitch, made of sand. [85-51 Isla del Aire – 108098]

PLATJA DE PUNTA PRIMA**

Punta Prima is the extreme south-eastern point of Menorca and can be very windy. It is approached either from Maó, through Sant Lluís and due south, or from the west along the coast road which joins the settlements between here and Binidalí.

The beach of fine white sand is about 100 m. wide, is enclosed between two low headlands and faces south-east to the Illa del Aire 1 km offshore. In high season the water can be slightly murky. Bathing at Punta Prima is only safe when the red flag is not flying: dangerous undercurrents can always develop at the 'corners' of islands. There is a Red Cross post for emergencies.

An ancient watchtower on the western headland (the Torre des Ganxo, meaning 'hook') is today surrounded by villas and apartments. Hotels in the resort include the Sur Menorca and the Pueblo Menorca, but the emphasis is on self-catering holidays. Ample supermarkets serve the apartments; bars and restaurants proliferate and three are on the beach. For relaxation, there are umbrellas and sunbeds for hire. Several sporting facilities are also on offer: windsurfing, sailing and pedaloes. Mini-golf and tennis are available nearby. [85-51 Isla del Aire – 097080]

CALA DE BINIANCOLLA
On the road between Punta Prima and Binibeca, the beach here suffered badly in the 1988/89 winter storms. The coast is rocky and the hinterland rather barren, but the cove offers the best shelter from the southerly winds in this very exposed part of the island. The fishing is good here, but the only bathing is from rocks. An *urbanización* mainly occupied by Spaniards is contiguous with that of Binibeca. [85-51 Isla del Aire – 082079]

CALA DE BINIBECA*
This small beach lies 1 km. east of the 'fishing village' of Binibeca Vell and is in fact adjacent to the *urbanización* of Binibeca Nou. One is not too aware of this, however, as the beach is enclosed by low headlands and backed by pines. Safe shallow water and soft sand make this spot ideal for children and non-swimmers. There is adequate parking beside the path to the cove and a picnic area in the pines: there is also the rare facility of a public lavatory. A small bar/restaurant stands on the rocks at the extreme left of the beach and pedaloes may be hired from it. Fishing can be enjoyed from the low headland beyond the bar, and there is a windsurfing school at Cala Torret just to the east. A small, low island, the Illot de Binibeca, lies just offshore. [85-51 Isla del Aire – 062083]

CALA DE BINISAFULLER*
Five km. south-west of Sant Lluís, the turning to this cove is 500 m. west of the road down to Binibeca. There is a rough parking area off the road just before you reach the beach, but there is also a rather larger area a little further on to the west. The narrow beach is of sand and crushed shells, but there are rocks soon after one enters the water. Bathing is safe, though not ideal for very young children. There is a landing stage for boats on the eastern headland and a sailing club operates from here; the Red Cross have a post on the western side. No umbrellas or sunbeds are available for hire here, nor is there a beach bar.

Two islets lie offshore, the largest being the Illot de Binisafuller, and the hinterland is dense *'maquis'* which is pleasantly fragrant. A scattering of cottages and some newer bungalows of the '*urbanización* Binisafua' are prettily set in the *maquis* with individual gardens; these are served by two restaurants, one of them with a swimming pool.

This uncrowded cove has one disadvantage: it lies directly under the flight path of Maó airport. [85-51 Isla del Aire – 044097]

CALA DE BINIPARRATX

Only 300 m. east of Cala de Binidalí, Biniparratx is by contrast totally secluded. A small rocky car park overlooks a gorge down which a reasonably easy path winds through gorse, juniper and cistus bushes. The beach is of pale grey, rather coarse sand; it is about 50 m. wide and sheltered by high cliffs on either side. Basically it is good for swimming and safe for children, but seaweed piled up at the shoreline became a problem in 1989, making the beach inhospitable throughout the season: at the time of writing the authorities are relying on the forthcoming winter to improve the situation before deciding whether they should take a hand themselves.

The snorkelling is excellent here and there are prehistoric caves in the western cliff face. Only one house, a bungalow on Cap d'en Font, overlooks the beach from a distance. There are no 'facilities' of any kind. [85-51 Isla del Aire – 031099]

CALA DE BINIDALÍ

A pretty little inlet 4½ km. south of Sant Climent, this beach not only serves the eponymous *urbanización* but also has a large car park which attracts day-trippers. The car park is on the western headland, from which the beach can be seen, but no buildings overlook the cove. The coastline here is very exposed, and during the winter of 1988/89 Cala de Binidalí became so silted up with seaweed and pebbles that its golden sand was invisible throughout the following season. It is to be hoped that this attractive beach will soon recover. A massive wall at the back of the beach was built as a protection against pirates. The Binidalí *urbanización* is not intrusive, the villas being low and very scattered. [85-51 Isla del Aire – 026099]

CALA ES CANUTELLS

Leaving Sant Climent in a southerly direction (by the Tramuntana restaurant), take a right turn after 2½ km. (signed 'Urbanización Ses Tanques'). Some of this development is complete; the new hotel Mar de Menorca will open in May 1990; work progresses on a limited number of villas. Until the recent creation of 'Ses Tanques', only a few old houses stood above the beach at Es Canutells. Steps lead down through a gap in the wall below the Bar Canutells to the small white sandy beach at the head of a narrow curving inlet. Bathing is safe in calm weather, but there is no safety flag: pedaloes can be hired but there are no other facilities. In the eastern cliff, a landing stage is used by fishermen, as are the caves alongside it. [85-50; 86-50 Mahón – 000120]

CALA EN PORTER★★

Reached either from Alaior (where the road is signposted

from the C 721 as it passes through the town) or via the PM 704 (Sant Climent road) which leaves Maó along the southern side of the industrial *polígono*, Cala En Porter is the oldest seaside resort on Menorca. It is now a major holiday town with hotels, villas, shops and restaurants, all of which are confined to the top of the high cliffs at the eastern side of the cove: the western cliffs are completely undeveloped.

The setting is spectacular: high cliffs on either side enclose a long inlet, with a green valley at its head. A stream, the *barranco de Cala'n Porter*, winds through marshland to enter the sea across a wide, deep beach of pale gold sand. Access to the beach from the town is by long flights of steps, difficult for the elderly or less energetic; there is, however, also a road which winds steeply down the western side to an area of car parking. At sea level there are a handful of shops, bars and restaurants; in addition, two beach bars operate in summer and hire out sunbeds, beach umbrellas and pedaloes. Bathing is safe here and the beach should be altogether ideal. Sadly, however, the sewage system constructed 14 years ago when the resort was developed has become inadequate and the sea water, in the summer of 1989, had a definite brownish tinge; though laboratory tests showed no dangerous levels of pollution, this nevertheless considerably marred the magnificent view of the cove from the cliffs above. The authorities say the problem is being dealt with as a matter of urgency (some 1,000 million pesetas are to be spent), and it is hoped that it will have been resolved by the summer of 1990.

Facing the open sea, high in the eastern cliff, is the large natural cave known as the Cova d'en Xoroi, which functions as a bar during the daytime and in the evenings as an unusual discotheque (see also pp. 25, 157). [84–50 Llucalary – 969142]

PLATGES DE SON BOU***
Approached by a newish road that leaves the C 721 400 m. west of Alaior and cuts through an impressive rock tunnel as it nears the coast, Son Bou is the longest beach on Menorca: some 3 km. long and, on average, 40 m. deep. The sand is pale gold and powdery and the very clear water gets deep only gradually, with some rocky outcrops. The sheer length of the beach means that it never gets overcrowded.

The eastern extremity of the beach is the headland of Cap de ses Penyes, honeycombed with caves and crowned by the fortified talayotic village of Llucalari. At the foot of the cliff can be seen the remains of an early Christian basilica, discovered in 1951. This building was a focal point of the fourth–fifth century village of Ses Canessies, by which name Son Bou was formerly known. The outline of the three-naved church is very clear: a remarkable feature is the deep font.

Hideous twin skyscrapers, the hotels of Los Milanos and Los Pinguinos, dominate the eastern end of the beach and serve as a telling reminder of the consequences of uncontrolled touristic development (the building of such monstrosities would never be permitted today). Around their feet new *urbanizaciones* are sprouting, which sprawl towards the ancient basilica. A large car park just west of the hotels is close to the easiest point of access to the beach.

Further west, the beach becomes wilder, quieter and less populous, thanks largely to a wide strip of marshland which cuts it off completely from the extensive villa development of San Jaime Mediterraneo on the low hills behind. The marshes harbour a thriving bird population which keeps well away from the rare paths leading to the dunes at the back of the beach; flooded after rain, these paths are normally usable with caution in summer. Many trees have been retained among the villas behind Son Bou, and these together with the colourful gardens give a pleasantly green aspect to the new development which has sprung up here. The Club San Jaime is its nucleus, with a bar/restaurant, disco, swimming pool and (extremely popular) water chute.

When the sea is calm, bathing and water sports are safe at Son Bou, but a wind can create dangerous currents and there have been tragedies here: watch for the red flag. The Red Cross post on the beach has a safety boat. On suitable days there are opportunities for windsurfing, ski-bobbing, jet-skiing and hiring pedaloes all along the beach; sunbeds and umbrellas are also available. In addition, no less than five beach bars and a shop cater for the large number of visitors to the island's longest stretch of sand. [84–50 Llucalary – 915175]

PLATJA SANT TOMÁS★★★

Separated from Son Bou by two headlands, the long sandy beach of Sant Tomás is really a continuation of it. The route thither, however, is quite different: from the main road (C 721) take the road south either from Es Mercadal or from the western edge of Ferreries to Es Migjorn Gran, then follow the road to the coast from there. (Both roads, incidentally, go through some of the prettiest pastoral scenery on the island.)

Sant Tomás beach, which is contiguous with that of Sant Adeodato further west, is a long narrow strip of soft white sand, backed by small hills covered with an ancient pine forest. Some villas have been built up the slopes, but the resort remains a thin ribbon of development, only two or three blocks wide. Three large hotels and a huge apartment block stand at the back of the beach and many holiday activities are centred on these. There are large car parks at each end of the resort. On the beach there are watersports facilities and a Red Cross station with safety boat – this is another beach where currents can be treacherous under certain conditions, so take note of the flag system; in summer a temporary beach bar hires umbrellas and sunbeds.

In the winter of 1988/89 the beaches of Sant Tomás and Sant Adeodato suffered dramatic damage when all the sand was stripped from both beaches almost overnight by freak storms. During July of 1989 a monumental effort was made to clear away the rocks with a dredger, lorries and men working 24 hours a day, and happily by August the beach was as sandy as ever. [84–50 Llucalary – 889189]

Sant Adeodato beach, with Sant Tomás in the background

PLATJA DE SANT ADEODATO (ADEODAT)★★

Reached like its neighbour Sant Tomás by the road through Es Migjorn Gran, Sant Adeodato lies to the right of the road when it meets the coast; here there is a small car park by the Bar Es Bruc, from which a path leads along the top of a small slope behind the entire length of the beach, which ends at the rocky point opposite the islet of Escull de Binicodrell a few metres offshore. Uniquely in Menorca, cultivated fields extend right up to the dry-stone wall behind the beach.

There are no buildings here, and, apart from sunbeds and umbrellas for hire, no facilities apart from the Bar Es Bruc. Like Sant Tomás, the beach became a bed of rocks after the 1989 storms, but it is now once again a narrow strip of pale gold sand and ideal for young families. [84-50 Llucalary – 885192]

CALA SANTA GALDANA★★★

One of the easiest beaches to get to by car: turn south off the Maó-Ciutadella road 300 m. west of Ferreries, and Cala Galdana lies 7 km. to the south, reached by a well-surfaced, fast road (PM 714) which descends steeply to sea level when it reaches the resort (large car park on the right at the bottom of the valley).

It is easy to see why Galdana has been called 'queen of the *calas*'. It is the perfect Mediterranean setting: a towering limestone amphitheatre, with pines growing out of the rugged cliffs at crazy angles, encloses a large west-facing cove with a horseshoe of pale gold, gently shelving sand. The water is almost always calm; in the morning it is emerald green, changing to aquamarine as the sun reaches into the cove.

Twenty years ago Cala Galdana was a virgin *cala* reached by a rough track: today it is one of the most popular resorts in Menorca and disfigured by two large hotels, the Audax at the western end and the really unforgivable Los Gavilanes, which rises from the beach right to the top of the encircling cliffs; a third hotel, the Cala Galdana, is slightly more discreetly situated. But even with these excrescences the view of the *cala* from the surrounding cliffs remains breathtaking. A small river, the Algendar, flows into the sea here; it can be smelly but for most of the year looks delightful and contributes to the charm of this spectacular beach.

In addition to the hotels, Cala Galdana has a range of holiday villas and apartments, as well as shops, restaurants and a discotheque, most of them a minute's walk from the beach. Opposite the Hotel Audax a footbridge crosses the river to an enormous rocky outcrop which resembles an island but in fact stands at the western extremity of the sands. A bar on the rock enjoys a panoramic view of the beach. Four other beach bars operate during the summer, and there are plans to make three of them permanent and to instal a lamplit promenade between them with illuminated areas of seating under the pines. Umbrellas and sunbeds are for hire, and there is a safety flag and Red Cross post on the beach. Bathing conditions are perfect and very suitable for small children. Snorkelling, windsurfing and the 'ski-bob' are popular here: there is a windsurfing school and the calm water is highly suitable for beginners. A diving school also offers tuition; motor boats are for hire, also canoes, pedaloes and water scooters. Near the car park is the Tobogán bar/pizzeria with mini-golf and a water chute. [82-49/83-49 Santandría – 820215]

PLATJA DE SON XORIGUER★★★

This resort and the three follow-ing are all reached from the road leaving Ciutadella for the south coast and usually signposted 'Cap d'Artruix' and/or 'Costa Sud' from the final section of the *contramurada* inner ring road. If coming from further east, however, there is no need to enter the centre of Ciutadella to pick up this road. Instead, swing right off the main C 721 Maó road at the second roundabout after entering the commercial zone (after the Leo factory on the right and an electricity substation on the left) in order to cross the carriageway onto a bumpy stretch that meets the old Maó road. Turn right onto this and at the next T-junction (by the pink-domed cemetery and opposite the costume jewellery factory), turn left onto an outer ring road which shortly after swings round to the right. Here turn right into the Carrer del Pare Huguet, which brings you to a small square, Plaça de Jaume II. The road to Cala En Turqueta and Arenal Son Saura is to your left; for Cala En Bosc and the west coast leave the square at the opposite corner by going right and then left: this brings you into the Carrer de la Pau which shortly after bears left to become the main road to the south coast at the Plaça Europa.

Just before reaching the light-house at Cap d'Artrutx, turn left to skirt thc marina at Cala En Bosc, (following signs to 'Club Falcó'.) This is a new coastal road leading to what were, until quite recently, a pair of remote beaches 500 m. east of the neighbouring resort. Today, touristic development has crept along the shore and the Hotel Club Falcó attracts watersports enthusiasts; the further beach, in particular, is very popular in summer.

A walkway suitable for wheel-chairs or push-chairs links the car park and the two beaches, the smaller of which faces east and the larger, south. Both have glorious white sand and a gradual slope into crystalline water: parts of the 'second beach' are dotted with rocks, but these are clearly visible under the water. The smaller beach has a rather primitive bar, the larger has a restaurant as well, and a shopping complex including a supermarket between it and the road. In addition to the usual umbrellas and sunbeds for hire, watersports are a speciality here. Windsurfing and water-skiing are on offer (both with tuition), as well as a particularly malevolent 'ski-bob'; parascending is available when conditions allow, and diving courses are also run by the Club Falcó. [82-49/83-49 Santandría – 721201]

CALA EN BOSC (CALA'N BOSCH)★★

Cala En Bosc lies at the end of the C 721, and is reached as described above. For the beach, turn left just before the built-up area, bearing left and then right in order to skirt the yacht marina. The beach is on the far side of the marina just east of the Cala'n Bosch hotel: there is ample parking nearby.

The cove faces south-west, with a deep area of sand surrounded by holiday accommodation (which, judging from the odd unpleasant smell in high season, has put undue strain on the drainage system). Apart from this occasional nuisance, the beach is attractive, with pinkish-white, granular sand, clear water

which deepens gradually and good snorkelling around the rocky eastern side. Bathing here is safe when the green flag is flying; there is a Red Cross post but no boat. Sunbeds, umbrellas and pedaloes may be hired, and there is a beach bar on the sand. [82-49/83-49 Santandría – 716201]

CALA BLANCA★★

Now quite a large resort, Cala Blanca lies at the end of a rather narrow turning to the right of the Ciutadella-Cap d'Artrutx road some 4 km. south of the city (just after passing the Grill Es Caliu on the left and about 1 km. south of the Santandría turning). The beach has very white sand and clear water, but can become overcrowded in summer. There is a large car park on the northern side and, at the back of the beach, a small area of shady pines beside the vestigial remains of a 'naveta'. There are several bars and restaurants on the low limestone cliffs each side of the cove, one with a water chute. Pedaloes, sunbeds and beach umbrellas can be hired, and bathing is safe for children and the elderly. For the more adventurous there are caves to explore in the cliffs, as well as diving from rock platforms along the sides of the cove and from quite a high makeshift diving board on the northern side. [82-49/83-49 Santandría – 714246]

CALA DE SANTANDRÍA★

Leaving Ciutadella as described for Cala En Bosc, the beach at Santandría is reached down a sharp turning on the right just under 2 km. south of the city. There is a sandy car park at the back of the beach opposite some caves in the cliff.

The inlet is long and narrow and has been described as the prettiest on the west coast of the island. The beach itself is larger than one would have anticipated and has soft white sand. In summer, however, it can get unpleasantly crowded. Bathing is safe: sunbeds, umbrellas and pedaloes are available for hire. Four bars and restaurants stand beside the beach and a smart hotel, the Ses Voltes, has a prime position overlooking the cove. On the northern side stands the modern Prinsotel La Caleta and to the south the *urbanización* Bolivia. Slightly inland, the restaurant Sa Cuadra is quietly situated in a valley where bamboos grow alongside the tables. [82-49/83-49 Santandría – 718258]

CALETA D'EN GORRIES (SA CALETA)

A small satellite cove of Santandría, the beach known locally as 'Sa Caleta' lies near the mouth of the inlet below the ruined defensive tower of Es Castellá. It can be reached either from Santandría or direct from Ciutadella by following the road past Cala des Degollador (below). Also prone to overcrowding in summer, the beach is sandy with rocky surroundings; it has a beach bar, sunbeds and umbrellas [82-49/83-49 Santandría – 712262]

CALA DES DEGOLLADOR★

It is remarkable to find such a pristine beach only 400 m. south of Ciutadella harbour (it can be reached by taking the road due south from the western side of the Plaça de S'Esplanada). The main beach is an 80 m.-wide stretch of white sand enclosed on three sides by a crumbling old wall. It is usually uncrowded except at weekends, when local families take advantage of the safe bathing. There are no beach 'facilities'. The beach's name of 'Platja Gran' seems bizarre until you walk a few metres along the northern side to discover a second beach, 'Platja Petita', only 3 m. wide and perfect for a single family. The north side of the inlet is undeveloped – one can walk across rough ground to the Torre de Sant Nicolau at the mouth of Ciutadella harbour; on the south lies the suburb of Son Oleo where desirable villas have their own moorings and sunbathing platforms on the rocks. Two bars and the hotel Playa Grande face south across the beach; on the southern side are the *hostal* Mar Blava, a further bar and a discotheque, Adagio's. Cala des Degollador translates as 'Executioner's Cove': there must be some gruesome story which explains its name. [82-49/83-49 Santandría – 714276]

CALA EN BLANES★

The first of a series of four resorts a short distance to the west of Ciutadella, Cala En Blanes is reached by crossing the bridge over the harbour, driving along the commercial mole to the far end and turning left onto the coast road when you emerge at the top. After passing the lighthouse, the road follows the coastline for 2 km. before reaching Cala En Blanes, where there is limited parking along the road behind the beach. The small resort consists of an *urbanización* of holiday villas and a large hotel, the Cala'n Blanes, which dominates the head of a pretty inlet. A small beach of pale sand offers safe bathing, sunshades and sunbeds but no sporting amenities. A beach bar, 'Sa Cova', occupies a natural cave on the eastern side. On the opposite shore a fairly level path leads past a few rather attractive villas to the Punta Cala'n Blanes. [82-49/83-49 Santandría – 694283]

CALA EN BRUT (CALA'N BRUCH)

Reached by taking a left turn (signed 'Playa') a few metres beyond Cala En Blanes and then bearing right, this cove becomes almost a fjord, culminating in a minuscule beach barely two towels wide: it is easy to imagine as the haunt of smugglers in times past. The entrance to the inlet is like a natural pool: rock platforms have been constructed at various heights around it for sunbathing or for diving from – fun for proficient swimmers. Limited parking is available on the road along the rim of the inlet and a bar/restaurant/discotheque overlooks the water. The hinterland is extensively developed with villas and apartment blocks. [82-49/83-49 Santandría – 691282]

CALA EN FORCAT

Shortly after Cala En Blanes the road westwards from Ciutadella enters the large *urbanización* of Los Delfines through an ostentatious concrete arch. There is no road access to the shore: steps go down from various points in the shopping parade to a sandy gorge which ends at the beach, or one can descend directly to it from the immense Hotel Almirante Farragut. The narrow, curving inlet of Cala En Forcat must once have been picturesque. Now the diminutive beach of coarse sand at its head is severely overpopulated in summer and dominated by the vast bulk of the hotel. Although the water is calm, shallow and very safe for children, it becomes distinctly murky in high season. The more adept swimmer can bathe from one of a series of rock platforms towards the mouth of the inlet and avoid the worst of the crowds. As the beach is so small there are no amenities save a couple of pedaloes belonging to the hotel. [82-40/83-49 Santandría – 685281]

CALES PIQUES

These two narrow inlets, looking like a smuggler's dream, cut into the western cliffs north of Cala En Forcat and at present lie just beyond the last line of development at 'Los Delfines'. The rocks offer good fishing and the minuscule beaches are sheltered though they only see the sun in the evenings. The more southerly beach has recently been enhanced by the addition of golden sand and rock platforms carved out of the side of the cove; the sand at the other is barely 2 metres wide. Both are reached by walkways and flights of steps leading from a recently constructed *urbanización* on the rocky slope above. [82-48/83-48 Ciudadela – 681287]

CALA MORELL⋆

From the *contramurada* ring road in Ciutadella the turning off immediately to the north of the main Maó road is signposted 'Cala Morell/Algaiarens/La lternatively, drivers n the east may avoid tadella by turning ₒᵤₜ at the Leo factory and rejoining the route on the other side of the industrial *polígono*.) Follow the signs through the outskirts of the city and some 5½ km. after leaving it, a left turn (also signed) brings you after 2½ km. to the *urbanización*, built in the Moorish style. Here a left turn at the roundabout brings you round the back of the beach (past some fine examples of funerary caves in the cliff to your left) to a small car park at the far side; from it a steep flight of steps leads down to the shore. The beach itself is of brownish grit, and swimmers may launch themselves more comfortably from the natural rocky platforms at the base of the cliffs. Here the inlet is only 60 m. wide: swimming and snorkelling from one side to the other can be accomplished with ease. No organized watersports are available, nor is there a safety flag; the natural harbour is of course used by private yachts. Although the water is shallow at the shoreline, the lack of sand makes the beach less than ideal for young children. No hotels have been built at Cala Morell, but there is an abundance of self-catering accommodation. High above each side of the beach a bar/restaurant overlooks the cove. [82-48/83-48 Ciudadela – 754343]

ARENAL DE S'OLLA ✓ (ARENAL DE SON SAURA, SON PARC)★★★

This glorious beach of pinkish white granular sand lies below the extensive *urbanización* of Son Parc which is reached from the PM 710 heading north from Maó to Fornells; the turning off it is clearly signed some 700 m. west of the 17 km. post. Within the development, the way to the beach is signposted, culminating in a brief stretch of rough track which leads to a large car park.

Arenal de S'Olla is a perfect beach, with lots of room even in high summer. The sand extends for 500 m. inland from the sea and, in August, drifts of sea daffodils adorn the bases of the dunes, which merge into a backdrop of pinewoods. The water is very clear and for a long way out is never more than 1.5 m. deep; bathing is safe for non-swimmers. Watersports of all kinds are available here: windsurfing, ski-bobs, jet-skis and water scooters (the intrusive noise of which is this beach's only defect), kayaks, pedaloes and a diving school. Umbrellas and sunbeds may also be hired. There is a restaurant and beach bar at each end of the beach, and a shop selling beach goods, newspapers and magazines. There is no safety flag but a life belt is positioned near the shop.

Despite continuing development in this area, the beach is overlooked by few houses and remains unspoiled. The somewhat monolithic Beach Club apartments are in disfiguring contrast to the red-tiled and green-shuttered houses along the ridge, but it is possible to tuck oneself under the dunes, look westward and be completely unaware of Son Parc. A 20-minute walk over the western headland brings you to the little cove of Cala Pudent (see p. 137) [85-48 Ses Covas Novas – 992323]

ARENAL D'EN CASTELL***

Since the early seventies this has become one of Menorca's leading resorts and it is still growing. It is approached from Maó by driving north on the Fornells road (PM 710), and turning right at the 15 km. post.

The popularity of Arenal d'en Castell is easy to understand: its beach and setting are both magnificent. An almost perfectly circular cove, half a kilometre in diameter, it is enclosed by high cliffs to the east and lower slopes to the west. The sand slopes gently into the sea, but shelves more steeply soon after reaching the water. (The eastern end of the beach tends to be slightly shallower and thus safer for children.) At this end the hotel Aguamarina overlooks the beach and there is a Red Cross post with boat and safety flag. There are also public lavatories nearby.

Unusually comfortable sunbeds are available all along the beach; umbrellas may also be hired. Among the many water sports on offer are windsurfing (with tuition), water scooters, ski-bobs, sailboats and pedaloes. By renting a small motorboat it is possible to explore outside the bay. A car park at sea level at the western end fills up quickly, but there is plentiful parking beside the road along the cliff top, whence long flights of steps lead down to the beach; there is also a shaded car park near the access path to the extreme eastern side of the beach which (most unusually) charges for the facility.

Three enormous hotels crown the cliffs, in addition to hundreds of self-catering apartments; accordingly, shops and restaurants proliferate. There are, in fact, no less than five bar/restaurants actually on the beach. At the western end of the resort the White Sands timeshare complex, with its attractive elevated swimming pool, occupies a prime position and overlooks a small section of beach cut off from the main strand.

As on many north-facing beaches, the colours of the sea and sand appear very intense at Arenal d'en Castell. [85-48 Ses Covas Novas – 010310]

NA MACARET

This is reached from the Maó-Fornells road (PM 710), turning north for Arenal d'en Castell at the crossroads 15 km. from Maó. Two km. along this road there is a further turning to the right for Na Macaret and Port d'Addaia. The sea penetrates the coastline in a long, narrow inlet, affording one of the most sheltered havens for boats in the whole of the Balearics. Na Macaret faces east onto the inlet and has a minute brown sandy beach lying in front of the village square (where there is ample parking). There are no facilities on the beach, but there are small shops nearby, and near the water's edge the bar/restaurant Na Macaret; there is another restaurant, the Acuario, in the square, and a bar a few steps along the small mole. The houses here are old and were built by people from Alaior who have adopted the place as a safe boating and bathing resort only 10 km. from the town. In summer the beach is also used by the families of yachting people berthed at Port d'Addaia. [85-48 Ses Covas Novas – 025304]

ES GRAU★★

From Maó take the Fornells road from the harbour front and turn right after 1 km. (signed 'El Grao 6.5 km.'). At the end of the road park on the left just before entering the square. The village is compact; a cluster of attractive small white houses scramble up the hillside and overlook an almost circular bay with a perfect curve of white sand. It has several bars and restaurants, two of them at the water's edge.

An island, the Illa d'en Colom, lies across the entrance of the bay and shelters it from the north-easterly wind. The water between the island and Es Grau is so shallow that only small boats (of which there are great numbers moored in the bay) can pass between them. This shallowness makes Es Grau an eminently suitable beach for young children, who can paddle and bathe in safety; but adult swimmers have to wade a long way out to sea. The Red Cross have a post on the beach and fly a red or green flag according to weather conditions. Windsurf boards and small boats may be hired but there are no sunbeds or umbrellas. Behind the beach at Es Grau are high dunes separating it from a zone of wetland which extends to the lake of Albufera with its exciting bird-life. Tamarisk trees grow in profusion here and the whole area is a protected nature reserve.

Boat trips to the Illa d'en Colom, where there are two more beaches, can be made from Es Grau (see p. 149) [85-49 Isla Colom – 083232]

CALA SA MESQUIDA★

Very popular at weekends with the people of Maó, this cove is only 4.5 km. from the capital and is reached by driving north-east along a clearly signed road (PMV 7101). Fork left for Sa Mesquida just after the 2 km. post, reaching the southern end of the bay past a cluster of holiday homes where the craggy islet of Sa Batería Amagada is linked to the shore by a footbridge.

Cala Mesquida is bisected by a rocky outcrop crowned by a small castle; the northern part of the cove is about 300 m. long, with dark red sand and bounded by the massive headland of Pa Gros. Bathing from the sand is good, although not ideal for young children as it shelves quite steeply. There is plenty of room for parking on the hard sand at the back of the beach. There is a beach bar here, but despite its proximity to Maó, this cove is unspoiled and has a feeling of remoteness.   [85-50/86-50 Mahón – 100192]

CALA ES MURTAR

The first beach north of Maó is reached by driving round the innermost edge of the harbour and taking the road north-east towards Cala Mesquida. Fork left 3½ km. after leaving the harbour and, 1 km. later, fork right. Cala Es Murtar has a small stony beach in a U-shaped inlet; there are a few houses around the small harbour, but no tourists. Excellent fishing and swimming is possible from the rocks. [85-50/86-50 Mahón – 107181]

LESS EASILY ACCESSIBLE

CALES COVES

To find this rather remote spot

drive 4 km. west of Sant Climent on the PM 704. Here take a left turn, signed 'Urbanización Son Vitamina'; an extremely pot-holed road, widened, presuma-bly, for future development, leads from the southern edge of this estate down to the water's edge at Cales Coves. Here there is a forked inlet with two shingly beaches linked by a rocky path along the cliffside. The area offers good snorkelling and swimming from the rocks, but the most interesting feature of Cales Coves is the honeycomb of ancient caves in all the surround-ing cliffs. Some have elaborate entrances, and one containing (severely eroded) Latin inscrip-tions can be found near the first beach. Many of these caves are inhabited nowadays, mainly in the summer months, but the authorities are anxious to stop this trend as the resulting pollu-tion is already a problem. [84-50 Llucalary – 982136]

PLATGES DE BINIGAUS

This beach cannot be reached directly by car. From Es Migjorn Gran (San Cristóbal), drive down to Platja de Sant Adeodato, park at the bar Es Bruc and walk 1 km. west: Binigaus beach beg-ins opposite the small rocky islet of Escull de Binicodrell. The sand here is fine and light grey with some shingle banks. Bathing is not recommended, as the offshore reefs can create a dangerous undertow, particu-larly when the wind is from the south or south-east. A beach bar is set up in the summer months but apart from this there are no facilities. The remotest extremity of the line of beaches running all the way to Son Bou, Binigaus is

favoured by naturists.

A major attraction here must be to walk up the stream behind the beach and find, among the prolific greenery of the gorge, a wealth of natural and prehistoric caves: most notable of these is the Cova dels Coloms, (p. 35) with the interior dimensions of a cath-edral. [84-49 Alayor – 876196]

CALA ESCORXADA★★★

The most easterly of a series of spectacular *calas* with high white limestone cliffs, a backdrop of pines and a beach of soft white sand, Cala Escorxada is little visited as it involves a long walk or the use of a boat. From Ferrer-ies, take the PM 713 road towards Es Migjorn Gran for approx. 8 km. and park on the right, just inside the double wooden gates on the farm road to Sant Roc. Walk past the farm-house, turn left at the first oppor-tunity and left again at the farm of Albranca Vell. After 1.75 km. turn right down an avenue of trees which passes the large house of Torre Vella on your left. From here the walk is another 3 km. through farmland and pine-woods before descending steeply to the beach. Cala Escorxada may also be approached from Calas Trebalúger and Fustam; a circular walk which visits them all is described in Dodo Macken-zie's *12 Walks in Menorca*. There is perfect bathing from the soft sand, good snorkelling around the rocky entrance to the cove and a safe anchorage for small boats. [84-49 Alayor – 858202]

CALA FUSTAM★★

This diminutive but beautiful beach can only be reached by sea or on foot, from either Cala Trebalúger to the west or Cala Escorxada to the east. In each instance the route follows the ancient 'Camí de Cavalls', a track which in medieval times and again in the eighteenth century ran around the entire Menorcan coast. The inlet is small and narrow, the sand is white and the cliffs are thickly wooded. On the eastern side of the cove is a large natural cave. [84-49 Alayor – 856202]

CALA TREBALÚGER★★★

From the military map it would appear that this cove is accessible by using farm roads leading off the PM 714 Ferreries-Cala Galdana road (at the 5 km. post), or from the Ferreries-Es Migjorn Gran road, 1 km. short of the latter town. However the motorist is confronted by locked gates at both points. The three practicable ways of reaching Cala Trebalúger, therefore, are by walking 6 km. from a point 1 km. north of Es Migjorn Gran (the route is described in Dodo Mackenzie's *12 Walks in Menorca* No. 2, walk 10), by following a rough and wooded coast path from the back of Cala Mitjana (itself a 1 km. walk from Cala Galdana) or, most painlessly, by boat. Actually getting down onto the beach at the end is tricky, involving scrambling down a small cliff.

This is a supremely beautiful and isolated spot: a glorious stretch of powdery white sand containing thousands of broken shells enclosed between pine-covered limestone cliffs. A fresh-water stream flows over the beach from the tranquil gorge behind; there are troglodytic dwellings in the gorge and, on

the beach itself, a large cave with two entrances and a rock arch-way. There can occasionally be a seaweed problem, as the beach is exposed to the south winds. For much of the year Cala Treba-lúger is populated only by a herd of black mules; but in summer it is a favourite anchorage for yachts and a port of call for boat excursions from Cala En Bosc and Cala Galdana. Conditions for swimming, snorkelling and sunbathing are all perfect; there are of course no beach facilities. A legal battle between prospective developers and conservationists is currently being waged over this beach; let us hope that Cala Trebalúger will not be stripped of its wild beauty.

CALA MITJANA★★★

This idyllic south-facing cove with its tiny satellite Cala Mitjaneta, facing east, is reached by walking for about 20 minutes from Cala Galdana through pinewoods. The walk begins from the Plaça de Na Gran off the road above the Gavilanes Hotel, where a clearly marked gate opens onto a woodland path. (Alternatively, another easy track begins from a clearing exactly opposite the 6 km. post on the PM 714 Ferreries-Cala Galdana road. Take the left fork at the first choice you are offered for the most direct way down; the track then goes through a gap in a wall and swings right for the descent to the beach.)

At the water's edge the white sandy beach is about 100 m. wide. It curves inland to meet the trees and is bounded by high wooded cliffs. The back of the cove can become seaweed-choked if the winter has been

The crystalline waters of Cala Mitjana

stormy, forming a stagnant, marshy area. An undoubted attraction at Cala Mitjana is the high limestone cliff to its eastern side, which overhangs the water and is full of caves. One such fissure can be entered by (non-claustrophobic) swimmers through a small crack which permits access to a tunnel running some 50 m. into the cliff – an eerie and exciting experience as the water makes unexpected slobbering and sloshing sounds and one cannot help thinking of the thousands of tons of rock just above one's head. Above the caves rears a natural arch into which steps have been carved by smugglers: the more daring young enjoy hurling themselves from the top into the pellucid waters below. Cala Mitjana offers perfect conditions for swimming and snorkelling; despite attracting plenty of visitors in summer, it remains an unspoiled and very beautiful place. [82-49/83-49 Santandría – 832211]

CALA MACARELLA★★★

The most usual way to approach this *cala* is by the well-trodden footpath which goes west from opposite the Hotel Audax at Cala Galdana. This is a very pretty walk taking about half an hour over wooded cliffs and through scented '*maquis*'. To reach it by car, however, take the Camí de Sant Joan de Missa from the outer ring road at Ciutadella (see p. 185) and follow it all the way to the hermitage of Sant Joan. Here turn left: 'Macarella' is written on the road at this point). Bear left at the junction near the farm of Torralbet and at the next junction keep left through gateposts with a sign reading 'Macarella da Santana'. The track deteriorates markedly as it turns due south, finally running down the wooded gorge of the *barranco de Macarella*. On the level ground at the end there is room to park behind the beach.

The pine-fringed cove is extremely picturesque; it is enclosed by lofty limestone cliffs, those on the western side containing three large caves. Used for burials originally, these now attract a contemporary troglodyte population during the summer months. The sand at Cala Macarella is very white, and the sea deepens only gradually; bathing is therefore ideal for young and old. During the summer there is a bar/restaurant at the eastern end of the beach (open for lunch 13.00–15.30) and sunbeds, umbrellas and pedaloes are available for hire. Touristic development here has been discussed but thankfully has not proceeded. The massive square mouth of the shallow cave known as Dos Pisos ('two storeys') can be reached by pedalo. [82-49/83-49 Santandría – 801215]

CALA MACARELLETA★★

Although not named on the military map, this near neighbour of Macarella has a perfect beach and is reachable on foot from there (20 minutes) or by a track from the farm and church of Macarella. From Ciutadella, follow the same route as for Cala Macarella until the junction just before the farm of Torralbet. Turn right here and follow the road south for 2½ km. Leave the farm of Macarella to your right and go down a wooded track for 250 m., fork left and after 50 m. you reach the *cala*, which faces due east.

The path from Cala Macarella climbs to the top of the western headland and crosses the back of it before winding down to the beach. There is a maze of paths on the headland: avoid bearing left too soon or you will emerge at the top of steep cliffs which offer a marvellous view of both beaches at once but from which it is impossible to get down to the *cala*. Your aim is to skirt the cove and emerge on the far side at the back, where there is access to the sand. Cala Macarelleta is totally unspoiled, with white sand and turquoise water. High limestone cliffs clothed with pines enclose it and deprive it of the sun after midday. [82-49/83-49 Santandría – 800213]

CALA EN TURQUETA★★★

Leave Ciutadella by the route described for Macarella above, but keep straight on when Sant Joan is reached (about 5 km.) and turn right after 1.5 km. (signed 'Camí de Son Camaró'). Continue for 4 km. until the rather forbidding farm of Sant Francesc where you are likely to be confronted by a locked gate. Leave the car here, negotiate the wall(!) and walk the last kilometre down an unmade road which follows a stream through pinewoods to the western end of the *cala*.

This is a semi-circular beach, divided in half by low rocks; the sand is soft and white and the very clear water deepens gradually. Rugged pine-clad limestone cliffs and woodland at the back of the cove complete a scene of outstanding beauty even by Menorcan standards. Conditions for a family picnic, for swimming off the rocks or sand, for snorkelling and boating are all ideal, but there are no beach facilities of any kind. This is a popular destination for boat excursions, which usually arrive in mid-afternoon. Several large caves to the east are only reachable from the sea.

There are shady woodland walks to Cala d'es Talaier and

Arenal de Son Saura from here, also up to the 'Atalaya d'Artruix' overlooking the beach, a look-out tower enjoying spectacular views of the south-west corner of Menorca and over to the mountains of Mallorca. The planning authorities have recently been under pressure to permit development at Cala En Turqueta, but local antagonism to the idea has been intense and fortunately no such defilement has yet occurred. [82-49/83-49 Santandría 783208]

CALA D'ES TALAIER★★

A thickly wooded promontory, the Punta des Governador, separates this beach from Arenal de Son Saura. To reach it, follow the directions to Son Saura (see below) then walk 500 m. beyond the eastern beach along a continuation of the same track: after passing a pond on the left, the path ascends to cross the neck of the promontory. It is also reachable by taking the road out of Ciutadella to Sant Joan de Missa and Cala En Turqueta: fork right at the junction where the church stands, then right again past several farmhouses; 500 m. after the farm of Marjal Vella turn sharp right to park in the driveway of the three-storeyed house called Mallaui. After passing through a pair of green gates, a track leads to the right of the property, through the trees on the western side of the hill of Artuiz and to the north-west corner of the beach.

This is a small beach overlooked by the low tower on the Atalaya de Artruix; there is a large flat rock at the mouth of the *cala* which gives shelter. The sand at Cala d'es Talaier is not as white as Son Saura, but fewer people come here, the water is crystal clear and bathing is superb. [82-49/83-49 Santandría – 772202]

ARENAL DE SON SAURA★★★

From the southern ring road round Ciutadella a minor road crossing the canal and going south-east is signposted 'S. Joan de Missa/Son Saura/Cala Turqueta'. Follow this route for 3 km. and just past the farm of Son Vivó, fork right. After a further 5 km., the drive gates of the fortified farmhouse of Torre Saura Vell necessitate a diversion onto an unsurfaced track which goes off to the left just before an archway. There are many well-maintained gates to open and close, but the way is unmistakable and leads after about 10 minutes rough driving to the coast, where there is parking alongside the track, some of it in shade.

This beautiful sheltered bay, facing south-west, is backed by pines; two long but very narrow stretches of gently shelving pure white sand are separated by a low wooded outcrop and a stream. The eastern beach is more popular as the western one tends to collect seaweed, but both offer safe bathing from soft sand, and the water remains shallow for a great distance. Except during summer weekends this is a very quiet place, though it is a favourite mooring spot for yachtsmen and boat excursions. There are no facilities for most of the year, but in high summer windsurf boards can be hired (1000 ptas an hour, no instruction available). [82-49/83-40 Santandría – 764203]

SES FONTANELLES

Leaving Ciutadella on the same road as for Cala Morell (see p. 182), there are three possible methods of reaching this cove, all of them fairly arduous. One alternative is to leave your car near the Cala Morell turn-off and walk north up a small lane which passes the farm of Binia-tramp – this entails a trek of some 10 km. and it is recommended that you follow walk no. 6 in Dodo Mackenzie's *12 Walks in Menorca*. Another option is to bear right at the Cala Morell turning and drive for a further 2 km. Here there is a locked Menorcan gate; climb this and follow the path downhill in a more or less northerly direction (Dodo Mackenzie covers this route also). The easiest option, however, is to approach from Algaiarens (see below). This is achieved by following a track from the eastern end of the Algaiarens beach which skirts the high headland between the two coves for approx. 1½ km. Cala Fontanelles is a small fishing haven, sheltered by the rock of Ses Ginjoles at the mouth of the inlet. The beach is dark and shingly and only rarely visited. [82-48/83-48   Ciudadela   – 781335]

CALA DE ALGAIARENS***

Although this beach is signposted both in Ciutadella, which you leave by the same road as for Cala Morell (see above, p. 182), and at the junction 5 km. northeast of the city, reaching it can be extremely difficult. About 2½ km. after this junction the road enters a pine wood and passes between gateposts bearing pro-

hibitive notices: '*prohibido el paso*', '*propiedad privado*', etc; indeed in high summer the gate may well be locked and manned. The owners of the farms in the La Vall region are anxious to conserve their area and protect it from indiscriminate camping (see also p. 183).

Assuming access is not barred, there is no legal reason not to drive on. There are no signposts to the beach, so the following directions should be followed with some care.

Keep to the metalled road (ignoring sandy tracks off it), until shortly after a 20 km.p.h. sign it comes to an end, just as a broad clearing opens on the left (with signs forbidding lighting fires and dumping rubbish). Turn into this clearing and choose the right one of two forks which lead out of it, a sandy track which soon passes a row of single-storey houses and continues through a field; 300 m. beyond the row of houses is another 20 km.p.h. sign where you should fork left, go through a set of gateposts and about 1 km. further on park under the trees. From here it is only 5 minutes walk to the back of the beach. Before plunging towards the sea, however, a pause among the pines and dunes will probably reward you with a sight of bee-eaters, goldfinches, blackcaps or whitethroats: the birds in the La Vall region are wonderful.

There are two coves at Algaiarens, both of golden sand, separated by low rocks; their names are Platja d'es Bot and Platja d'es Tancats. Both shelve gently and offer perfect bathing. A small stream enters the sea across the former beach, which is the one nearer the car park, and the water is said to be drinkable. No 'facilities' of any kind may be found here and the bay offers no sheltered mooring for boats. The setting is tranquil and remote and some naturism is practised. [82-48/83-48 Ciudadela 788335]

CALA DEL PILAR★

Driving west from Ferreries on the C 721 as far as a point 250 m. beyond the 34 km. post, take a right turn (unsignposted) as if heading for the farm of Alputzer Vell. This wide, white road, enclosed by walls, winds through farmland and passes a number of farmsteads before going through two gateways after which it becomes a rough and narrow track. Beyond here, in a sandy grove of ilex and wild olive trees, there is room to park the car. A helpful wooden sign indicates the path to Cala Pilar; from here it is a pleasant walk of some 15 minutes on a sandy track through woods and aromatic scrubland. The path is easy to follow as long as you ignore all forks to the left; it emerges at the top of some high reddish dunes. From here there is a steep descent down a sandbank to the beach, which is small and pretty with reddish gold sand and red sandstone outcrops on its western side. From the headlands to the west and east rough paths lead to the isolated coves of Macar d'Alfurinet and Ets Alocs respectively.

Although little visited, there is a small bar by the beach during the season. The bathing is good and fishing can be enjoyed from the rocks at each end of the beach. The islet of Escull d'es Barco lies just offshore. [82-48/83-48 Ciudadela – 836341]

CALA ETS ALOCS

The purple-flowered chaste-tree, known as 'aloc' in Menorquín, blooms in autumn on the damp land at the back of this cove and gives the place its name. The beach is rocky, but has only narrowly escaped development: an *urbanización* was planned here but never built. Now this stretch of the coast is a conservation area.

Access to Cala Ets Alocs is difficult. One can walk over rough country from Cala Pilar, or alternatively take the same route as for Cala Calderer, but just before the farm of Santa Elisabet, fork left along an abandoned track which leads to the cove. [84-47/48 Fornells 843342]

CALA EN CALDERER

About 700 m. west of the 31 km. mark on the C 721 west of Ferreries a minor road heads for the north coast past the farms of Santa Teresa and Santa Cecilia. On the right rises the steep hill of Puig de Sant'Agueda, crowned by the remains of a Moorish castle. As the bedrock changes to sandstone, the road becomes unmade and bumpy until it passes through an iron gate just after the farm of Santa Elisabet. Although still unmade, the surface is now more even; pass through three more gates, two of them enclosing the farmhouse of So N'Ermitá, and drive on to a bluff where the road ends and there is room (just) to turn the car. A rocky path descends from here to Cala Calderer, which has lowish red sandstone cliffs, golden sand and a pebbly shoreline. The Illas Bledes are visible from the path.

(An alternative route is from Es Mercadal, taking the Camino de S'Alairó towards Binimel-lá and then, by careful map-reading, making for the farm of Sant Jordi. From here a walk of little more than 1 km. leads down the valley to the beach.) [84-47/48 Fornells 868346]

CALA BARRIL
Accessible only from the sea or by walking along the cliffs from Cala Pregonda or Cala En Calderer, this is a circular cove facing the Illes Bledes. The beach is a mixture of smooth boulders, seaweed and dark sand; it is not a bathing spot, but the fishing is excellent. [84-47/48 Fornells – 878354]

CALA PREGONDA***
Road access to Cala Pregonda is currently forbidden by the land-owner, but the beach can be reached by a fairly easy walk of about 20 minutes from Binimel-lá. Follow the route to the latter beach as described below and park by the reedy lagoon. Once at the beach turn left along the back to find a sandy track aiming at a small rise surmounted by a low wall on which a '*coto privado*' notice can just be seen. Climbing the wall just to the right of a large stone marked '1915' will bring you to a broad track leading down to an area of salt-flats and then a small pebbly cove, usually covered in flotsam. After crossing these and breasting a large dune at the far end, you find yourself in a further cove, sandier than the last (Cala de Salairó). Cross the back of this and skirt a tamarisk grove towards a small headland of dark sandstone. This must be climbed, making for a wall along the top; as you approach, you will be relieved to see an opening in the wall come into view, on the other side of which you find yourself on the road leading down to the beach. Although the land behind the beach belongs to the farm of Son Ametler, the foreshore is public (as in the whole of Spain), and a path down the slope bears the welcoming notice '*paso por playa para visitantes*' ('visitors' path to beach').

Cala Pregonda is outstandingly beautiful. The bay is recognisable from afar by its curious sandstone stacks; the sandy beach is the colour of ripe corn and lies at the foot of hills clothed in pine and tamarisk. A small island with its own golden beach lies opposite, and alongside is a stack resembling a hooded monk making a speech. This rock gives its name to the cove: *pregonda* means 'proclamation'.

The clear water is perfect for swimming: it quickly reaches a depth of about $1\frac{1}{4}$ m. (consequently it is not ideal for very young children) and thereafter deepens only gradually. Small boats have no difficulty in landing here by day, but rocks at the entrance to the cove make sailing hazardous at night.

This part of Menorca's coast has been declared a region of natural beauty; nevertheless, both in 1986 and 1989 abortive attempts were made to build alongside the beach. Three well-established houses stand here which pre-date the conservation decree, but with luck there will be no more. There are, of course, no beach 'facilities' of any kind. [84-47/8 Fornells – 888348]

CALA DE SALAIRÓ★

Less than 10 minutes walk from Binimel-lá, as described above; a remote and sheltered cove with pinkish gold sand tumbling in dunes to a flat beach, ideal for swimming and sunbathing away from everyone else. Regrettably, the back of the beach has become rather littered with flotsam but the water is clean and bathing very good. [84–47/8 Fornells – 895343]

PLATJA DE BINIMEL-LÁ

From the C 721 the most direct route is to cross Es Mercadal to the Fornells road, turning left 50 m. out of the town onto an unmarked road just before a bridge. A right fork some 2¾ km. later, and a left at the T-junction which follows, will take you past the start of the road to Cap de Cavallería; 2 km. after this, turn right (signposted) onto a rough but extremely wide sandy track. After 1500 m. a left fork leads down a slope towards the beach (the last stretch of this track is particularly tyre-punishing). Here there is a large parking area (sometimes frequented by some rather predatory mules).

As both parking and access are easy here, this is a popular week-end spot. Children are attracted to a freshwater lake behind the reddish dunes. The beach itself is of coarse red sand and pebbles with gravel at the water's edge and curves attractively on either side of a small stream. It is, unfortunately, very prone to accumulations of seaweed and flotsam after a northerly gale, and in August 1989 was frankly dirty. Care should be taken when bathing from the beach as there are low rocks lurking below the surface. The water gets deep too quickly to be safe for young children. The main beach is exposed to northerly winds, but to the east of the bay a series of small sandier beaches are more sheltered and private (and attract nude sun-worshippers). These beaches can either be reached by scrambling along the shore, or by ignoring the left fork in the road as you approach Binimel-lá and carrying straight on until a second large parking area appears below the road, from which they may be reached more directly. In summer a temporary beach bar provides refreshment as well as hiring out pedaloes, sunbeds, umbrellas and windsurf boards. There is no safety flag nor Red Cross post here.

But beach fanciers are unlikely to be content with the dubious attractions of Binimel-lá, when with the expenditure of only a little extra energy Cala Pregonda, one of the finest beaches on Menorca, lies a few minutes' walk away. [84-47/8 Fornells 899342]

CALA MICA

This small north-facing beach of rather dark sand lies between the beaches of Binimel-lá and Ferragut; it can be reached by walking from either of them, the walk from Ferragut being easier. A track to it also leads due north, past the farms of Ferragut Vell and Ferragut Nou, from the minor east-west road between Platja de Tirant and Binimel-lá. Fishing from the rocks and bathing from the sand can both be enjoyed here in complete solitude. [84-47/48 Fornells – 910347]

PLATJA DE FERRAGUT/ CALA ROTJA (CALA DE CAVALLERIA)★

These popular beaches can be reached by a track running off the road to Cap de Cavallería, reached from a turning some 5 km. north of Es Mercadal on the road to Fornells and then turning right through a gate (rather faintly marked 'Cavallería') after 4 km. The fork down to Platja de Ferragut goes off to the left (not signposted) exactly 2 km. after going through the gate. After leaving the Cavallería road the track descends, its surface deteriorating as it does so. It is possible to take a car all the way down, but more prudent to leave it at the top of the last slope and walk the last few hundred metres.

These two beaches, separated from each other by an area of low rocks, are of dark honey-coloured, very fine sand and backed by extensive sand dunes. Popular with local people at weekends but often deserted at other times, they offer a long stretch of sand, which is never too crowded. There are no amenities. [84-47/8 Fornells – 917350/918351]

CALA TORTA

To the west of Port de Sanitja lies the headland of Es Brau which forms the eastern boundary of this large cove. No definite path leads to it but walking from the road to Cap de Cavallería or from Sanitja is unproblematic. The beach may be shingly or of darkish sand depending on the currents. Although unlikely to be a deliberate choice for a day out, Cala Torta is usually deserted and not an arduous walk [84-47/ 48 Fornells – 923360]

CALA VIOLA DE PONENT

Also known as Cala Ses Galeres, this tiny beach is also reached from the Cavallería road described above (but ignoring the fork to Platja de Ferragut and continuing towards the end of the headland for a further $3\frac{1}{2}$ km., where a track leads down to the beach on the left). A minute, almost circular, limestone cove, it has shallow clear water but very little sand and, often, a distressing amount of litter and flotsam. It is little visited and, of course, has no amenities. [84-47/ 48 Fornells – 931370]

PLATJA D'EN PALET (ES MACAR GRAN)★

A visit to this beach involves a walk of some $4\frac{1}{2}$ km. in each direction but is well worth the effort. The route is admirably described by Dodo Mackenzie in 'More Walks in Menorca' under the title 'Peppermint Rock Beach'.

Having driven north from Es Mercadal, follow the directions given for Cala Tirant until you are 1 km. down the unmade road which leads to it. Here a path goes off to the left towards the farm of Binidonaire, after which it continues northward to meet the coast just west of Punta Negra. The cove nestles beneath this lofty headland: a wild place at which there is rarely another visitor. Fine sand is scattered with pink and white-striped pebbles of the smoothest texture, whence Dodo Mackenzie's nickname for the beach. [84-47/48 Fornells – 935348]

CALA TIRANT★

Between the capes of Fornells and Cavallería, this sizeable

beach of coarse, ochre-coloured sand is backed by dunes, wetland and a large mere. It is reached by turning off the Es Mercadal-Fornells road 5 km. north of Es Mercadal. A country lane winds through fields of wild flowers for approx. 2 km. before reaching a junction where a huge white block announces the turning down a wide unmade road to the sea. This road was built to serve the small apartment development at Cala Tirant which overlooks the beach on the western side.

There is a large car park and a bar on the high ground on the left; this bar is open in early and late summer but in the peak months business is transferred to a beach bar on the sands. The main beach is very long and exposed to the north wind; a considerably smaller beach at the eastern end is used by members of the Menorca Beach Club on the 'Playas de Fornells' *urbanización*. Windsurfing and catamaran sailing are available with or without instruction; sunbeds and beach umbrellas from the beach b very shallow for out; young chil safely here, and surfers learn the art, but it is frustrating for swimmers. There is no flag nor Red Cross post, but a lifebelt hangs next to a list of Red Cross and police telephone numbers.

A path along the rocks leads to the smaller beach at the eastern side. Although Platja de Tirant itself lies in front of open countryside, the view from it is completely dominated by the still growing conurbation of 'Playas de Fornells'. [84-47/8 Fornells – 943335]

CALA PUDENT★ ✓

A walk of scarcely 1 km. leads to this quiet and picturesque haven: the rocky path begins at a rough wooden gate in the wall at the western end of Arenal de S'Olla (Son Parc) beach and crosses a rocky headland, fragrant with cistus, rosemary and Mediterranean heath; it skirts the back of

The tranquil scene at Cala Pudent

...attractive, rocky cove, full
. flotsam, then climbs a small
rise from which it is an easy
scramble down to Cala Pudent.
A long inlet providing a safe
anchorage for small boats, the
cove has a beach of soft white
sand. The water is clean, warm
and very shallow. This is a good
place to come to for solitude, as
even in high season it tends to be
visited only by a handful of
Menorcans in their boats.

PLATJA DE MONGOFRE NOU★

This beautiful golden beach lies
in the very inaccessible area east
of Port d'Addaia. To get there,
follow the instructions for Cala
Presili below, but just short of 2½
km. after leaving the Maó-
Fornells road, turn left, passing
the farm of Santa Rita on your
right after 750 m. Continue along
this unmade road for 2½ km. and
fork right, skirting an area of
wetland on your left. Pass a
further area of marsh on your
right and then a small lake. Park
near the farm of Mongofre Nou
and walk approx. 750 m. north-
west to the beach, which is surrounded by dunes and pine trees.
[85-49 Isla Colom – 039287]

CALA DE S'ENCLUSA

There is no way to reach this cove
except by the coastal route from
Cala Caldes, itself very remote
and about 1 km. to the east. The
sand is fine and lighter in colour
at S'Enclusa and the beach has a
pretty setting beneath the pine-
clad headland of Es Savinar. [85-
49 Isla Colom – 042284]

CALA CALDES

This cove lies up a deep inlet and
faces due north. It can be

reached from the road to Cap de
Favàritx (PM 715) which leaves
the Maó-Fornells road a little
under 9 km. from Maó. Some 3
km. north of this junction, park
the car near the gates of the
minor road which forks left to the
farm of Mongofre Vell: the walk
from here is about 3 km. along a
well-defined track. The beach is
tiny, of dark sand dotted with
tamarisk trees: a lonely spot.
From the western side, a coastal
path leads to Cala de S'Enclusa
after about 1 km. of rough walking. [85-49 Isla Colom – 050282]

CALA PRESILI★

This is the first of a series of
coves best reached from the
headland of Cap de Favàritx. To
get there, drive north from Maó
on the PM 710 (Fornells) road,
fork right onto the PM 715
(signed 'Cap de Favàritx')
between the 8th and 9th km.
marks, and follow this road
almost all the way to the end.
From a point about 1 km. short
of the lighthouse a rocky track
goes off to the right: it is just
drivable, but the experience is
not pleasant in an ordinary car,
and the walk to Cala Presili from
here is only about 1 km. Backed
by high dunes, it is a quiet cove
with white sand and good
bathing. Platja de Capifort is
visible to the south and can be
reached on foot with little effort.
[85-49 Isla Colom – 073279]

PLATJA DE CAPIFORT★

This long strip of white sand can
be approached either from Cala
Presili as described above, or
from Cala Morella Nou to the
south. There is no access by road
and so the beach is always quiet
Bathing and sunbathing are both

excellent. [85-49 Isla Colom – 073275]

CALA MORELLA NOU★

Twin sandy beaches lie between the Cap d'En Tortuga and Cap de Monsenyer Vives headlands south of Cap de Favàritx. Access is difficult but this peaceful spot may be reached by walking along the coast via Cala Presili as above. Alternatively, there is a turning to the right off the road to Cap de Favàritx approx. 2½ km. after leaving the Maó-Fornells road which leads to the farm of Morella Vell, where you should park the car. A track leads north-west from here, leaving the farmstead of Morella Nou well to the left, and reaches the coast at the more northerly of the beaches. [85-49 Isla Colom – 075268]

CALA DE SA TORRETA★

This wild, sandy beach, backed by pines, lies on the east coast north of Es Grau (see p. 148) and can be reached on foot by following the path which leads from the northern end of the bay there (approx. 1½ km.). More adventurously, take walk no. 8 in Dodo Mackenzie's third book, 'More Walks in Menorca'. It is likely that, even in July and August, there will be no one else there. Bathing is good here and the surroundings delightfully peaceful, but after a 'tramuntana' has been blowing there can be rather a lot of seaweed on the beach. A picturesque fisherman's cottage with a thatched awning over-

looks the beach from its southern end. [85-49 Isla Colom – 072247]

FONDEADERO DE LOS LLANES★★

An exciting way to reach this delightful spot is to follow the Dodo Mackenzie walk mentioned above. Alternatively, walk along the coast north from the bay of Es Grau, whence it is the first beach you come to; from this route, panoramic views of the Illa d'en Colom may be enjoyed along the way. The cove is little visited and utterly peaceful, with clean white sand and crystalline shallow water; the bottom becomes rocky, however, a little distance further out, so swimmers should beware of scraped knees, while snorkellers will be in their element. It offers a sheltered anchorage for small boats and enticing bathing conditions. An ancient defensive tower crowns the northern headland. [85-49 Isla Colom – 079072]

CALETA DE BINILLAUTÍ

From the PMV 7102 from Maó to Es Grau, fork right after 2¼ km. onto a farm road. From here the journey is better done on foot past the farms of Milá d'Arrera and Binillautí Nou; after 3 km. the track ends where a solitary dwelling stands with its back to the sea. The cove is semi-circular and sheltered by black rocks; the beach is shingly and is more favoured by anglers than swimmers. [85-49 Isla Colom 097204]

TOURING MENORCA

1: MAÓ AND THE EAST

The briefest glance at a map of Menorca is enough to show that circular car tours of the island are not a practical proposition. The island's single arterial road runs from Maó to Ciutadella, through the three inland towns of Alaior, Es Mercadal and Ferreries, and in general all other parts of the island are reached via turnings off it; after visiting an area there is only rarely an alternative to returning to your starting point by the same route. Except for a small stretch linking a number of resorts in the south-east, there is no coastal road.

All the touring routes suggested here, therefore, take the main road (C 721) as their starting point, and it has seemed most sensible to arrange them according to the towns on that road from which they are most conveniently reached. Almost all involve some back-tracking, but none involves large distances – so several tours can be made on a single day if you wish. Menorca offers a great variety of landscapes and so many points of interest, archaeological, historical and scenic, that we hope you will want to explore the island as much as you can. But the routes need not be slavishly followed. A reasonable map of the island (see pp. 6 for recommendations) may suggest alternatives: beaches and the main archaeological sites are listed separately, and in the gazetteer (p. 187–198) we try to give (necessarily brief) descriptions of all the points of interest on the island.

MAÓ (MAHÓN)

Junio, Julio, Agosto y Puerto de Mahón
Los mejores puertos del Mediterráneo son

The harbour of Maó is its glory: an inlet nearly 6 km. long and up to 900 m. wide, with a deep-water channel that increases from 15 m. at the mouth to almost 30 m. further in; it is the largest natural harbour in the Mediterranean and the second largest (after Pearl Harbor) in the world. The harbour is the reason for Maó's existence; it is also the natural feature that has contributed most to Menorca's turbulent history and to the shaping of the island's destiny from the earliest times to the present.

Older guidebooks almost invariably recommend that the visitor first approach the city from the sea, and this is undoubtedly the best way to let Maó introduce itself. The modern tourist, however, is more likely to arrive by air and thus to approach the capital from the landward side. But the traffic system in Maó is complicated, and the easiest course for a newcomer to the city in a hired car is to make straight for the waterfront (which involves a left turn at the roundabout in the industrial estate on the Ciutadella road before reaching the city itself) and to park there. Thus it is still possible to appreciate some of the natural grandeur of the harbour before making the ascent to the main town.

At the time of writing the harbour road is being widened with the aid of an EEC grant: piles have been sunk in the water onto which the new roadway will extend to become a gracious tree-lined promenade. Already, however, parking is possible all along the waterfront, and in the (free) car park of the Estación Maritima (where there is a bar/restaurant, a shop and the booking office of the Compañía Trasmediterranea shipping line). Near the Estación are the landing stages for a number of boat trips round the harbour (see p. 107), and the showroom of the Xoriguer gin distillery, into which the public is welcome to wander for a tasting of the various traditional gin flavours and liqueurs. Also nearby is the small aquarium, entrance to which is also usually free (the place is in fact a bar, with the tanks of exhibits used mainly as exotic decoration). Further east the waterfront is lined with restaurants and shops, often housed in old boathouses and warehouses; there are a couple of ceramic factories, too, in which you can watch the craftsmen painting the china in a workshop at the rear of the shop.

A little further to the east, you reach the twisting road up to the centre of town, the Costa de ses Voltes or Abundancia*, with a broad stairway running straight up the centre. The waterfront road meanwhile continues right round the headland to reach the large cove of Cala Figuera, where there are many more restaurants, including some of the city's best.

Walking up the steps which cross and recross the Costa de Ses Voltes, past a large bust of Admiral Miranda, you find yourself in the middle of a city whose architecture and narrow, steep streets feel at first more British than Mediter-

---

*Like the place-names of Menorca, in recent years almost every street name on the island has been changed, causing more than a few problems for the visitor – especially when some streets are still marked with the old name, some with the new and not a few with both! The new names are used here, as they are on the latest edition of the Archaeological Map, a recommended purchase.

The market, Maó

ranean. Many older buildings in the central part of Maó are
eighteenth-century, built during one of the three periods of
British occupation, and the architectural styles favoured by
the occupying power proved influential: Georgian fanlights
and cast iron balustrades are seen, sash windows are quite
common and there are some fine bow windows, which are
found nowhere else in Spain. Indeed '*winder*' and '*boinder*',
the words used to describe them, are unique to the
Menorquín dialect.

At the top of the steps is the small Plaça d'Espanya and
to your left, the Plaça del Carme, dominated by the large
and spacious church of the same name; just below the
church, however, the cloisters no longer fulfil their original
contemplative function but are the scene of Maó's lively
market. The market is well worth a look: in the dappled
light, the massive pillars of the cloister still stand among the
tables of produce, and architectural details surmount and
embellish the more permanent stalls housed in niches in the
walls. Above the market is Maó's conservatory of music and
an exhibition centre. The fish market is separate, occupying
a green, ornamental circular structure lower down the hill;
it is usually all but sold out by noon.

To the right from the Plaça d'Espanya, a steep street leads
up to the Plaça de la Conquesta. This square stands on the
site of the old castle of Maó; in the centre is a statue of the
young King Alfonso III who drove out the Moors from

Menorca in 1287. Also here is the Casa de Cultura, once housing the museum and library of the city but currently undergoing restoration: the archaeological and fine arts museum collection has regrettably not been accessible to the public for several years, as it is being transferred to a specially designed new home in the cloisters of the church of Sant Francesc (at the time of writing it was hoped that this transfer would be completed by the summer of 1990).

Two other small streets from the Plaça de Espanya lead to a smart pedestrianized shopping street, the Carrer Nou: at one end is the Plaça Reial, site of the American bar, a popular meeting-place, a few yards from the English library (at 2 Costa d'en Deià round the corner – see also p. 33) and the busy S'Arravaleta, lined with benches abuzz with the gossip of elderly gentlemen.

At the north end of the Carrer Nou is the Plaça Constitució, site of the largest and most important church in the city, Santa María. Rebuilt between 1748 and 1772 on the site of an earlier building founded by Alfonso III (and possibly of an earlier mosque), it has a plain but imposing exterior. Inside there is a large single nave and an organ, built by the Swiss Johann Kyburz in 1810, the fame of which extends beyond the island and even beyond Spain. It has over 3000 pipes and four keyboards, and recitals on it are often given on weekday mornings, usually starting at around 11.45; during the International Music Festival in August/ September each year there are further opportunities to hear its powerful sound. At the end of the square is the neo-classical town hall, originally built in 1633 and restored in 1788, with an external stairway leading to a first floor loggia; there is a wrought iron cupola on the tower, surmounted by a clock which was imported from England by the British governor Sir Richard Kane. The ancient coat of arms of Mahón is carved on a wall as you enter and in the vestibule is a stone tablet recording the granting of the status of a *municipium* to the city by the Romans.

From here, one may wander in almost any direction to explore more of the city. Going past the town hall and bearing left will bring you to the Carrer Isabel II, where some of the more elegant (if a little dilapidated) town houses of the city can be seen. The large courtyard on the right leads to the headquarters of the military governor, a building also used by Kane. Just past it is the narrow lane called Es Pont d'es General, said to be the only surviving Moorish street in Maó, and at the end of the street looms the massive bulk of the eighteenth-century church of Sant Francesc, once a convent. Beside the church a balcony permits a glimpse down to the harbour beneath.

Carrer Sant Roc, Maó, leading to the ancient Puente de San Roque

At right angles to the town hall, the Carrer Sant Roc leads to the only remaining fragment of the old city walls, a sixteenth-century Gothic tower and gateway in the Plaça Bastió: its position indicates the outer limit of the city in the seventeenth century. Alternatively you can follow the busiest of the roads leading away from the harbour from the Plaça Constitució, the Carrer Hannover, which runs steeply uphill and out of the old part of the city to reach the enormous square built when Maó first outgrew its confining walls, the Plaça de S'Esplanada. This dignified leafy square has room in its central park for a children's playground, a bandstand and fountains (and, on certain days, a morning market). It is bordered by largely eighteenth-century buildings housing shops, cafés and restaurants; the western side, with an obelisk commemorating the dead of the Spanish Civil War, is occupied by the army barracks. The tourist office is here, at no. 40, as are taxi ranks, and most of the island buses run either from here or the Avinguda Josep M. Quadrado to the west. Should you feel confident enough of your skill in dealing with the traffic and one-way systems of Maó to have reached the Plaça in a car, there is a large free car park off the road leading south from it to Sant Lluís.

MAÓ HARBOUR

A tour of the harbour in one of the numerous excursion boats is highly recommended. Most depart from opposite the Xoriguer gin distillery and showroom; information about times is available there, and from notices along the quay. Most of the boats offer a tour of about one and a half hours at a cost of *c.* 700 ptas (children half-price) with commentary in English and Spanish. Similar trips can be taken most afternoons from Cales Fonts in Es Castell, including what is probably the most entertaining of them all, the harbour cruise in the boat *El Pirata*, which departs daily at 14.30 (tickets and information from the Dinkum bar at the far end of the waterfront, tel: 367017): this has a lively, amusing and impressively multilingual commentary and makes a stop on the Lazareto for a *pomada* and/or a swim.

Waterfront cottages and the church of Sant Francesc from Maó harbour

From the water the Santa María church dominates the view of Maó: also prominent are a number of hotels on the skyline. Just east of the town, the Georgian villa which is now the Hostal Almirante was home to Admiral Collingwood, Nelson's second-in-command, who stayed here during the Peninsular War (dying, indeed, on his way back to England). Other British-built buildings can be seen overlooking the harbour, distinctively painted in dark red: one is the old customs house. From his house Collingwood had a clear view of the large villa of **Sant Antoni** (also known as the Golden Farm), prominent on the northern side of the harbour. It is here that Nelson is supposed to have stayed during a brief visit to Menorca though there is no evidence that he came ashore at all, and he was certainly not accompanied by Lady Hamilton! The house is now owned by a Barcelona family and is not open to the public.

Within the roadstead there are three islets: furthest in is the **Illa del Rei** ('Island of the King'). A Roman villa once stood here (its fine mosaic floor is stored in Maó museum); the island gained its name in 1287, when Alfonso III landed there – it thus became the first part of Menorca to be liberated from Moorish dominion. Later the British built their military hospital here and it was given a new name, 'Bloody Island'. The Spanish continued to use it as a hospital until 1964, since when the island has been home only to a population of rabbits. The buildings on the island were built by the British in 1771, about the same time as Es Castell was being constructed. The Illa del Rei is the scene of a dramatic firework display during the last fiesta of the year in September.

Further out towards the sea lies **Illa Plana** ('Flat Island'). Historically this was Maó's quarantine island – a very necessary facility in a port visited by ships from every quarter, carrying potential infections which could be (and often were) devastating for the small island population. Later it became a US naval base and it is now used by the Spanish navy. The largest island in the harbour, the **Lazareto,** was a peninsula until 1900, when a canal was cut to separate it from the land. This was done to prevent escapes, for the Lazareto had taken over as the isolation hospital from the Illa Plana in 1817. The walls around the island are of double thickness and very high, to prevent infection being carried to the city by the wind. Inside the complex there is a curious circular chapel, with the altar in the middle and small barred cells around the outside for the worshippers. Today it is used by the Spanish health service as a holiday island and may be visited only on certain days of the year. There used to be a further islet in Maó harbour.

The eighteenth-century naval station buildings in Maó harbour

'Rat Island', but this was blown up in the 1930s as it presented a hazard to shipping.

On the northern side of the harbour lies the main naval station and shipyard, built out onto mud-flats by the British in the eighteenth century. Nearby is a non-Catholic cemetery: its population is largely American (the US once used Maó harbour as their main training base), and a warship of the Sixth Fleet visits the cemetery once a year to repaint and maintain it.

Two deep coves penetrate the northern side, **Cala Rata** and **Cala Llonga**. This stretch of the shoreline is largely occupied by the villas of the wealthy and (in some cases) celebrated. In recent years the waters of Maó harbour have been considerably cleaned up; fish and even lobster are now caught and both *calas* produce shellfish: mussels are farmed, and at Cala Rata the small clams known locally as *escopinyas* (very popular on the island and inevitably ascribed aphrodisiac properties). Harbour excursions also pass the ladies' bathing-station, a pink building with direct access to the water, where ladies of an earlier time could enter the water fully clothed, concealed behind grilles. The harbour mouth is protected by the lofty headland of La Mola, where there is an extensive military base; during the Spanish Civil War it was used as a prison.

Having reached the mouth of the harbour you may be taken past the site of Fort San Felipe and into the pretty Cala de Sant Esteve, with its curious cave-dwellings disguised to look like normal houses. The fort, once one of Europe's great fortresses, was systematically demolished by the Spanish in the 1780s, and very little visible remains except the mouths of several large tunnels which ran beneath it to reach the harbour. Nearby an obelisk commemorates the site of Saint Philip's Town, a settlement which grew up round the fort; no other trace of it survives, as the land was cleared for tactical reasons and Georgetown (Es Castell) built in its stead. On the opposite side of the *cala* may be seen the ruins of a smaller fort, the Marlborough Redoubt.

NORTH FROM MAÓ

Es Grau – Illa d'En Colom – Cap De Faváritx

The starting point for an exploration of the north-eastern corner of Menorca is the end of the Maó harbour (Cala Serga), reached by following the waterfront road or, from the western direction, by turning left at the roundabout in the industrial *polígono* signposted 'Puerto'.

From here one road continues to skirt the harbour, leading eventually to the beach at Cala Mesquida (p. 126) or, by taking a right turn some 2 km. beyond the crossroads, past the terracotta-painted Georgian mansion of Sant Antoni, where legend incorrectly has it that Nelson stayed. This road continues towards La Mola, the headland north of the harbour (no entry to the military zone at the end), with opportunities to go down to the coves of Cala Rata and Cala Llonga and enjoy excellent views of Maó.

The main route north, however, is the PM 710 Fornells road from Cala Serga, passing Es Vergers, the flat land where Alfonso III defeated the Moorish forces (now an area of intensive market-gardening), and the monument to Sir Richard Kane. After 1 km., the first main turning to the right (signed 'El Grau') is worth taking. The road goes through undulating, fertile countryside, passing a little under 3 km. later the doomed holiday development of Shangri-la. Once a desirable *urbanización* with a golf-course and well-spaced villas with views of the lake, the complex was recently declared to have been illegally built on land designated as a conservation area, and, in an impressive demonstration of radical planning, its houses are shortly to be blown up and the area allowed to revert to a wild state. Meanwhile the region, although still occupied, has a forlorn and overgrown air as it awaits its fate. Beyond it is the freshwater lake of **S'Albufera**, declared an ecological zone in 1986 and now a bird watcher's paradise. Small paths lead around its tranquil shores, from which some of the many migratory species of birds which alight here can be seen. **Es Grau**, the fishing village at the end of the road, is a delightful spot. Usually quiet, it overlooks a large bay of extremely shallow water with a long deep beach of palest grey sand (see p. 126). Park the car by the beach before you enter the village.

This beautiful part of the island has a tranquil, almost Scottish appearance. One can walk through the village onto the rocky headland of Sa Cudia beyond for good views of the Illa d'en Colom, and there are agreeable walks in both directions along the coast. There are several restaurants and bars in the village, including the very pleasant Tamarindos, right by the water's edge. Plans for further building on Sa Cudia have been aborted, the island government having bought up the designated land in order to protect the area.

Just outside the bay of Es Grau lies Menorca's largest offshore islet, the **Illa d'en Colom**. From late May to September, boat trips go back and forth to the island throughout the day (ask for details at the Bar Ca'n Bernat in the village or simply wait on the rocky platform round the corner from the beach, but before the main fishing harbour, where the boat calls). Tickets cost 400 ptas return and the boatman will offer you a choice of two beaches on the island, *sol o sombra* (sun or shade). On Illa d'en Colom itself traces have been found of an early Christian basilica; there are also the remains of mine-workings last used in the eighteenth century for the extraction of copper. The eastern coast has rugged cliffs and in the centre are some remarkable rock formations, including one reminiscent of the parting of the Red Sea. Illa d'en Colom is owned by the Roca family of Maó, who spend their summers in its only house, near the southerly beach.

Returning to the Maó-Fornells road and turning right, after 1600 m. a fork goes to the left: this is the remaining section of the original road built from end to end of the island by the British governor Sir Richard Kane in 1713–20 (see pp. 85). It bypasses Alaior to the north before being subsumed by the modern C 721 at Es Mercadal. Six km. further on the Ermita de Fatima, built as recently as 1955, stands on an eminence to the right of the road; a small chapel with a plain white interior, it is a popular venue for Menorcan weddings. After a further 1 km., a turning to the right (signed 'Faro de Favàritx') is the beginning of a scenic route through some of the most ancient terrain on the island to one of Menorca's many headlands. (This is also the road to take to reach the archaeological site of Sa Torreta – see pp. 66.) At first the countryside is pastoral with thousands of wild flowers in spring. Only as you approach the lighthouse does the landscape change, becoming quite suddenly arid and rocky, and, at the extremity of the headland, turning into slate cliffs which crumble into the sea: this wild quarter is almost uninhabited. South from **Cap de Favàritx**, three headlands (the furthest of which is in fact Cap de Mestral on the Illa d'en Colom), and a row of fine beaches can be seen; the nearest, Cala Presili, can be reached by a ten-minute walk along a track that leaves the road 1 km. before the lighthouse – it is a narrow beach of fine sand, usually unfrequented. A scramble over the next headland brings you to Playa Capifort; further south still are the beaches of Cala Morella Nou and Cala de sa Torreta, both inaccessible by road (see pp. 138–9).

Returning to the main Maó–Fornells road once again, one can either turn left and retrace one's steps to the capital, or if time permits, turn right to explore more of northern Menorca. From here, a stretch of about 6 km. runs through thinly-populated, lush countryside of woods (mainly ilex and pine) and fields, past verges ablaze with poppies and wild mustard in the spring; there is a petrol station on this section of the road. At the 15 km. post a crossroads offers to the left a route to Alaior. Turning right here, however, leads to the deep inlet of Port d'Addaia, a favourite haven for yachtsmen, the quaint, rather old-fashioned little resort of Na Macaret and Arenal d'en Castell, one of Menorca's premier beach resorts. These are described on pp. 158–60 'North From Alaior'.

SOUTH FROM MAÓ

Es Castell – Cala de St Esteve – Sant Lluís – Cala d'Alcaufar – S'Algar – Punta Prima – Binibeca

The road south-west from Maó passes the head of the deep inlet of Cala Figuera, reaching the elegant satellite town of **Es Castell** (Villacarlos) a few minutes later. Laid out on grid pattern, this township was planned and largely built by the British during their second occupation of 1763–82. Originally named Georgetown, Es Castell was required to house British troops and personnel based in the nearby Fort San Felipe (the French had built Sant Lluís for similar reasons a few years earlier), and the town remains the favoured area of residence for British expatriates today. (It was renamed Villacarlos, or strictly Villa Real de San Carlos, when the Spaniards took over Menorca in 1782 and is still most commonly referred to by this name.)

The town consists of a series of straight streets (with names such as 'Stuart' and 'Victori') meeting at right angles around a central square. Originally the parade-ground, the square is enclosed by the elegant façades of the British barracks (still in use) and dominated by the clock tower

The main square and Town Hall, Es Castell

the Georgian town hall. At the southern edge of the town you will find the pretty harbour of Cales Fonts which has become the main centre for dining out in the area – a dozen eating places line the waterfront there. It makes a pleasant place to lunch or for an evening out. Cales Fonts is also the departure point for some of the boat trips around Maó harbour (see p. 145). Another cove in the town is Cala Corb ('Corpse' – so-named because the currents tended to wash up the bodies here of escapees from the quarantine islands in the harbour or of unsuccessful cases from the military hospital on Bloody Island); it is also lively at night, with two bars by the waterside which specialise in Menorquín and flamenco music respectively.

A turning to the right just before Es Castell is the best way to visit the prehistoric village of Trepucó (see p. 65), which incorporates the tallest surviving taula on the island.

Leaving Es Castell by the same road, continue south-east past the cemetery and the Sol d'Este *urbanización* (the most easterly houses in Spain) on your left. Here there is a small crossroads, which you go straight over, turning right shortly after (not signposted) just before a '*zona militar*' barrier which leads to the barracks on Punta de Sant Carlos, the site of the old San Felipe fort. (The fort, Menorca's chief stronghold for most of the turbulent eighteenth century and at one time one of the most elaborate fortresses in Europe, was thoroughly demolished by the Spanish in 1807, though parts of the labyrinth of underground passageways beneath it still exist, some with openings onto the harbour. Today the ruins cannot normally be visited.) This road leads round **Cala de St Esteve**, a deep, narrow inlet with a few villas surrounding it; some of them are in fact caves hollowed out of the cliffside but with stuccoed façades added to resemble ordinary houses – the TV aerials projecting from the rocks above are the giveaway! There is no beach here, but bathing off the rocks at the mouth of the *cala* is popular. The place owes its name to St Stephen the first Christian martyr: according to legend his remains were temporarily interred in a chapel here while on their way to Spain in 417 AD.

At the far side of Cala de St Esteve there is a car park below the remains of the **Marlborough Redoubt**, a strongly fortified outpost which faced Fort San Felipe across the mouth of the inlet and covered the approaches to it from the south and east: in it a force of 50 are said to have held off an attack by 700 men. One corner tower remains, with surrounding walls and various foundations still visible; a walk up the slope towards a tower (Torre d'en Penjat) at the top affords good views of the surroundings and of the high headland of La Mola at the other side of the harbour mouth.

Retracing your steps to the Es Castell-Sant Lluís road and continuing south-west brings you after a little under 2 km. to the sign for the sprawling, pretty village of Trebalúger. It has a tower, and a well-preserved talayot reached from the Camí Vell, signposted from the Sant Lluís road shortly after the main road into the village. Trebalúger marks the beginning of the so-called 'Golden Triangle', the residential area favoured by many of the wealthier citizens of Maó (and by many expatriates).

About 1 km. further on you approach the 'white town' of **Sant Lluís**. Founded by the French in 1761 on farmland, it is an attractive small town of narrow (mostly one-way) streets meeting at right angles. Today a bypass runs round the outside (culminating in an ostentatiously magnificent

The remains of the Marlborough Redoubt

roundabout which was the talk of the island when first constructed) and the town is usually quiet and sleepy. In the main street, the Carrer Sant Lluís, old men sit in the road outside the Centro Deportivo, and the lofty tower of the neo-classical church dominates the two-storey houses of the town. Dedicated in 1761 to the memory of Saint Louis (Louis IX), the church forms one side of a small square with a fountain; its west façade bears the arms of the French royal family. In a small square opposite stands the tiny town hall and an obelisk erected by the Comte de Lannion, a sensible Breton who was Menorca's first French governor and founded the town. Another local landmark is the gaily painted blue and white tower of a windmill, the Molí de Dalt, higher up the street opposite the Plaça Nova. Still in working order, the mill now houses a collection of old agricultural implements and is open to the public 9.30–13.30 and 18.00–21.00, Monday to Saturday, 10.00–13.00 on Sundays. Continuing southwards, 1½ km. out of Sant Lluís, a left turn leads down to the quaint old fishing village at **Cala d'Alcaufar**, a small rocky inlet dominated by the tower on its southern headland; here there is a small beach (see p. 113) surrounded by simple cottages and a single hotel, the Xuroy, which is the oldest tourist hotel on Menorca. Just before the village a fork to the left leads to the large tourist development of **S'Algar**; the complex includes two hotels, the huge San Luis and the smaller S'Algar, and numerous villas and apartments, as well as restaurants and the Club S'Algar; this has a swimming pool and offers a wide range of water-based activities with an impressive selection of boats, etc., for hire. There is bathing in the sea here too, but only from man-made rock platforms.

A pleasant walk may be made from the top of the S'Algar complex, along a path which runs through ilex groves beside a stream, to the **Rincó des Rafalét**, a dramatic coastal cleft with 50 m. high cliffs and clear, deep water. The cliffs are striated with red and grey-blue rock and caves at sea level can be explored by swimmers or in a small boat. An enormous detached rock partly protects the entrance. Rincó des Rafalét is a favourite with painters and photographers.

Returning to the road from Sant Lluís, keep going south, bearing left (signposted) to reach **Punta Prima**, which has a good sandy beach (p. 114) facing the barren little Illa de l'Aire. Punta Prima is an unassuming resort, with several hotels and a range of apartments. Its exposed position means it can often be windy, however, and swimming here can be dangerous under certain conditions. East of the beach stands the well-preserved Torre des Ganxo ('hook') from the far side of which the only stretch of coastal road on Menorca begins.

Here the coast is mainly rocky and lined with villa developments. There are small beaches at Calas Binibeca, Binissafuller, Biniparratx and Binidalí (see pp. 115–16 for descriptions); the last two are quite deep inlets. 'Bini' means 'son of' in Arabic, but most of the modern villas in this area are not particularly Moorish, the exception perhaps being the elaborate 'fishing village' at **Binibeca**, an island showpiece designed by a Catalan architect in an amalgam of vernacular Mediterranean architectural styles, after which the whole thing was smothered in whitewash. Binibeca

An alleyway in Binibeca Vell

features a small harbour beside which tiny alleys lead to the houses of the 'village' and flights of steps wind in and out apparently at random with apartments at several levels. The village incorporates a church steeple but you will hunt in vain for the church! Oddly, this award-winning complex faces one of the most aesthetically offensive buildings on the island: a brown stone block of flats on the other side of the harbour, its rectangular outlines emphasized in spring by plantings of mesembryanthemum in a particularly vicious pink.

The coast road turns inland some 5 km. west of Binibeca passing several fine farmhouses on a ridge looking out to sea and a turning to the left which leads to the beach at Es Canutells (p. 116), before arriving at the market town of Sant Climent (San Clemente). From here one can either turn left to visit the resort of Cala En Porter and the archaeological sites of Cales Coves, So Na Caçana, Torre Llisá Vell and Torralba d'en Salort (see 'Archaeology', pp. 69–72), or head back towards Maó by turning right. This road takes you past the airport and the impressive talayot at Torelló (p. 68).

2. THE INLAND TOWNS

ALAIOR

The third largest town on Menorca, Alaior (Alayor) lies on the main C 721 road some 11 km. west of Maó. This stretch of the road is rich in opportunities to visit archaeological sites: outstanding are Talatí de Dalt (see p. 68) and the navetas at Rafal Rubí Nou (p. 69) and Biniac-Argentina, all within a few metres of the road. Indeed the *término* (county) of Alaior is probably the richest in prehistoric remains on the island.

Arabic in origin, the name was formerly that of a farm, Ihalor, on the land of which the town was founded in 1304 by Jaume II of Mallorca, who made it the centre of one of the seven regions into which the island was then divided. The town lies mainly on the northern side of the main road. Built on steep hills with the large church of Santa Eulalia (completed in the seventeenth century on the site of Jaume II's original building) crowning the highest, the town has an impressive air from a distance. Many of the houses are dignified, with heavy stone doorways and ornate balconies. The other church, San Diego, was gutted during the civil war: also seventeenth century, it is adjoined by the attractive cloisters of the Franciscan convent, now converted into flats and known as Sa Lluna: an intriguing view of this peaceful

Alaior: the Sa Lluna cloisters

courtyard, completely secluded from the street, can be glimpsed by climbing the staircase visible through an open doorway next to the church. During the summer this unusual setting is used for concert recitals and displays of folk-dancing.

Alaior owes its prosperity and progressiveness to the rich agricultural land surrounding it. In addition, it is home to the island's important cheese and ice-cream industries Coinga, the largest producer of *queso de Mahón*, has its factory one block south of the main road (signposted) visitors are welcome to enter a courtyard (signed 'Venta de Quesos') at the back of the factory and buy cheeses, milk and butter direct from the shop there. (Guided tours of the factory can also be arranged.) The equally famous 'La Menorquina' ice cream factory is next door (see also p. 20) A shoe industry also flourishes in the town, with the emphasis on shoes for men.

SOUTH FROM ALAIOR

Cales Coves – Cala En Porter – Platges De Son Bou – Torre d'En Gaumes – San Jaime Mediterráneo

Two roads lead to the south coast from Alaior, one to each of the two important resorts that lie within the *término*, Son Bou and Cala En Porter.

The latter is one of the oldest seaside resorts on the island and enjoys a magnificent setting above a beautiful cove surrounded by lofty cliffs. The road down to Cala En Porter leaves the C 721 (signed 'Cala Emporter') just after it has reached Alaior and runs through undulating agricultural land passing a succession of important archaeological sites (fully described on pp. 69–71). About 6½ km. south of Alaior this pleasantly quiet road meets the main road from Maó to Cala En Porter. Here a left turn followed almost immediately by a right brings you to the rough track which leads down to the narrow, forked inlet of **Cales Coves**, site of the fascinating cave necropolis described on p. 71. A right turn onto the Maó road leads to the town of **Cala En Porter**, which is mostly built on top of the high cliffs to the east of the inlet. Here there are shops, restaurants and apartments covering quite a large area. The sea itself is reached either by steep steps down the cliff or by a road which curves down the back of the inlet to end in a small parking area behind the beach. Apart from its sea-bathing Cala En Porter has an unusual attraction in Sa Cova d'en Xuroi, a complex of natural caves high up in the side of the cliff to the east of the *cala*. Legend has it that Xuroi ('one-eared') was a Berber pirate, shipwrecked on the island, who abducted a girl from Alaior and kept her in this cave for ten years, producing four children; one winter, footprints revealed by an unusual snowfall gave away his secret and the girl was rescued by her family, at which Xuroi and his eldest son threw themselves into the sea. During the summer, the caves are open from 11.00–21.00 daily (the 250 ptas admission includes a free drink), and at 22.30 they reopen as a discotheque. It is a remarkable setting: stairways with occasional balconies lead down the cliff to reach a series of caves with secluded seating areas, a small dance floor overlooking the sea and sophisticated lighting. Best of all, the noise from the disco can disturb no one apart from the sea-birds and the odd passing vessel!

The remains of the palaeo-Christian basilica at Son Bou

Alaior's other beach is the **Platges de Son Bou**, over a mile long and the largest unbroken stretch of sand on the island. There are two roads to this section of the coast, of which the newer goes directly to Son Bou, leaving the C 721 a few metres west of the Alaior town boundary. This road also leads to one of the most interesting and important prehistoric sites on Menorca, that of the extensive talayotic settlement of **Torre d'En Gaumes**, which is clearly signposted to the left approx. 4 km. south of Alaior (see pp. 72–3). Nearer the coast a number of ancient caves with elaborately-decorated façades are visible from the road.

Apart from its magnificent beach (p. 117), Son Bou has interest as the site of one of the most accessible early Christian basilicas on the island; its remains are easily discerned just to the east of the two large hotels, relics of a time before the hazards of unbridled tourism had been realised, which disfigure one end of the beach. Enclosed by a low wall, the plan of the church is plainly visible and closely matches that of North African examples from the fifth century AD: there are three naves, and at the apse end, three chambers in one of which stands the heavy baptismal font, made from a single block of stone carved into four lobes. In the cliffs above the basilica can be seen several caves, while at the top are the remains of the defensive walls of the prehistoric village of Llucalari.

To the west of the hotels is the village development of **San Jaime Mediterráneo**, attractively set among trees and gardens on the low hills that back the beach (but frustratingly cut off from it by a wide belt of reedy wetland which is impassable for much of the year). The Club San Jaime, the entertainment centre of this development, has, in addition to a good restaurant (paella on Sundays) and swimming pool, a satisfactorily high double water-chute which is a great attraction to children from all over the island. A further road northward goes from here: older and in less good condition than the Son Bou road, it meets the C 721 two km. west of Alaior. On it are the *urbanización* Torre Soli Nou and the only official camping site in Menorca, Camping Son Bou (see p. 16).

NORTH FROM ALAIOR

Port d'Addaia – Na Macaret – Arenal d'En Castell – Son Parc

To visit the coast and countryside to the north of Alaior

follow signs saying '*playas*' from the centre of the town; you should emerge at the north-western corner on the Carrer es Camí Nou, a narrow road bounded by walls with white-washed tops, which takes you out of the town past the cemetery, and within a short distance meets the surviving stretch of the island's original main road, the Camí d'en Kane (see p. 85). Here turn left, then right almost immediately for the road to Arenal d'en Castell, Port d'Addaia and Macaret.

This is a scenic road, narrow (there are occasional passing places) and bounded by dry-stone walls for almost all its length, which takes you through a very rural and thinly populated part of the island. Points of interest on the road are the Coto Social de Caza, an area reserved for hunting (see p. 101) and a small monument by the roadside which commemorates Miguel Barsola y Cardona, a local farmer who died a valiant death while leading a small band of local people in repelling a band of Moorish pirates attempting to land at Arenal de S'Olla (Son Parc) in 1644.

After about 7 km. you meet the main Maó–Fornells road, which you should go straight over, following signs to Arenal, etc. This is a very different scene – a broad, modern highway shaded by pine-topped cliffs. After about 2 km. a turning to the right leads to the deep inlet of **Port d'Addaia**; the road passes through a small shopping centre (snack bars, hairdresser, bookshop, supermarket, car rental office, chandler and launderette) and an area of villa development where a further turning to the right (signed 'Puerto de Addaya') brings you down to the yacht basin. The natural shelter the inlet provides makes it a favourite anchorage with small boats (and not so small). Today it is a place for serious sailing enthusiasts: a peaceful scene, people messing about with boats in an atmosphere far removed from the bustle that must have taken place here when the British fleet chose Port d'Addaia as its invasion bridgehead in 1798.

Diving and fishing expeditions can be arranged in the yacht harbour for approx 6000 ptas for a full day (10.00–18.00), run by the Diving Centre Menorca North. There is also a twice-daily (10.30 and 15.30) boat service to the beach at Son Parc (Arenal de S'Olla).

Back on the higher road, a right turn leads past more villas to a car park at the end of the headland; from here there are good views of the mouth of the inlet with its reefs and islands (S'Illa Petita, S'Illa Gran d'Addaia and the tiny S'Illa de ses Aligues) with Punta Mongofre in the background. Over the water to the west lies the fishing village of **Na Macaret**. To visit this small resort, return past the shops to the crossroads where a right turn soon brings you to the new roundabout signalling the beginning of the large Ses Coves Noves development. Go straight on here and shortly afterwards follow signs saying 'Playa'; keep right at the next fork and you will find yourself in a small square behind the little beach. There are three restaurants here, the Na Macaret facing the water, the Acuario behind and, a few steps along the mole, the Bar Llaud: the latter runs a boat trip (one and a half hours) to Arenal d'en Castell, Son Parc, Cala Pudent and Punta Pantiné (900 ptas per adult, children half-price) at 11.30 and 16.00 (groups of ten or more can also arrange boat trips here to the destination of their choice). In contrast to the other resorts in this area, Na Macaret is quaint, quiet and unassuming. The square is lined with small two-storey holiday cottages of a distinctly old-fashioned style, and the beach is small, with brownish sand and no facilities.

Returning to the new roundabout, the Ses Coves Noves development looms ahead – this is a part of Menorca which has been zoned for almost unrestricted touristic development. Here turn right to reach the flourishing resort of **Arenal d'en Castell**.

One of Menorca's most popular holiday destinations, Arenal d'en Castell's main appeal is its magnificent setting – on a steep slope ringing an enormous beach that forms the greater part of an almost perfect circle (p. 125). The resort is dominated by three large hotels, one of which, the dark red Aguamarina, looks right onto the sands and somewhat mars the view. The sheer size of the beach here means that, although popular, it is never unpleasantly crowded. There are plentiful facilities for watersports, etc., and though the water can be a little colder than at some other Menorcan beaches, the bottom is sandy and the sea shallow for at least 10 m., making Arenal d'en Castell a perfect beach for families with young children. The whole of the headland to the north and east of the resort is zoned for further development, with a few villas and many roads already in place.

Returning to the Maó-Fornells road a right turn (signed for Fornells and Mercadal) takes you past the donkey safari site (see p. 109) and almost immediately after it, the Restaurant Sa Barraca d'es Carboner, half hidden among the trees to the left of the road: here a hearty meal or snack can be enjoyed in the shaded courtyard outside this old charcoal-burners' hut, which also has a children's play area. One km. further on, a road to the right leads to the resort of **Son Parc**, the site of Menorca's only golf course (see p. 101). As you enter the development a left fork takes you to the course, while the other skirts it to bring you to the main holiday village; there are shops, several restaurants and a large number of villas, mostly hidden among the pine-woods. From the centre a further left turn goes to the beach, which lies just to the west of the development: it has a large unsurfaced car park reached down a rough track and over a bridge (p. 124). Properly called Arenal de Son Saura (or de S'Olla to distinguish it from another beach of the same name on the south coast), the beach is north-facing and very deep with extensive dunes behind. If you seek greater privacy the usually deserted cove of Cala Pudent is only some 20 minutes' walk along the coast (p. 137).

Back at the main road, turn right if you wish to see more of the north of Menorca: this road takes you through rolling country, which is a mass of flowers in spring, towards the Es Mercadal-Fornells road, where the route described on pp. 164–5 may be taken or the C 721 regained at Es Mercadal. Alternatively retrace your steps to Alaior (by turning left here and right at the crossroads for Arenal d'en Castell), or for variety take the right turn towards Fornells and Es Mercadal and turn left some 2 km. along it onto a quiet and pretty road that skirts the eastern slopes of Monte Toro and passes the barbecue area of Sa Roca (popular with coach parties in the evenings) before meeting the Camí d'en Kane about $1\frac{1}{2}$ km. short of the turning to Alaior.

ES MERCADAL

The 9-km. stretch of the main road westwards from Alaior is increasingly dominated by the approaching bulk of Monte Toro, Menorca's highest eminence. Shortly before it reaches the next inland town it passes a popular geological phenomenon, **Sa Penya de s'Indio**: this is a curious sandstone outcrop to the south of the road, which very much resembles the head of an Indian brave in profile.

The town of **Es Mercadal** (Mercadal), founded in the fourteenth century, is more or less at the centre of the island and was once, as its name implies, important as a central market on Menorca. Nowadays its chief industry apart from agriculture is the manufacture of biscuits, in particular the macaroons known as '*amargos*' (which can be purchased from the *pastelería* Villalonga on the corner of Sa Plaça at number 11, or, if closed, from a small shop at 44 Carrer Nou); also sugared biscuits called '*ca's sucrer*'. The town also makes the most 'down-market' shoes on the island, the sandals known as '*abarcos*' constructed of cowhide with a rubber sole said to be made out of recycled car tyres and to be guaranteed by the manufacturers for 50,000 km. Much of the best agricultural land on Menorca lies around Es

The prominent windmill at Es Mercadal, which now houses a restaurant

Mercadal. It is a quiet, shuttered town overshadowed by Monte Toro looming immediately to the east.

Enter the town beside the prominent windmill and fork right to arrive in the main square of Sa Plaça (previously Plaça de la Constitució). The main thoroughfare, the Carrer Nou, leads from here. Many of the shops are in it, though others are scattered through the town, often in streets which appear to be purely residential (as do many of the shops themselves, until you peer inside). A small alley, the Carrer Obispo Severo, leads to the tranquil Plaça Església, dominated by the parish church of San Martín. From here the Carrer Forn leads to the Carrer Major, in which the *ayuntamiento* stands: a tunnel, the Plat de la Sala, leads through to Carrer Denmig, where a *farmacia* and the Post Office are situated. Es Mercadal has a large school, as befits so central a town, the Colegio Nacional Mixto Virgen de Monte-Toro, and two excellent restaurants specializing in authentic Menorcan cuisine: the Ca N'Aguadet in Carrer Lepanto at the south-western edge of the town, and the Molí d'es Recó, pleasantly situated within the old windmill you pass as you enter the town. Other restaurants include the unassuming Restaurant Jeni, which is also an *hostal* (1 star), open all the year round.

MONTE TORO

The road up to **Monte Toro** is clearly signposted from Es Mercadal. The distance to the top is 3.4 km. and walking up is pleasant if you have the time. The 'mountain' is virtually at the geographical centre of the island; while not enormous, it is visible from almost any part of Menorca and the top is high enough to afford magnificent views of all four coastlines – making one very aware of being on an island. Mallorca's mountains are also visible on a clear day. From this vantage-point, too, the geological duality of the island (agriculturally prosperous limestone south and thinly-populated, rugged Old Devonian north) is clearly apparent. On Monte Toro itself, vertical cliffs drop sheer on the southern side; the hill is almost certainly hollow with caverns, as many streams gush from it to water the surrounding countryside.

The Moors originally named this hill 'El Tor' (the height). But the modern name is more popularly explained by a legend: before there was any man-made path to the top, it seems, the people of Es Mercadal saw an unexplained light shining from the summit; a party climbed up to investigate but their way was barred by a precipice guarded by a bull (*toro*). Instead of attacking them, however, the bull miraculously cleft the rock and led the villagers to an image of the Virgin Mary at the top of the hill. In gratitude they built a chapel there to shelter the Virgin and added an effigy of a bull at her feet; this is the shrine to the Virgin of Monte Toro which crowns the summit today. (There are several versions of this story!)

Monte Toro is seen as a spiritual centre still: around the shrine an Augustinian monastery grew up, part of which survives in the seventeenth-century renaissance-style church. From this church the bishop of Menorca blesses the fields on the first Sunday in May. A convent now occupies the former monastery and the nuns run a café and gift shop. On the crest of the hill a fine statue of Christ with arms outstretched stands on a high plinth bearing the legends '*Reinad en Espana*' and '*Reinad en Menorca*' on opposite faces ('May He reign in Spain, May He reign in Menorca').

The summit of Monte Toro is much visited, especially on Sundays, but there is ample car parking at the top. Distressingly, a radar and TV relay station disfigures the crest of the hill: a forest of aerials obscures the statue and a Moorish defence tower has been engulfed by pylons. Approaching the chapel you pass a small statue of Father Pedro Camps, born in Es Mercadal, who founded the town of St Augustine in Florida in 1768 and is chiefly celebrated for maintaining the Catholic faith in Florida during the British occupation of that state. Camps died in 1790 and is buried under the main altar of the cathedral in Ciutadella. The church itself is white and hung with tapestries; a massive gilt altar screen is complemented by the coffered wooden ceiling over the apse. Beside the pretty courtyard is a long refectory building, beamed and decorated with colourful tiles; the cafeteria in similar style has a terrace on which one can look out over southern Menorca while enjoying a drink.

NORTH FROM ES MERCADAL

Fornells – Sanitja – Cap de Cavallería – Binimel-lá

Re-entering Es Mercadal from Monte Toro take the first turning to the right (signposted 'Centro Villa/Fornells'). This road leads to a T-junction with the C 723 at which you turn right for Fornells. The road proceeds through undulating countryside with many small hills, meeting the main road from Maó after 5 km. Shortly after this the first glimpses of the enormous bay of **Fornells** begin to appear on your right.

The bay is a vast shallow inlet over 4 km. long between the Cap de Fornells and the large barren headland of Sa Mola; almost landlocked, it appears from many points along the shore to be a lake. Fornells itself, a small fishing village, lies at the mouth of the bay on the western side, watched over by a seventeenth-century fort built as a defence against pirates: its garrison saw action during the British invasion but it is now crumbling away. Fornells is exposed to the north wind and the winters are often stormy; a breakwater gives protection to the small fishing fleet. During the rest of

The waterfront at Fornells

the year it is delightful to stroll along the edge of the bay, to fish in the shallows or to sail out to the islets of Sargantanes and Ravells. Fishing is still important but nowadays Fornells is more dependent on tourism: it has become a smart place to eat seafood (especially the expensive *caldereta de langosta*) in the wake of patronage from King Juan Carlos who occasionally sails over from Mallorca to sample a bowl from the restaurant Es Pla on the waterfront. There are several other seafood restaurants in the village, as well as three *hostales*, a limited range of shops, a small supermarket and a post office.

New development is going on to the north of the village, where all the villas and apartments have wonderful sea views. Fortunately there has been no building on the eastern shore and a couple of tiny beaches tempt yachtsmen and windsurfers. Fornells itself has no beach apart from a minuscule stretch of sand in front of Es Pla, where children paddle among shoals of minnows while their parents eat. There are other beaches at the far end of the bay: Cala Rotja, composed of red salt flats, and Cala Blanca, full of bizarrely shaped white rocks. South of Fornells village on the western side, a windsurfing school at Ses Salines takes full advantage of the ideal conditions for beginners that the bay affords. The wetlands at the southern end of the bay are excellent bird-watching country: groves of tamarisk and fennel are punctuated by small pools which attract waders.

Leaving Fornells you may wish to have a look at the 'Playas de Fornells' development on the western side of the headland. To do this, turn right under a large arch and follow the road round through the development. Many of the villas are built in vernacular style with interesting chimneys, beamed and railed verandahs and established gardens. A restaurant, Jaspers, occupies its own little headland, and there are other facilities at the Menorca Country Club (members only), including a swimming pool. The beach is minute, but a path leads from it to the public beach of Cala Tirant (see p. 136), a few metres round the corner.

Three km. south of Fornells along the bay, where the sails of wind surfers make a colourful picture with Monte Toro looming behind, there is a crossroads. Here a left turn takes you towards Maó, with the opportunity to visit Son Parc, Arenal d'en Castell and Port d'Addaia as described on pp. 159–61. Turn left also if you are interested in exploring the southern shores of Fornells bay on foot or in seeing the recently excavated remains of the palaeo-Christian basilica of Fornells.

(To do this you should go through the gateway to the

farm of Salinas 1 km. east of the crossroads and follow a sandy track through pines and tamarisks; fork right at the first opportunity and just under 1 km. further on you will reach two sheds on opposite sides of the track (which has by now become distinctly rough). Park here and enter an opening in the wall on the right which leads to an overgrown path between walls, terminating after about 50 m. in another opening to the left; go straight ahead through a gap in the hedge and the ruins are in the field ahead of you. The remains of the church are extensive but, for the layman, not especially informative; the star-shaped font has been roughly covered for its protection. There is more excavation to be done here, but the site is wonderfully deserted and atmospheric. Walkers can continue along the track to reach the large but now crumbling villa of S'Albufera; through woodlands to the north of the house, tracks lead to the south-eastern shores of Fornells bay.)

Turn right at the crossroads (following signs to Binimel-lá and Cala Tirant), however, if you wish to visit the beaches of the north coast and rugged Cap de Cavallería. This is a narrow but metalled lane on which after 2 km. a large sign painted on a huge white block announces the approach to the beach (p. 136) at Cala Tirant 2 km. away to the right, which you may wish to visit. One km. further on, keep right at a junction and 900 m. after that, turn off onto a gated road (signed 'Cavallería', but the sign is almost obliterated) on the right.

This is an unmetalled, rather rough road, but quite drivable with care. Exactly 2 km. along it, a fork to the left

The farmhouse of S'Albufera, near Fornells, magnificent even in decay

(not signposted) leads to a group of beaches properly known as Cala Rotja (or Cala de Cavallería) and Platja de Ferragut (separated from each other by a rocky area) and, some distance further west, Cala Mica (pp. 135–26). These remote beaches of dark sand are popular with Menorcans at weekends but never get too crowded. The island that now comes into view is the Illa des Porros off the extreme north of the island. Leaving the fork to the beaches behind, the road continues through further gates and over cattle grids, until soon the lighthouse at the tip of **Cap de Cavallería** comes into view. The track bears left to skirt the farmhouse of Santa Teresa, whose driveway, flanked by castellated walls outlined in white, goes up the slope to your right. There are several large caves below the road here.

Now a tower comes into view, overlooking the small harbour of **Sanitja** with a few fishing boats. This placid inlet is in fact one of the oldest centres of civilization on the island. The Phoenicians were here and later it became the Roman port of Sanitsa (or Sanisera) referred to by Pliny. In 1900 the remains of two Roman villas were discovered beside the harbour, and they are worth visiting if you are so inclined.

To reach them follow a steep little track leading down to your left just after the turning off to Santa Teresa. After a few hundred metres the track ends at a makeshift barricade, where you can park the car to cross the barricade and follow a small stream, crossing it via stepping-stones when you can go no further. Follow the wall on your right as far as the opening at the other side of the field, and go through this opening to cross an area of rushy marshland, past a large boulder and through another opening in the far wall. From here a track leads up a small slope, bearing right, and at the top you will find the ruins of the first villa, its foundations quite well preserved. A gap in the next wall brings you to a second, larger villa where further remains can be seen, including underground water channels and the base of a column. The area is only partially excavated and there may well be further evidence of Sanitja's Roman past awaiting discovery.

Some 2 km. after the farmhouse of Santa Teresa you reach a final set of gates; suddenly this is limestone country again, with scrubby moorland on either side of the road. To your right the tower on Sa Mola de Fornells appears. Here there is another small beach (Ses Galeres), sadly littered. At the end of the road, no entry is permitted to the lighthouse courtyard itself, but it is possible to park on the left of the road about 20 m. before you reach the gates and explore the headland.

This, the most northerly point on Menorca, is a wild and rugged area which for much of the year is scoured by the northerly *tramuntana* wind which sends impressive clouds of sea spray high into the air. The terrain is rocky but not difficult to walk on with stout shoes. Looking back, there are magnificent views of the central hills – from here one would think Menorca was a mountainous island. By the western side of the lighthouse enclosure a little path leads to the cliff edge, a sheer drop of 89 m. Nearby is an extensive network of caves (you will need a torch if you wish to explore them), which have doubtless served a military function on more than one occasion, and an excavated area which was probably a powder magazine. West across the Cavallería headland are other enclosed military constructions, which can provide much needed shelter on a windy day. On the eastern side of the headland, dramatic cliffs enclose the small cove of s'Olla, where the sea roars and the limestone strata stand out clearly. Again, the drop is vertiginous and the edge is best approached with care!

Returning by the same road, turn right when you have passed the last gate; the lane continues through a pastoral landscape, where the bizarre shapes of the few trees testify to the unremitting force of the *tramuntana* wind. After 2 km. a signpost to the right reads '**Binimel-lá**': the road to this large beach is a rough track but extremely wide (almost, indeed, dual carriageway at times). A left fork 1500 m. along it leads down a slope towards the beach (see p. 135), where there is parking beside the reedy pool. A broad stretch of coarse sand and gravel, with pebbles nearer the water's edge, Binimel-lá is an uncrowded beach, backed by an extensive area of sand-dunes. Its chief appeal for many, however, is that from here one can walk to the idyllic cove of **Cala Pregonda**, which cannot be reached by road (see p. 134 for directions). In recent years the landowner here has come in for considerable criticism for building a few houses near the beach and there is a possibility that he may be forced to remove them. But even with the building, the setting of Cala Pregonda is exceptionally beautiful, with woods behind the two rocky islands in the cove, one of which features a curious sandstone stack somewhat resembling a bewigged judge in profile, but traditionally seen as a monk making a proclamation (*pregonda*).

Cala Pregonda marks the western extremity of the territory that can be reached by going north from Es Mercadal. There are various possibilities for the return journey: one can retrace one's steps eastward, either as far as the Fornells crossroads or for only 2½ km., where a narrow road off to the right leads straight to Es Mercadal (or reaching the town, bear right to find the main C 721). Alternatively one may continue westwards on the lane after emerging from the Binimel-lá turning for 400 m., where a left turn at a T-junction leads to Es Mercadal. The most dramatic and interesting route back to the centre of the island, however (for intrepid drivers only), is to turn right at the T-junction mentioned above onto the 'Camí de Tramontana', a lane that ceases to be surfaced at the farm of Son Rubí: 200 m. after the metalled surface ends, turn left down a slope, making for a prominent white farmhouse perched on a rise. The high hill now on your right is Sant'Agueda (264 m.), site of the Roman-Moorish fortress. The track deteriorates as it passes the entrance to the farm of Sant Joan, but it is worth persisting through the gates of the next farmyard (Sant Antoni) and up a steep section, at the end of which the metalled road resumes; at the top (200 m.) there are spectacular views of northern Menorca from the farm of Son Vives, whose gates the road now passes. A short stretch along the crest is followed by a correspondingly steep descent (speed limit 10 km.p.h.). Thereafter it is a few minutes only until, passing the magnificent villa of Hort Sant Patrici (now the home of a major cheese production business, Nura Ramada Diplomada), you reach the main (C 721) road just to the east of Ferreries.

FERRERIES

Ferreries is the third of the inland towns on the main road between Ciutadella and Maó; sheltered from the north by the hill of S'Enclusa (at 275 m. the second highest eminence on the island), it is the highest town (150 m.) on Menorca and for many years enjoyed the reputation of having one of the highest birth rates in all Spain – families with over a dozen children were quite normal. Like Alaior and Es Mercadal, the town was probably founded in the fourteenth century: its name may derive from the earlier presence of a blacksmith's ('*ferreria*' in Catalan), or possibly from the name Sa Fraria, indicating the erstwhile siting of a convent here.

Entering it from the main road, the Avgda Virgen del Toro leads to the large (it incorporates a football pitch!), irregularly shaped central square, the Plaça Espanya, on the north-west side of which some tumbledown houses of great age are still standing. West and north of the square is an old quarter of steps and alleys, many of them pedestrianized, where an unimposing house door may often reveal a surprisingly large supermarket or shoe shop within. Here also is the elegant little Plaça de l'Església (the sign naming it after Generalísimo Franco has yet to be obliterated) on one side of which stands the nineteenth-century Ermita San Bartolomeu, with a square belfry: the interior is dignified, painted white and cream and almost entirely devoid of ornament except for the gilt wood of the massive altar. Also in the square is the *ayuntamiento* and the police-station beneath a musically chiming clock. Ferreries has a surprisingly large selection of shops, though little to offer the tourist. The manufacture of high-quality furniture is a major industry of the town.

SOUTH FROM FERRERIES

Two roads from the town lead down to the south coast: one to the popular resort of Cala Santa Galdana, the other, through the pretty country town of Es Migjorn Gran, to the beaches of Sant Adeodato and Sant Tomás.

Cala Galdana road: Cala Galdana – Macarella – Macarelleta – Cala Mitjana

A fast modern road leaves the main C 721 300 m. west of Ferreries, reaching the coast after 7 km. at the popular resort of **Cala Galdana**. Still one of the most beautiful coves on Menorca, despite some insensitive development, there is an excellent beach here (pp. 119–20) and a small number of shops and restaurants, mostly to the west of the small stream which flows through the resort even in high summer (and is Menorca's only permanent river). In addition to its own attractions, Cala Galdana is an excellent starting-point for several walks. Behind it lies the stunningly beautiful Algendar gorge with its remarkable microclimate and wildlife (see p. 36), while an easy 30-minute walk westwards along the coast (the path begins in the pinewoods above the Audax hotel) brings you to the undeveloped beaches of **Macarella** (pp. 129–30), and, over the next headland, **Macarelleta** (p. 130). In the other direction, too, a stroll through fragrant woods will bring you to the equally perfect beach of **Cala Mitjana** (pp. 128–9).

At the south-eastern corner of Cala Galdana steps have been cut into the cliff which climb the 50 m. to the top (or you may prefer to avail yourself of the lifts in the Los Gavilanes hotel!). From the cliff top the view of this lovely cove is breathtaking, but care should be taken with young children or vertigo sufferers, as there is no fence to keep you from the precipice.

Es Migjorn Gran road: Es Migjorn Gran – Sant Adeodato – Sant Tomás

At the western edge of Ferreries a turning to the south off the main road signposted 'San Cristóbal' leads through some of the most attractive countryside on the island. Trees abound, and the road climbs and descends through undulating country that remains green even in high summer. Some 1500 m. after leaving Ferreries there is a magenta sign intended to indicate the archaeological site of **Son Mercer de Baix**, which you may wish to visit (undeterred by someone's determined efforts to obliterate the sign!): if you do, turn right here, onto a gated road which climbs through woodland to reach a plateau; it passes the farm of Son Mercer de Dalt (and, a few hundred metres further on, a 'hypogeum' or underground cave on the right just before the first gate) before reaching the farmhouse of Son Mercer de Baix, where a path to the right brings you to the site. The main attraction here is a well-preserved naveta, unusual in having supporting pillars within the lower chamber.

After the Son Mercer turning the road continues through a pastoral landscape before descending through a rock cutting to approach the large village of **Es Migjorn Gran** (San Cristóbal). It is well worth stopping here for a brief visit. The main road almost bypasses the town, forcing you to the right as you approach, and sweeping you on to a junction where a right turn will take you further south (the traffic system seems deliberately designed to discourage casual visitors!). Park, therefore, before you reach the junction, and walk into the heart of the village, which lies ahead of you and to the left.

Landscape south of Ferreries

Like an Andalusian hill town, Es Migjorn Gran is a compact huddle of mainly white houses, set in peaceful, narrow streets from the ends of which there are attractive views of the surrounding countryside; its hilltop setting also makes the village pleasantly cool in high summer. As so often in provincial Menorca, the shops are scarcely distinguishable from private houses, refusing to reveal their function until you are right on top of them. Founded in 1769, Es Migjorn Gran is a friendly, quiet town, only the sound of the occasional sewing machine behind a cottage window giving a clue to the busy life of the villagers. In the Pla de l'Església stands the solidly built church of San Cristófol: inside, the altar is raised on a marble dais, and surmounted by a large pillared structure of dark wood; the apse is painted with a striped rising sun motif. In the Carrer Sant Llorenç running down the south side of the church, the Galería Migjorn at no. 15 holds regular exhibitions of work by local artists, both expatriate and Menorcan, while in the Carrer Sant Jaume, halfway down, you may find a tiny street market. On the other side of the church the Carrer Gran runs the whole length of the village: there is a *farmacia* here, and at the western end, near the Ferreries road, the tiny but justly celebrated restaurant of S'Engolidor (58 Carrer Major), where island cuisine is served on the terrace of a typical Menorcan town house.

The village is surrounded by laboriously terraced fields. Leaving it (by turning right at the main road round the southern side) brings you almost immediately past a large cave by the side of the road. Shortly after passing the prominent farmhouse of Santa Clara, a turning to the left leads to the talayotic village of Santa Monica; more interesting, however, are the remains at Sant Agustí Vell, reached via a sandy track to the right (not signposted, but recognizable by the gate posts set some distance back from the road) some 800 m. further on (see pp. 73–4).

After a further 2 km., the road reaches the coast at the beach of **Sant Adeodato**, with further east the larger and more developed beach of **Sant Tomás**, now the site of an *urbanización* with several hotels, apartment blocks and villas. Sant Tomás has one of the finest beaches on Menorca, but early in 1989 disaster struck when a freak storm completely removed all the sand from both it and the beach at Sant Adeodato (to the consternation of the holiday companies, whose brochures depicting unbroken stretches of golden sand had already been distributed). By July of that year, however, the sand was back, laboriously replaced by the authorities, and it is to be hoped that the storm of 1989 will indeed prove to have been a freak occurrence.

Off the beach of Sant Adeodato lies a small island, the Escull de Binicodrell. The beach is backed by dunes and a pleasant stroll can be had to the beach of **Binigaus** at the far end. There is no development here. Sant Tomás, by contrast, offers the three-star Sol hotel Los Cóndores, the 4-star San Tomás and the Hotel Victoria Playa at the far end of the resort with all facilities. Villas are being built up the low hill behind the resort, but development is now being firmly restricted on this part of the island; there are restaurants, mini-golf, tennis courts and medical facilities.

Returning towards Es Migjorn Gran, bypass the town to your left and keep straight on the road to Es Mercadal (as you leave the town, notice a fine example of a country villa bearing the date 1887). This is another pretty road, running through farmland and past terraced valleys and finally skirting the hill of Puig Mal. Alternatively, a right turn $3\frac{1}{2}$ km. from Es Migjorn Gran will take you to the C 712 nearer Alaior past the talayotic village of Turmadenc d'en Capitá on the crest of a hill.

NORTH FROM FERRERIES

Ferreries is not a particularly convenient starting point for an exploration of Menorca's north coast. There is one dramatically scenic stretch of road which leaves the C 721 from a point just east of the town, but this is described elsewhere (p. 169). The only northerly excursion worth making from the town is the visit to **Sant'Agueda**, the hill fortress first constructed by the Romans and later taken over by Menorca's Moorish overlords until their defeat in 1287.

Going westwards from Ferreries on the main road and soon after passing the turn-off to Cala Santa Galdana, the road flattens out with a small range of hills ahead on the right and two large farmhouses. Exactly 3.3 km. from Ferreries take an unsignposted road to the right which makes for these hills (there is a white farmhouse on a rise to your right); 4 km. further on you come to the gate-posts of the farm of Santa Cecilia. Park here, where the path up to the fort begins at a gate on the right of the old white schoolhouse beside the road. The narrow track is lined with fragrant cistus, the Mediterranean vegetation around you presenting a marked contrast to the green, English-looking landscape of the Pla Verde stretching out to your left. After ten minutes on this rocky track the first traces of an ancient paved road begin to appear, with steps from time to time, and shortly after there are glimpses of the defensive walls at the top of the hill. Vestiges of the old paved way become re frequent as you ascend (pausing to ponder the mystery an abandoned veteran car halfway up!); the labour involved in making the road is exhausting merely to contemplate. After about 25 minutes you reach the fort on its summit (at some 264 m. high, the third highest eminence on Menorca). Little remains apart from a few fragments of the encircling walls and towers and a deserted farmhouse, but the views in all directions are stunning, especially of the wild north coast. There are traces of Roman, Arab and later occupations, but they are difficult for the layman to discern. The twisted trees, mute witnesses to the ferocity of the *tramuntana*, tell a more vivid tale than any man-made traces at the spot that for 500 years was Menorca's major stronghold. The walk up to Sant'Agueda and back will take you a minimum of an hour, plus the time you spend wandering around at the top.

It is possible, by driving on past Sant'Agueda, to reach the north coast at the beach of Cala En Calderer (p. 133). The road deteriorates as it goes north, becoming a rough track at the farmhouse of So N'Ermitá, from whose land one can scramble down to the beach.

3. *CIUTADELLA AND THE WEST*

CIUTADELLA (CIUDADELA)

'*Maó may have more people, but Ciutadella has more souls*'.

Dignified, aristocratic Ciutadella is the architectural show-piece of Menorca. In contrast to the busy streets and Georgian style of Maó, Ciutadella is Mediterranean, Catholic, ancient and secretive; scarcely a building in the city reflects the years of British and French occupation.

The centre of Christianity on the island ever since the religion was introduced, Ciutadella remained a religious capital even under the Moors and the natural city home of the island aristocracy and intelligentsia. In 1722, when Sir Richard Kane moved the capital of Menorca to Maó, these elements remained behind, with the result that this small city is full of palaces and churches, as well as practically the only remaining traces of Arabic architecture on the island. Like Maó, it has a harbour; but Ciutadella's is one of the smallest in the Mediterranean.

Today a ring road encircles the old city, changing its name as it progresses from Avinguda Francesc de Bonja Moll, through Avgdas de la Constitució, El Conqueridor Jaume I, to Avinguda Capità Negrete. This road follows the line of the old walls (*contramurada*), which ringed the city until the middle of the eighteenth century: a small portion of the original battlements survives, overlooking the harbour at the north-east corner of the Plaça d'es Born. From whatever direction you approach Ciutadella you are likely to encounter this ring road, and if uncertain where to park it is best to turn left along it until you reach the Plaza Colón (recently renamed Plaça de S'Esplanada), a gracious tree-lined square at the western end of the ring road. Turn right up the side of the Plaça and you may be lucky and find a parking place there; if not, turn left at the end into the broad avenue Camí de Sant Nicolau, lined with fragrant Indian bead trees, which heads out along the southern shore of the harbour; here you are almost certain to be able to park at some point.

From the northern end of the Plaça de S'Esplanada a short walk brings you to Ciutadella's main square, the Plaça d'es Born (meaning 'palisade'), once used for jousting and similar chivalric pursuits. Unusually impressive for a provincial square, the 'Borne', as it is often called, is dominated by an obelisk in the centre which commemorates the citizens of the city who died during the Turkish invasion in 1558 under Mustafa and Piali (see p. 82). On the western side of the square stands the town hall (*ayuntamiento*), a crenellated structure with a squat tower which replaced the original building destroyed by the Turks. Here, in addition to the mayor's offices and a severe council chamber lined with portraits and coats of arms, there is a cafeteria on the second floor which leads to a small grassed area from which an excellent view can be enjoyed of the harbour below. Also, on the ground floor there is a small historical museum, unfortunately closed at present for restoration.

Directly opposite the *ayuntamiento* is the first of Ciutadella's palaces, that of the counts of Torre-Saura – a long neo-classical frontage with a high arched loggia at each end and a tall arched doorway in the centre leading to the inner courtyard. Built in the early nineteenth century, the palace contains large reception rooms and is said to house a fine collection of paintings. There are other palaces in the Borne, too, as well as the half-baroque, half-Gothic church of Sant Francesc at the south-east corner.

The alley by the side of the Torre-Saura palace (Carrer Major d'el Born) leads into the heart of the old city, a delightful area of narrow streets and little squares from which all traffic is excluded. Almost immediately upon entering it you pass the Palacio Salort on the right. Open to visitors from 10.00–14.00 on summer weekdays, the palace

Façade of the Torre-Saura palace, Ciutadella

is worth a visit (150 ptas): there is a fine ballroom with a frescoed ceiling, a mirrored chamber and an interesting kitchen – clearly the nineteenth-century aristocracy in Ciutadella lived in some style. A little further into town is the cathedral of Menorca, Santa María, a severe, reserved building in the Catalan-Gothic style that seems well suited to the character of the people of Ciutadella. Built on the site of the main mosque on the island, it was declared Christian within days of the Catalan conquest of the island in 1287, and the Christian structure had completely replaced the mosque by 1362 (though the tower on the north side, part of it probably originally a minaret, still contains a typically Arab ramp). The church was granted its cathedral status in 1795. On the outside is a high windowless wall (which may have been added after the Turkish raid in 1558); behind it and above, thick buttresses, square in shape and made of the golden stone so common in the city, separate the windows. Inside, most of the interior fitments and decorations were destroyed by republican extremists during the civil war; but the interior is serene and beautiful, consisting of a single lofty central nave, bathed in light, with a pentagonal apse, a massive gilt wooden arch over the altar and a dozen small side chapels in renaissance style.

Opposite the main entrance is the Olivar palace, housing an art collection as well as a library and archaeological collection. From the west door of the cathedral, the Ca'l Bisbe (previously Calle Obispo Torres) leads to the neo-classical bishop's palace with an arcaded gallery; at the end of this street stands the palace of the Squella family (where Admiral Farragut spent a night in December 1867) in the

Ses Voltes, Ciutadella

Mid-morning in the Plaça d'Alfons III, Ciutadella

Staircase in the seventeenth-century Saura town house, Ciutadella

Carrer Sant Sebastiá; in addition to its elaborate wrought-iron balcony, the palace boasts a superb staircase inside, but this is rarely visible. A right turn opposite the Squella palace brings you to the delightful 'Ses Voltes' area of the town, a series of arcades shading the shops and restaurants behind with very Moorish arches. This in turn leads to the lively Plaça Nova (previously Plaza d'Espana), a small square from which further streets lead to the Plaça d'Alfonso III on the *contramurada*, a popular rendezvous with a small garden in the middle and cafés and restaurants around the sides. You have now walked right through the old city, having reached the point where the Mahón Gate, one of five original entrances to the city, once stood: none of the gates now survive.

Turn back and wander at leisure through the old streets between this and the Borne. The market, in an arcaded square, is just to your left, and there are numerous palaces and churches to look out for, including (to the left of Ses Voltes as you return towards the cathedral) the delectable little chapel of Santo Cristo in the Carrer Bisbe Vila, built in 1667 with classical columns and a small octagonal dome; nearby are the cloisters of the old seminary. In the same street another church is now the headquarters of Radio Menorca, while an imposing town house has been converted into a bank. At the end of this street the Carrer Santissim is the setting for two palaces, the grand but plain Martorell palace, and the elegant home of the Saura family: the latter, now an antique shop, features a graceful stairway in the courtyard (dated 1718) and imposing full-length

Doorway of the Església del Roser, Ciutadella

windows with neo-classical mouldings on the frontage. Returning towards the cathedral via the Carrer Roser will take you past the ornamental pillared façade of the church of Our Lady of the Rosary, which was transformed by the British into a Protestant church for the benefit of the troops.

Blessedly traffic free, the old town is ideal for a leisurely stroll, during which your eye will be caught over and over again by gracious façades and small architectural details. There are pleasant cafés and restaurants and an excellent ice-cream parlour. North of the Borne and accessible via a flight of steps is the harbour – a narrow, steep-sided inlet only some 1000 m. in length. It can experience severe storms: on occasion there have even been minor tidal waves which have flooded the harbour and cleared it of the small boats which throng it. A lively spot, particularly in the evenings, the quaysides of Ciutadella harbour are nowadays lined with restaurants and music bars; many of them make use of caves hollowed out of the cliff behind, which served originally as warehouses.

Ciutadella is no museum piece, however. It is the nucleus of the important shoe industry on Menorca, and a thriving centre of business activity. Costume jewellery and leather are two other industries which provide employment. The city also has several excellent and unusual shops. From the port there are regular sea communications with Alcudia in Mallorca and thence to Barcelona.

NORTH FROM CIUTADELLA

Three roads lead from Ciutadella to the north-western corner of the island. In general this quarter is bleak and rocky, but there are a few (small) beaches and much touristic development to the west of the city. The road heading north-east goes to the resort of Cala Morell, which has some interesting caves as well as a reasonable beach, and a little further on, to the lush agricultural area of La Vall and the enormous beach of Algaiarens.

Cala En Blanes – Cala En Brut – Cala En Forcat

The road to the far west of the island leaves Ciutadella via the harbour, which can usually be reached by driving down the Costa del Molí near the town hall (sometimes this road is closed, however, in which case the harbour must be approached from the innermost end, driving down into the Pla de Sant Joan from the northern end of the ring road near the Francesc tower). Once down in the harbour, cross the bridge over it and turn left along the commercial mole at the far side (this is where the boats for Mallorca and Barcelona go from). Bear right as you climb up from the harbour and turn left at the crossroads. This road takes you past the Ciutadella lighthouse (with a good view of the Sant Nicolau tower at the far side of the harbour) and follows the coast, arriving after about 1 km. at the deep inlet of **Cala En Blanes**: the small beach (see pp. 122–3) at the end is dominated by a sizeable hotel on the other side of the road, with a scattering of pretty villas along the rocky sides of the *cala*. There is a small bar here, 'S'a Cova', hollowed out of the rock beside the beach.

At the next crossroads, go straight over and follow signs to 'Playa' to the left; a right turn shortly afterwards leads round the cove of **Cala En Brut**. Here there is scarcely any sand at all, as the rocky sides come together into a steep crevice, but the shore has been extensively worked into a series of cemented bathing platforms of all sizes and at many different levels; bathing at Cala En Brut is popular, but only with more adventurous swimmers and divers.

Two blocks inland, pick up the main road again and shortly afterwards a left turn leads through the archway entrance of the large resort development of Los Delfines, with health centre, car hire, restaurants, supermarkets and a large range of shops. The complex centres on the tiny cove of **Cala En Forcat**, once doubtless a charming inlet but now overshadowed by the enormous Hotel Admiral Farragut, from which it is most directly approached. The area of slightly gritty sand, though deep, is narrow; the beach (p. 123) can become unpleasantly overcrowded and the water less clear than one expects on Menorca (though the crowds can be avoided to some extent by making use of a series of rock platforms carved out of the sides of the cove, which is long and sinuous).

It is odd that this relatively ill-favoured corner of Menorca should have been designated as an area for mass tourism; a little further round the coast are two further minute beaches (one is scarcely 2 m. wide), **Cales Piques**, which are clearly destined for the same fate as Cala en Forcat. Roads as yet empty but fully equipped with street lighting cover the surrounding area and new walkways lead across the rocky headlands. A little further north is **Cap de Bajolí**, Menorca's most westerly point: in a cave were discovered the skeletal remains of the giant land tortoise (see p. 59). Near the cape is a spectacular limestone arch (see p. 35).

Return to Ciutadella by the route on which you came (it is quicker in reverse, since Cala En Brut can be bypassed altogether, but as the bridge over the harbour is one way you will be compelled to drive up the back of the harbour to the end of the *contramurada* ring road). If you are feeling adventurous, however, visit the archaeological site of the **Torre del Ram** near the hippodrome: it has a naveta and an artificial burial cave. Situated due north of the Los Delfines complex, it is reached from a road which will take you back to Ciutadella by a slightly different route. Though barren and windswept, the landscape here is far from featureless: stone sheep and cattle shelters (*ponts*) litter the fields in this part of the island, giving the area a vaguely Middle Eastern air.

Punta Natí - Cala Pous - Cala Morts

The area due north of Ciutadella is among the least

interesting on the island. Leading only to the **Punta Natí**, the barren north-west corner of the island, the road commences in the Camí de Son Salomó at the northern end of the ring road (where a left turn would take you down to the harbour) and goes through rocky fields between high dry-stone walls, with only the occasional '*pont*' to vary the view – there is one magnificent one, seven tiers high; it also passes Ciutadella's rubbish dump. The only thing to recommend the route is the archaeological site of **Torre Vella d'en Lozano**, featuring a number of talayots with rooms built onto them, one of which has access to a lower chamber. There are also the remains of a hypostyle chamber and several circular buildings. The site is just south of the farmhouse of Torre Nova and is reached by a turning to the right just over 2 km. north of Ciutadella. From the lighthouse at the end of the road, the only two coves in this part of Menorca can be reached by walking eastwards over a rocky and rather desolate landscape: the sculptured hollow of **Cala Pous** and, 200 m. further on, the sheer cliffs of **Cala Morts**. Neither has a sandy beach. On this lonely coast the French ship *General Chanzy* was wrecked during the night of 9 February 1910 with the loss of 157 lives: there was only one survivor.

Cala Morell – La Vall – Algaiarens

By far the most interesting and scenic route north from Ciutadella takes you to the resort of Cala Morell and the agricultural area of La Vall. The road is signposted from the ring road one block north of the point where the road from Maó enters. (It may also be reached, if coming from the east, by turning off the main C 721 just by the Leo factory in the industrial estate before you reach Ciutadella.) Follow signs on a round about route through the outskirts of the city to reach open country.

A little over 5 km. out of Ciutadella is the picturesque Torre d'en Quart, with a farmhouse attached to the ancient tower; already the countryside is much greener and less forbidding than it is further west. The turning for Cala Morell is 1 km. beyond the tower, past the little farmhouse of Clariano on the left. After a few minutes the road enters the resort, build around a small inlet surrounded by bare rocky cliffs. **Cala Morell** is modern and growing along roads lined with whitewashed posts somewhat resembling snowy owls. At each side of the beach there is a (small) car park: the eastern one is a good viewpoint from which to examine the fascinatingly sculpted red sandstone of the Cul de sa Ferrada (see p. 35). Beside the road down to the beach there are some splendid prehistoric burial caves with elaborately carved façades.

Back at the road from Ciutadella, one can continue north-east towards the isolated agricultural region known as La Vall. A quiet lane bordered by dry-stone walls and trees reaches, after 2½ km., a gate bearing the sign '*propiedad privada – prohibido el paso*'; unless the gate is locked and/or manned (which is often the case in high summer) there is no legal reason why you should not proceed nevertheless. As so often on Menorca, questions of right of way are a grey area; but since Algaiarens is signposted from as far away as Ciutadella and the road serves a sizeable section of the island, it is doubtful if the local farmers have any real right to prevent you from visiting this area. They are, however, probably sincere in their claim to be limiting access to the magnificent beach at Algaiarens in the interests of conserva-tion (fearing rubbish dumping and irresponsible camping with the attendant fire risks). If the gate *is* manned, you may find the guard is willing to let you through all the same, if you discuss your intentions amicably (this is particularly likely if your hire car bears a local registration!).

Once through the gates, there are no signposts to **Algaiarens**, which is reached by a succession of tracks through countryside that teems with bird-spotting oppor-tunities in spring and early summer (see p. 132 for route). The beach itself is large and often deserted. Round the headland to the west there is a further beach at **Fontanelles** to which it is possible to walk (see walks 5 and 6 in Dodo Mackenzie's *12 Walks in Menorca* No. 2 for details).

From Algaiarens it is possible to follow a series of rough and sometimes gated tracks on through the lush and low-lying **La Vall** region, by bearing generally right past the farms of Sa Font Santa and Almudaina. If your car is adequately sprung and you have the military map as a guide, you should end up back on the C 721 some 6 km. west of Ferreries. Otherwise return to Ciutadella the way you came.

SOUTH FROM CIUTADELLA

Cala des Degollador – Cala Santandría – Sa Caleta – Cala Blanca – Cala En Bosc – Platja De Son Xoriguer

The west coast south of Ciutadella is rocky and barren, but punctuated by two attractive coves, both now popular holiday resorts, Santandría and Cala Blanca. Leaving the old town by the Carrer de Mallorca due south from the end of the Plaça de S'Esplanada brings you first to the city's own beach, **Cala des Degollador** (p. 122), at the end of an inlet between Ciutadella and the suburb of Son Oleo. From here the main road (PM 721) to Cap d'Artrutx at Menorca's south-western corner is one block to the east. Alternatively bypass the city by following the instructions for Platja de Son Xoriguer on p. 120.

Cala Santandría, one of Menorca's older resorts (and the scene of the Duc de Richelieu's landing in 1756) is signposted to the right 2 km. further south (just past the Restaurant La Cabaña). This is a deep, attractive *cala*, with a satellite cove on the northern side, **Sa Caleta**, and a defensive tower at the mouth. Today, the beach can become unpleasantly crowded in high season; both sides are lined with villas and apartments and there are a number of hotels and restaurants.

Some 2 km. further south off the same road lies **Cala Blanca**, nowadays a sizeable resort scattered along the rocky shoreline on either side of its pleasant beach. The older half is buried in shady pinewoods to the south of the beach, with a large hotel and several restaurants. More recently, development has spread north along the rocky shore, where new apartments, small villas and shopping centres, linked by poorly surfaced roads, are still being built: the number of supermarkets is impressive, but this part of Cala Blanca has a somewhat dreary and unfinished air. Behind the beach there are the remains of a naveta, though one could be forgiven for not noticing it, as scarcely two stones remain together.

Southwards the road becomes straighter, bending only at the military base at So N'Olivaret where there is a large talayot to the left of the road. Just before the lighthouse at Cap d'Artrutx, a turning to the left leads to the increasingly chic resort of **Cala En Bosc**, where there is a marina entered through a narrow passage from the sea and lined with smart shops and restaurants. Most of Cala En Bosc faces a rocky shoreline: its beach is the far side of the marina east of the large Hotel Cala'n Bosch. The resort is popular with Germans and this is one of the few places on Menorca where British tourists may feel outnumbered! Menorca's electricity arrives from Mallorca in this south-western corner and great pylons march away from here towards Ciutadella. A number of boat excursions leave from the marina: there is a glass-bottomed boat offering short trips along the coast for *c.* 800 ptas: it leaves daily at 10.00 and 15.00. The motor vessel *Heide Maria* makes regular excursions as far as Cala Trebalúger, where the crew cook and serve a generous paella before returning, looking in at several lovely coves on the way back with opportunities for a swim at some of them (commentary usually in German): in 1989 the cost of this excursion was 2600 ptas per person (children half-price).

Nearby to the east is the newly developed and extremely popular **Platja de Son Xoriguer** (p. 120), where a wide range of watersports is available.

Arenal De Son Saura – Cala En Turqueta – Cala Macarella – Son Catlar – Torre Llafuda – Torre Trencada – Naveta d'Es Tudons

South-west of Ciutadella, a network of lanes and tracks fans out across this pleasantly pastoral, rather flat corner of Menorca (they are excellent for cyclists). Almost all of them begin from the Camí de Sant Joan de Missa, reached from the centre of the city by turning south from the *contramurada* into the Carrer de Sant'Agueda, three blocks south of the junction with the main Maó road, and going round the small, one-way Plaça de Jaume II so as to leave at the opposite corner. Most become rough tracks but lead eventually to a glorious beach: among the gems of Menorca's southern coast reached via this road are **Arenal de son Saura**, **Cala En Turqueta** and **Cala Macarella** (see pp. 129–31) – even Cala Galdana can be reached by country tracks (the military map is recommended!). Other highlights of this sector include the church of **Ermita de Sant Joan de Missa** itself, and the extensive archaeological site of **Son Catlar** (pp. 75–6). After visiting the latter it is possible to combine a swim at Arenal de Son Saura (directions on p. 131) with a glimpse of the fortified farmhouse of **Torre Saura Vell** (walk down the elegant tree-lined drive from the archway, pausing if you wish to rest on the stone benches thoughtfully provided halfway along, to peer through the farmyard at the tower); also perhaps to walk westwards from the beach at Arenal de Son Saura, then north after 700 m., for a look at the astounding, Stonehenge-like *Llindar* (lintel) at **Son Saura Nou**, one km. inland.

Before leaving the Ciutadella area, do not neglect the three important archaeological sites nearby, all easily reached from the main road to Ferreries: **Torre Llafuda**, **Torre Trencada** and the **Naveta d'Es Tudons** (pp. 74–5).

FURTHER READING

Bannerman, D.A. and Bannerman, W.M., *The Birds of the Balearics* (London, 1983)

Bonner, Anthony, *Plants of the Balearic Islands* (Palma de Mallorca, 1985)★

Colom Casasnovas, Guillermo, *Biogeografia de las Baleares: la formación de las islas y el origen de su flora y de su fauna* (2 vols., Palma de Mallorca, 1978)

Foss, Arthur, *Ibiza and Menorca* (London, 1975)

Garcia, L. Pericot, *The Balearic Islands* (London, 1972)

Hepburn, Ian, and Mule, X.M., *A Bird-Watcher's Guide to Mallorca and the other Balearic Islands* (Perry, 1990)

Hoskin, M., and Waldren, W., *Taulas and Talayots – What They Are, Where They Are* (Cambridge, 1988)★

Mackenzie, Dodo, *12 Walks in Menorca* (Maó, n.d.)★

Mackenzie, Dodo, *More Walks in Menorca* (Maó, 1989)★

Maps, Jim, *Complete Guide to Menorca* (Maó, 1965)

Mata, Micaela, *Conquests and Reconquests of Menorca* (Barcelona, 1984)★

Olives, R. Miguel, *5000 Años en Cosas de Menorca* (Barcelona, 1986)★

Olives, R. Miguel, *Calas y playas de Menorca* (Barcelona, 1988)★

Pasarius, T. Mascaró, *Mapa arqueologico de Menorca* (Ciutadadella, 2nd ed. 1989)★

Polunin, Oleg *Trees and Bushes of Britain and Europe* (London, 1976)

Polunin, Oleg, and Huxley, Anthony, *Flowers of the Mediterranean* (London, 1972)

Pons, Margarita Orfila, et al., *An Archaeological Guide to Menorca* (Maó, 1984)★

Sastre, Llorenç, *Menorca en velo* (Maó, 1989)

Sloss, Janet, *Menorcan Cooking* (Cheltenham, 1987)★

Taylor, David Wilson, *Minorca* (Newton Abbot, 1975)

Watkinson, Eddie, *A Guide to Bird-Watching in Mallorca* (Alderney, 3rd imp. 1986)

Titles marked ★ are widely available in bookshops in Menorca.

INDEX AND GAZETTEER

on S coast 6½ km. S of Ferreries; accessible only by boat or on foot via 2 routes, each of them quite lengthy 127–8

Cala Galdana (Cala Santa Galdana) one of Menorca's premier resorts, set in and around an exceptionally beautiful limestone cove 7 km. SW of Ferreries; large beach with safe bathing from soft white sand, ideal for children; full range of watersports, hotels, restaurants and apartments; scenic walks, boat excursions 9, 14, 15, 24, 25, 26, 34, 36, 39, 80, 99, 100, 102, 104, 106, 107, 109, **119–20**, 128, 170, 173, 185

Cala Llonga inlet in N side of Maó harbour opposite Es Castell; mollusc-farming and prosperous villas 147, 148

Cala Macarella pretty pine-fringed beach 2 km. W of Cala Galdana (qv), by walking from which it is best reached (access possible, but difficult, by road); safe bathing, caves in cliffs 104, **129–30**, 170, 185

Cala Macarelleta sandy, east-facing satellite cove of Cala Macarella (qv) 104, **130**, 170

Cala Mesquida (Sa Mesquida) beach resort 4½ km. NE of Maó; dark sand, defence tower 22, 40, 87, 90, **126**, 148

Cala Mica small remote beach of dark sand 8½ km. N of Es Mercadal; only accessible on foot from Binimel-lá and Ferragut (qqv) **135**, 167

Cala Mitjana S coast beach of white sand with limestone cliffs and caves, 6½ km. SW of Ferreries; reached on foot from Cala Galdana or from the Ferreries road 35, **128–129**, 129, 170

Cala Mitjaneta minute, east-facing satellite cove of Cala Mitjana (qv) 39, **128–9**

Cala Molins inlet 10 km. NE of Alaior, just west of Port d'Addaia; the resort of Na Macaret lies on one side 104

Cala Morell beach resort 8 km.

NE of Ciutadella; villa accommodation and rock tombs in the cliffs 26, 34, 35, 104, **123–4**, 132, 180, 182–3

Cala Morella Nou remote double beach 10½ km. N of Maó 138, **139**, 150

Cala'n Bosch see Cala En Bosc

Cala'n Porter see Cala En Porter

Cala Pous Fissure in northern cliffs adjacent to Cala Es Morts (qv) 181, 182

Cala Pregonda spectacular sandy beach on N coast 9 km. NE of Ferreries; no access by road, but can be reached on foot from Binimel-lá (qv) 35, 104, **134**, 135, 168

Cala Presili sandy beach in extreme NE of Menorca, just S of Cap de Faváritx 138, 139, 150

Cala Pudent small, unsullied cove in a shallow-water inlet a few minutes walk to W of Son Parc (qv) 124, **137–8**, 137, 160, 161

Cala Rata inlet in N side of Maó harbour roadstead, surrounded by attractive villas and accessible from road to La Mola 147, 148

Cala Rotja (Cavallería) see Ferragut, Platja de

Cala Rotja narrow inlet at S end of Bay of Fornells; shallow water and reddish mudflats 165

Cala Ses Galeres see Cala Viola de Ponent

Cala Tirant large cove 6½ km. N of Es Mercadal; sandy, with extremely shallow water 34, 102, 106, 107, 135, **136–7**, 165, 166

Cala Torret resort area 4 km. S of Sant Lluís, recently favoured by celebrities; windsurfing and other facilities but no sandy beach 106, 115

Cala Torta large, little visited cove 9½ km. N of Es Mercadal; reached on foot from the Cap de Cavallería road **136**

Cala Trebalúger unspoiled S coast cove of white sand and wooded limestone cliffs 6.5 km. S of Ferreries; accessible only with difficulty on foot, but visited by boat excursions from Cala En

point of Menorca; lowish slate headland with lighthouse 13 km. due N of Maó 45, 59, 66, 87, 103, 138, 139, 148, 149, 150

Ferragut, Platja de long sandy beach to W of Cap de Cavallería, 9 km. N of Es Mercadal 135, **136**, 167

Ferreries (Ferrerias) inland town 29 km. NW of Maó on the lower slopes of S'Enclusa (*qv*); shoe and furniture manufacturing 7, 9, 15, 16, 25, 27, 34, 36, 51, 74, 75, 94, *97*, 98, 102, 109, 111, 112, 118, 119, 127, 128, 133, 140, **169-70**, 171, 172, 173, 183

fiestas 27, 31, 96-8, *97*, 146

fish 18, 59, 100

fishing 100, 115, 123, 126, 132, 133, 134, 135, 139, 159

Florida 87, 89, 163, 164

flowers 1, 36, 44-9, 75, 105, 124, 137, 149, 150, 161

flying 3, 100

folk dancing 95, 156

Fondeadero de los Llanes small, sandy, usually deserted beach 1 km. NW of Es Grau (*qv*), whence it can be reached on foot **139**

football 101, 169

Formentera 1

Fornells fishing village at the mouth of the large Bay of Fornells; historically of strategic importance for Menorca's defence, now celebrated for its seafood restaurants 9, 14, 18, *19*, 23, 24, 27, 35, 40, 52, 66, 79, 83, 86, 98, 106, 107, 109, 124, 125, 126, 135, 137, 138, 139, 148, 149, 150, 159, 160, 161, **164-5**, *164*, 168

Fornells, Bay of enormous shallow, almost land-locked bay nearly 5 km. long; windsurfing, sailing and birdwatching 34, 49, 59, 65, 103, 106, 164-5

Fort San Felipe fortress begun in the 16th century and developed under the British into one of the most formidable defensive complexes in Europe, but almost totally destroyed by the Spanish in the 1780s; ruins now incorporated in a military

base 4 km. SE of Maó 17, 65, 82, 84, 85, 86, *86*, 87, 88, 147, 150, 151

France 29, 34, 37, 78, 86, 87, 89, 103

Franco, Generalísimo 90, 170

French occupation 17, 65-6, 77, 86-7, 106, 150, 152, 153, 174

furniture making 92, 170

Galissonnière, Marquis de, 87

gas 30

gates 41, 42, *42*

geology 34-6, 163, 181, 182

Gibraltar 84, 86, 87, 88

gin 17, 20, 89, 141, 145

G.O.B. 44

golf 101, 160

Greeks 77, 78

Gruta na Pulida vast system of natural caves beneath Sa Mola de Fornells 35

Hamilton, Lady Emma 89, 146

health care 28

history 77-90, 140

hitch-hiking 10

Horizonte residential development 1 km. SE of Maó that has in recent years become a sizeable suburb of Es Castell 22, 25, 65, 91, 104

horse racing 101

hotels and *hostales* 10-15, 114, 115, 117, 119, 120, 121, 122, 125, 128, 129, 153, 158, 160, 162, 165, 170, 173, 180, 181, 184

hunting 101-2, 159

hypogeums 64, 76, 171

Iberians 77

Ibiza 1, 34, 82, 99

ice cream 20, 91, 156, 179

Illa de l'Aire flat island off SE corner of Menorca opposite Punta Prima; uninhabited, with automatic lighthouse and unique indigenous lizard 35-6, 59, 84, 104, 115, 153

Illa del Rei island in Maó harbour, site of the first landing by Alfonso III in 1287; subsequently used as a quarantine island and by the British as a military hospital (when popularly renamed 'Bloody Island') but now deserted 79, 81, 85, 146